Linda Quiquivix, 2024

All original Zapatista communiques in this book can be found at https://enlacezapatista.ezln.org.mx

The Handala paragliding sketch as the frontispiece was inspired by an Unknown Artist, 2023

The paper for this book likely comes from a tree nobody asked consent from, for which we ask forgiveness in these times.

This report back regularly uses the word *compa*, a shortened version of the Spanish words *compañera*, *compañero*, and *compañeroa*. It has several uses in Spanish, including coworker and comrade. The word compa in this book describes someone who accompanies in struggle side by side, from below and toward the common.

This book was midwived over six years by an Iranian compa and volunteer-edited by Palestinian, Egyptian, and Mexican compas. The charcoals used in the illustrations were gifts from the fires of anti-Zionist Jewish shepherds, a border-transgressing Indigenous compa, and the midwife's Palo Santo stick.

Learn more about this book at **wildoxbooks.org**

We welcome your comments, questions, corrections, and complaints.

Palestine 1492
A Report Back

Linda Quiquivix

Wild Ox Books
Occupied Chumash Lands

Heart of the sky

Heart of the earth

Heart of the water

Heart of the air

Heart of the fire

Our heart

My heart

To the product of 500 years of struggles

To the enslaved

To the displaced

For the captives

For the war resisters

For the martyrs

For the maroons

For the creation of the world anew

For a free Palestine

Dearest Reader,

Palestine 1492 is a report back of what I see from 500 years of the struggle for life in words, maps, and images in the seven cardinal directions and in the spiral that is time.

In Maya geography, there is east, west, south, and north, and there is also earth and sky. In the middle there is you, a meeting place between the physical, spiritual, emotional, and mental that together make up the social, a meeting place between earth and sky.

East, the physical, begins this report back by orienting us in a corner of Mother Earth still holding a stubborn insistence on life: Palestine.

West, the spiritual, helps diagnose an illness of a wounded, imbalanced, and dangerous world imposed globally since 1492.

In the South, the emotional, Chiapas nourishes our courage from below in a time of World Wars and global rebellions.

In the North, the mental, we flip the world on its head but not to remain, to help plan our common escape.

Throughout, I share conclusions Palestinians, Zapatistas, Panthers, and jaguars have taught me along this journey: this world itself is unethical and changing it is difficult, even impossible. If after reading you also believe this to be true, may we dismantle this world together and help build the world anew from below and in common,

together and side by side,

Linda Quiquivix

⦂‖ B'AQTUN, ⊕ K'ATUN, ·‖ TUN, ·‖‖ WINAQ, ‖ Q'IJ, ⋮ TZ'I'
SEPTEMBER 19, 2024

OCCUPIED ABYA YALA

I also dedicate this book

to those who asked me not to write it

 EAST

Palestine from Below

Palestine Diary, 2010–2011	2
When the Rooftops Are Streets	48
To Die Standing	64
Panthers and Jaguars	90

 WEST

Palestine from Above

Speak of the Devil	104
Wounded Europe	112
Jerusalem Next	130
A World Cut In Two	136
The Last Crusade	150
Palestine Counter-Maps	180
The Wretched of the Empire	196

⫸ SOUTH

THE FOURTH WORLD WAR

The Third World War		204
Capital		216
Downward Assimilation		226
Globalization from Below		236
Dying in Order to Live		246

⫷ NORTH

A WORLD WHERE ALL THE WORLDS FIT

Above vs Below		272
Side by Side		290
Strategy and Tactics		302
The Common		314

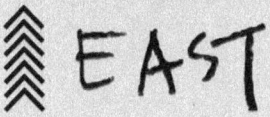 EAST

Palestine from Below

> "All of this stuff is not Palestinian history. It's the occupiers' history," says Jihad. "We have been occupied by Israel, then the Romans, then the Greeks, then the Turks, then the British, and then Israel."

> "So, what would you consider Palestinian artifacts?" I ask the Palestine from below.

> "Well, just little things nobody wants to pay for."

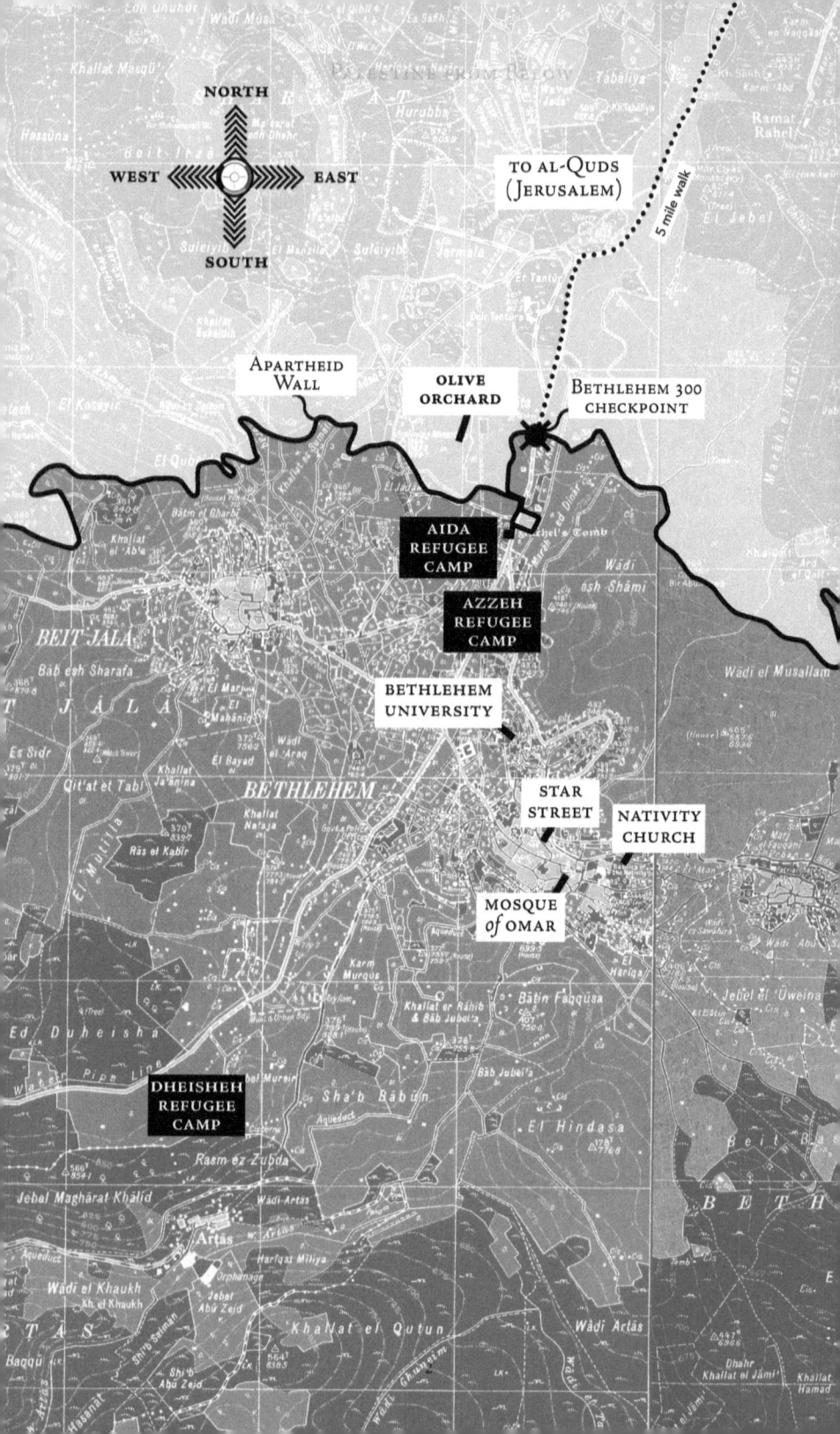

Palestine Diary, 2010–2011

·

There's a little store between the Nativity Church and the Mosque of Omar called the Shop of John the Baptist. There, I finally spot a postcard of Bethlehem to send back home. Most I've seen are of Jerusalem, most I've seen are of *al-Quds*.

"*Qadesh?*" I ask in my best Arabic. How much?

"One shekel."

The store is run by Yahya, whose name is pronounced John in English. He introduces me to his friends Mohammed and Josef. They ask if I am Arab, and I say no, I'm Guatemalan. "Do you know Guatemala?" I ask.

Mohammed nods. "It's very poor."

They ask about my name. "Quiquivix is an Indigenous last name," I share. "How do you say 'Indigenous' in Arabic?"

"What is that you mean?" they ask.

"You know, the Brown people who the White people kill, like in America."

"Ah," says Josef, "*al-Naas al-Asliyeen*, the First Peoples."

"Not here!" Yahya hugs Mohammad. "Look, he is my brother. He is Muslim. I am Christian. We are brothers!"

I nod, "We have a lot to learn from you."

"Yes, if everyone learns from Palestinians, there will be peace in the world," Yahya says and everyone agrees.

They ask what brings me to Palestine. "I'm researching Palestine's maps and borders," I reply. "And learning Arabic."

I hand Yahya one shekel for the Bethlehem postcard, say thank you, and start to head out.

"Come back," Yahya says. "You want to sit? We help you with your Arabic homework."

"Thank you, I will return *inshallah*," I reply. If God wills it. A phrase I've always known in Spanish to be pronounced as *ojalá*.

• •

My Arabic teacher Khalil is drawing on the board the long and winding road to get to *Ram Allah* ("God's Height") from where we are in *Beit Lahm* ("the House of Meat"), a little town pronounced in English as Bethlehem.

The State of Israel forbids most Palestinians in the West Bank from traveling on the straight road through the sacred city between Bethlehem and Ramallah, a city known as *al-Quds* ("the Holy One"), a city known in English as Jerusalem.

al-Quds is only five miles away from Bethlehem and then from there, only eight more miles to Ramallah.

"You have to go through *Wadi al-Nar*," the Valley of Fire, Khalil points to the irrational, winding journey on the board, "cross the Container Checkpoint..."

"I think I'm going to be sick..." I find myself saying out loud.

"QiQi, if you want to live with the people you have to be like the people," Khalil tells me, disappointed.

I am grateful for his reminder.

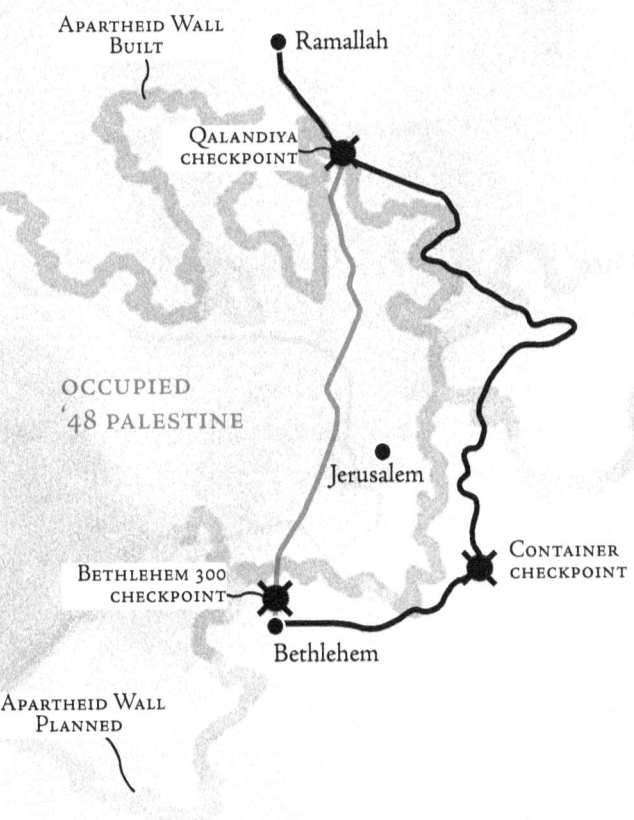

• • •

Crossing the border into the West Bank from Jordan means crossing the River Jordan near Jericho, on a bridge named after the soldier who captured Jerusalem for the British Empire in 1917 in a war the Empire called the "Peaceful Crusade." "Peaceful" is a word fascists often use to mean peaceful only for them. The State of Israel controls all of Palestine's entry points, and foreigners empathizing with Palestinians are often turned away. I wondered how it would go for me this time.

The soldier's first question, always their first question, "Where is your father's name from?" was to make sure I'm not Palestinian.

"Mexico," I answered. The soldier smiled at "Mexico." I was grateful I had thought to stop answering their questions with "Guatemala." The soldiers never know Guatemala, and they don't like it when you teach them.

The soldier seemed fine that I was going to Bethlehem along with Jerusalem to research "Holy Land maps of the nineteenth century made by American and other Western Christians." I had practiced that, how to describe my doctoral research to Them without once referencing Palestine or the colonial present and be denied entry.

"Do you know anyone in Jerusalem?" the soldier asked. I gave the name of my colleague's sister who lives in Malha. I had only met her once, at his wedding, but he told me to mention her and to pronounce Malha in a Hebrew accent.

Malha is an Israeli settlement southwest of al-Quds, built on the remains of a Palestinian village, al-Maliha, "the Salted One," who they say is named after the spring in the village that contains salty water.

Al-Maliha was ethnically cleansed of Palestinians by

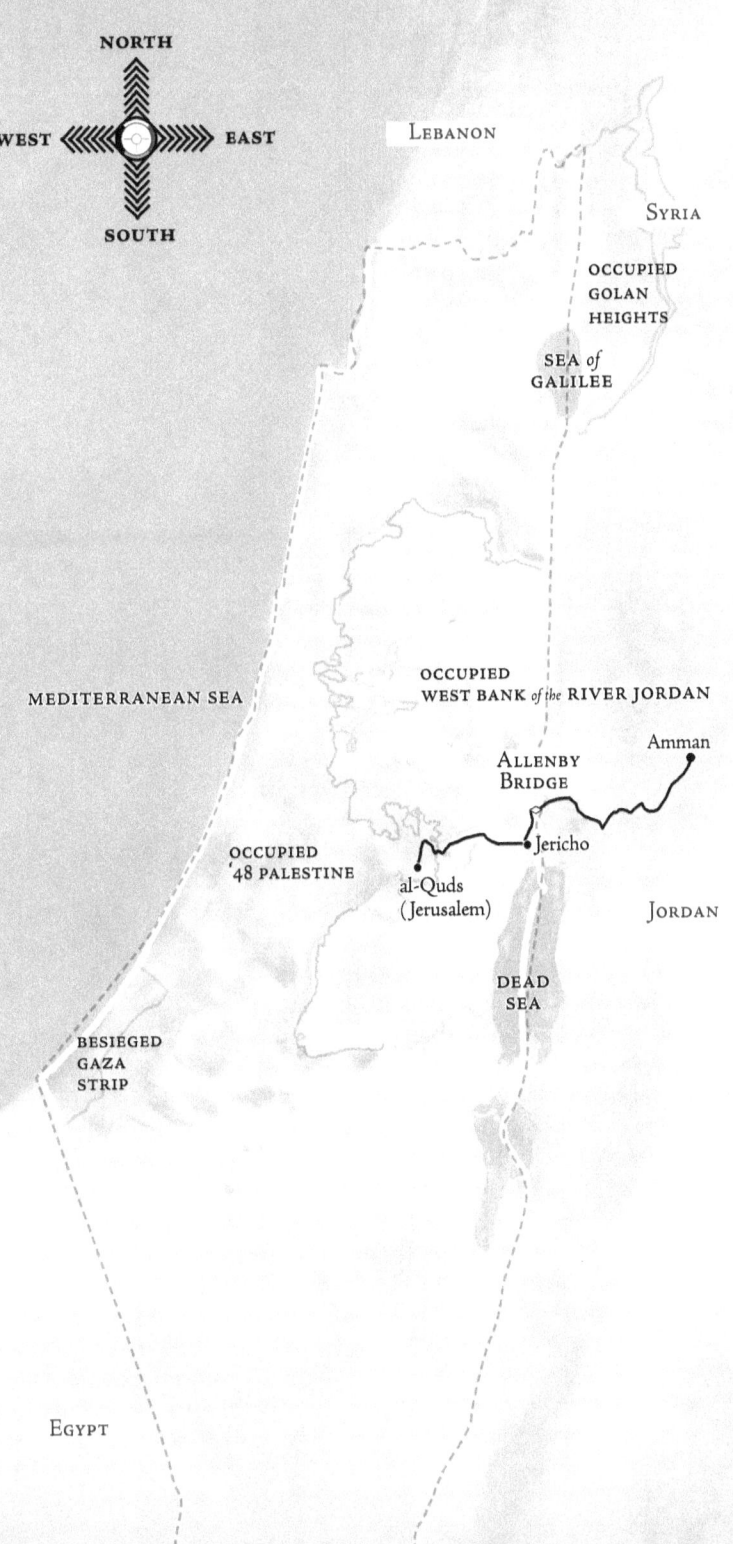

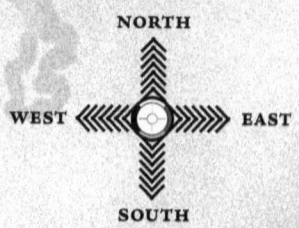

OCCUPIED WEST BANK

OCCUPIED '48 PALESTINE

Deir Yassin
Jerusalem
al-Maliha
Beit Jala
Bethlehem

~2 miles
~3 miles
~5 miles

AIDA, AZZEH & DEHEISHEH REFUGEE CAMPS

OCCUPIED WEST BANK

Zionist paramilitaries during the *Nakba*, the Catastrophe of 1948 that resulted in the creation of the State of Israel through the erasure of Palestine and the expulsion of Palestinians. After learning about the Zionist massacre of Palestinians in the neighboring village of Deir Yassin, the people of al-Maliha had fled for safety, assuming, as many Palestinians who did the same during the Nakba, they would return home once the war ended. The war hasn't yet ended. Both Deir Yassin and al-Maliha had signed non-aggression treaties with the Haganah, the Zionist paramilitary that became the regular military, the now badly named Israel Defense Forces (IDF). "Defense" is a word that fascists also like to misuse.

In its prior formation as the Haganah, the IDF signed treaties with Palestinian villages during the Nakba like they did with Deir Yassin, but a different Zionist paramilitary, the Irgun, massacred Deir Yassin villagers nevertheless and attacked al-Maliha a few days later, leading its people to flee, many toward Bethlehem and to neighboring *Beit Jala*, a name that means "Home of the Grass Carpet" in Aramaic, the language of Jesus of Nazareth.

Generations after the Nakba, many of al-Maliha's people are still living in Bethlehem and Beit Jala, still as refugees, many still in refugee camps, not giving up on the return home. There are three refugee camps in Bethlehem created by the Nakba: Aida, Azzeh, and Dheisheh. Some of al-Maliha's people live in Aida Camp. Some of their homes were taken over by Israeli settlers who still live in them today. Other homes in al-Maliha, the State of Israel completely destroyed.

Israel's Malha today is one of the more upscale colonies, with a soccer stadium, a hi-tech industrial park, and a zoo. They say its indoor shopping mall was the largest in the Middle East when it opened in 1993, before the days of Dubai.

Israel's Malha sounds like many places in the United States, meaning it's easy to shop and be distracted from the blood under one's feet.

Only a couple more questions and the soldier let me in. Palestine.

••••

When we were little, our grandmother used to get angry at the *telenovelas*, at the *musalsalaat* in Arabic, at the soap operas, whenever the good character died a tragic death and evil lived past the final episode, which happened a lot. "*Hierba mala nunca muere*," she'd announce to everyone in the room. Bad weeds never die. She would sometimes add, *Dios tarda pero nunca olvida*, God takes a while but never forgets.

Israel's Ariel Sharon is a *hierba mala que nunca muere*. An asshole that never dies. My mother, a sweet lady who cusses really nice would have nightly called him *un maldito desgraciado*, a fucking disgrace, all before the first commercial break.

In 1982, Ariel Sharon, Israel's war minister at the time, helped orchestrate the slaughter of thousands of defenseless Palestinian refugees living since the Nakba in Sabra and Shatila Refugee Camps up in Beirut. It was a collaboration between the fascists of Israel and the fascists of Lebanon.

The Sabra and Shatila Massacre revealed to many that Israel is the aggressor, not the victim, tarnishing its reputation. The backlash led Israel to conduct something to resemble an internal investigation, finding Ariel Sharon responsible, dismissing him as Defense Minister, demanding he never hold public office, then voting him in years later as Prime Minister.

The first time I had the honor of touching Palestine's soil and encountering her people was four and a half years prior. As

NORTH
WEST
EAST
SOUTH
LEBANON
SABRA & SHATILA
REFUGEE CAMPS
Beirut
SYRIA
OCCUPIED
GOLAN
HEIGHTS
Haifa
MEDITERRANEAN SEA
OCCUPIED
WEST BANK of the RIVER JORDAN
OCCUPIED '48
Jerusalem
BESIEGED
GAZA
STRIP
RAFAH
CROSSING
Beersheba
JORDAN
EGYPT
SINAI
PENINSULA
FROM CAIRO
Taba

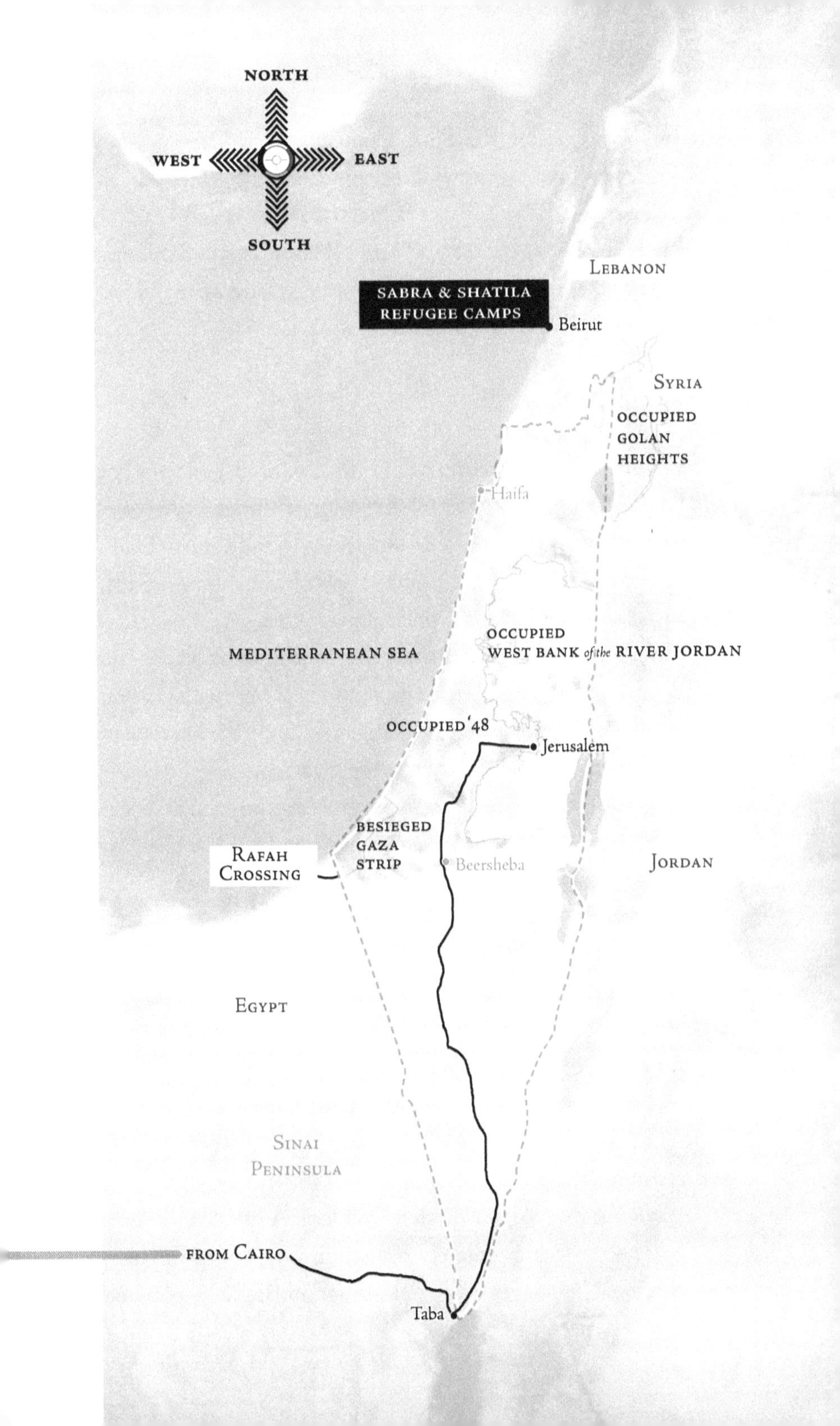

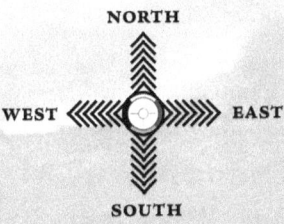

our bus was crossing the Sinai Peninsula from Cairo toward the border at Taba, we were all learning Ariel Sharon had just suffered a stroke. That day was January 4, 2006.

It is now the year 2010 and Ariel Sharon is still alive, in a coma being kept alive, in a permanent vegetative state. *Hierba mala nunca muere*, I hear my grandmother say.

I can't stop staring at two-year-old Little Nellie, listening to her *teta* Mary, her grandmother, tell her a lot of things in Arabic I cannot understand but Little Nellie seems to fully grasp. *I have been studying Arabic longer than you've been alive*, habibti, querida, darling, *and you understand a million times more.*

I am renting a room from Mary for three months before I go off on my own. Mary and three generations of her family live on Star Street, steps away from the Nativity Church, the Mosque of Omar, Manger Square, and three refugee camps.

They say conversation and repetition are important when learning a new language. I feel this must be true. Over the past two weeks I have engaged in the following conversation with Palestinians so much, I don't have to think before replying anymore:

"*Min ween inti?*" Where are you from?

"*Amreeka.*"

"*Inti arabiyeh?*" Are you Arab?

"*La, min asl guatemalee.*" No, I'm Guatemalan.

Right about here is where they pause, give a sweet chuckle, and gesture to their own face.

"*Ana bashbah arabiyeh?*" I offer. Do I look Arab?

They nod and immediately transition into fluent English, one of several languages every Palestinian in Bethlehem seems to know.

"You studying Arabic?" they ask.

"*Na'am.*" Yes, I reply.

"*Al-Arabi sa'eb.*" Arabic is difficult, they warn.

"*Na'am.*" Arabic is *sa'eb* indeed, I nod.

Saif, who runs a textbook store, tells me that his father, *Allah Yerhamo*, may God have mercy on his soul, used to say that you're not a man unless you know two languages.

I have encountered Saif, whose name means "sword", in my search for a first-grade textbook in Arabic, aiming to keep up with the six-year-olds of Palestine by the time I return home.

"And when you know four languages," Saif continues, "that's when you become a real man." He apologizes for the gendered life advice. It confirms my suspicions that no Palestinian is impressed that I speak two languages fluently, so I'm going to stop mentioning it. Who does impress Palestinians is the priest everyone keeps bringing up who knows no less than eleven languages—No! Twelve. There's a debate.

"Here, take this dictionary," Saif suggests as I'm about to leave. "*Al-Arabi sa'eb.*" Arabic is difficult.

⁘

On Star Street lives a little girl who speaks Arabic, English, and Spanish all in the same sentence. Her name is Suad, which means "happy." She's getting confused, her mother says and asks Suad to pick one language.

I introduce myself. Suad's mother, Maria, is from Chile and is Christian. Suad's father, Sameer, is from Bethlehem and is Muslim. They've been living in Bethlehem together for five years but will probably move to Chile in January or February. Sameer is having trouble finding paid work, and Chile might be easier.

It has the largest Palestinian community outside the Middle East, many of whom are from Bethlehem and Beit Jala.

Maria says she doesn't leave the house much and is happy to have company over. We are sitting on the roof of their building, and the view of Palestinian homes, church bells, and mosque minarets along the rolling hills is breathtaking. And then an Israeli settlement looking like a spaceship has landed on a mountain top breaks up the landscape.

Maria, Sameer, and Suad's house is the only Muslim house on all of Star Street, they share with me. Sameer excuses himself to pray, and I ask Maria what it's like in a mixed marriage where she's Christian and he's Muslim. She says Sameer is really good about it and doesn't mind at all that she and Suad go to church.

I think I learned how Suad speaks three different languages all in one sentence: her dad also speaks Arabic, English, and Spanish all in one sentence. I like listening to Sameer. He speaks about reality, about racism and genocide around the world and throughout history, to which Maria responds, "*Sameer, pareces al Che con esa platica de comunismo,*" Sameer, you sound like Che with all that communism talk.

"*No es cosa de comunismo,*" Sameer replies. It's nothing to do with communism. "*Es cosa de* imperialism, *khalas.*" It has to do with imperialism, period.

⋮

I've started watching the *musalsalaat* in Arabic with Mary and her daughter Lucy, who watch soap operas every night. The overacting helps me understand the Arabic sometimes, but the topics can be difficult.

The other night on the soap opera, for example, the working-class Suzanne sat her mother down for some shattering news about her relationship with the upper-class Ziad, whom she had been lying to about her socio-economic status. In that night's episode, Suzanne had just returned from the doctor and shared some news that caused her mother to faint. It's how I learned to say "I'm pregnant." *Ana haamel*, she had said. Suzanne then announced at the dinner table to the rest of the family that she was *haamel*. One brother erupted, chasing a screaming Suzanne into the kitchen, their mother and younger sister chasing after him. The other brother remained seated, stunned. Then, without saying one word, he got up, grabbed a butcher knife, and stuck it into Suzanne's stomach! "*Ya haraam!*" Mary exclaimed at the television. Something evil or sinful had just occurred. This had never happened before in my grandmother's *telenovelas*. The episode ended and we turned off the TV. It was time for bed.

The next morning, I sat with Mary in her little store. She sells eggs, candy, soda, milk, chips, bread, toiletries, alcohol, and cigarettes. A lot of cigarettes. The neighbors are the best part about the store. Sometimes they come inside, say their hellos, and end up sitting in one of the chairs Mary keeps out. They stay for 10 minutes, sometimes an hour. When they leave, someone else comes to take their place.

The delivery guy was among the first this morning. He dropped off some soap, took a seat, and lit up a cigarette. He and Mary casually discussed things, I didn't know what. Something to do with *masaari*, money. Then they started talking about me, which I could tell because they were looking at me. Where is she from? Is she Arab? Are you sure? She's studying Arabic? Arabic is difficult.

After the delivery guy left, two tourist police officers came in. They took a seat, lit up a cigarette, asked who I was, where

I was from, was I Arab, was I sure, Arabic is difficult.

After they left, a neighbor came into the store and sat down in a huff. She was fanning herself from both the heat outside and some sort of anxiety. The conversation started out politely. Good morning. How are you? I am fine thank you. Who is this? Where is she from? Is she Arab? Are you sure? Arabic isn't too hard. She's learning in Arabic script? Arabic is difficult.

Then the conversation's speed and volume steadily increased. The neighbor became upset, and I could only catch a few familiar vocabulary words: *banaat* (daughters), *masaari* (money), *majnoona* (crazy, in the feminine form).

Mary could only reply intermittently, "*La'! La'!*" No! No! every time the neighbor paused for air.

This continued back and forth for a long time without me understanding a word for a while until I heard *sharmouta*, whore. I knew that word. Nadeem back home had taught me that word.

"*Ya haraam! Ya haraam!*" shouted Mary, almost falling from her seat. It upset everybody present for several more minutes until the conversation died down and the neighbor said her goodbyes. It was 11:30AM, and it was time for lunch. Mary eats lunch at exactly 11:30AM in front of a *musalsal* downstairs, and at exactly 12:30 NOON she turns the television off and takes her *siesta*, her mid-day nap. It's a non-negotiable schedule.

As Mary and I walked downstairs, I asked in English so it was clear I wouldn't be imposing, "Is it okay if I sit with you in your store again?"

"*Na'am habibti, na'am!*" she exclaimed. Yes my darling, yes!

"*Beheb ajles hon… hada zay musalsalaat.*" I love sitting here… This is like the soap operas. "*Musalsalaat haqeeqiya!*" she laughed as we walked down the stairs. Real-life soap operas.

Walking in the door tonight, I thought I smelled *menudo*. Tripe.

It was Sunday, a special day. It was special because Mary's daughter, Nellie, after whom Little Nellie is named, had cooked *karshaat*, Arabic for tripe. I asked what the special occasion was, and Nellie replied that *karshaat* was the special occasion. The day becomes special because you have cooked karshaat.

I hadn't heard of karshaat before, so I emailed Fayyad back home, whose mother Suhaila introduced me to many of my first Palestinian dishes up near Jenin on an earlier trip, in their village named Rummaneh, which means "pomegranate." When Suhaila had me taste a regional spice called *za'atar*, it was at her kitchen table when I decided I would name my first born Za'atar. Za'atar is a mixture of sumac, sesame seeds, olive oil, and either thyme or oregano that there's a lively debate about and that I don't get involved in.

I looked up karshaat and found an article in *This Week in Palestine* revealing that karshaat is cooked once or twice a year and is a highly ceremonious, intimate meal, and that Palestinians trust only the "ritual cleanliness" of their mother's, sister's, or wife's kitchens. I showed the article to Nellie, and she confirmed it was correct. And that yes, there is no way she would ever eat karshaat at a restaurant, "It's disgusting!"

Nellie had taken five days preparing this meal. Her sister Lucy shared that one reason Palestinians don't usually invite foreigners to eat *karshaat* is because many react disgusted to eating tripe, an insulting response to such a special invitation. This explained why everyone in the living room had paused to look at me when I first walked in the house, awaiting my reaction to the scent of karshaat and looked relieved when

I responded that it smelled like home. I was humbled at the invitation to enjoy karshaat with the family that night: tripe stuffed with lamb that swims in a yogurt soup made out of *jmeed*, hardened yogurt.

After dinner I rushed back to my email and saw Fayyad had already replied, "That's awesome, I have not eaten karshaat in forever," he wrote. "You'll earn your stripes that way."

••••

Sitting with Mary in her store again, I learn she was born in Bethlehem and was six years old at the time of the Nakba of 1948. Her father, sister, and brother were killed in Israel's 1967 invasion of the West Bank, the so-called Six Day War. They were at Bethlehem University when Israel dropped a bomb right on top of them. Mary's brother was also injured with gashes on his arm and leg. She was at home.

I ask Mary how her husband died. The Israelis killed him, right here in this house, she said. They came looking for their sons, teenagers during the First Intifada. Her husband went upstairs to answer the door when the soldiers buzzed. They beat him fatally on the head. He was in the hospital 21 days before he died. The year was 1990. The day was June 18.

Mary shows me a picture of her father. It is a wallet-sized black-and-white photograph with the ridges around the edges. He wore a light suit, a patterned tie, and a dark sweater vest. He had glasses, and his hair was combed back with few gray strands as highlights. Mary looks just like him.

Mary also points to a photograph of her husband. It is one I see every day, a color photo that hangs above the store register.

I had an interview this morning for a volunteer position in Aida Camp's Lajee Center. Everything I've heard about Lajee so far, I like. They don't work with any of the political parties, and I don't either. Lajee is looking for someone to host an art class with the kids. I only know a little Arabic, and Yousuf suggests that little kids are great to practice with. They love to teach adults, and when you mess up, instead of scold you they are eager to help.

I keep hearing the voice of Mayssun from Shatila Camp: *The camp isn't a zoo. Don't be a foreigner asshole.* Lajee seems to know this well. They sent another foreigner to size me up before I interacted with anyone else. Rich is a British photographer who has been working with Lajee for years. He didn't seem thrilled to meet me and even seemed suspicious of me at first, which makes be think we're going to get along.

Rich recently came out with a book about Aida Camp's stories of struggle. At the end of my interview, he let me borrow his only copy. I promised to return it that evening at his book talk at the Peace Center in Manger Square.

Rich is different from other foreigners here. At his talk, he made something clear to everyone present: his book is made up of stories by Palestinian refugees about life as refugees, these aren't "Richard's adventures in Palestine." When during the Question & Answer period someone asked about his plans for the future and how his work is coming along, he answered that he wasn't there to talk about his personal life, but wanted to discuss Israeli apartheid, the failure of the international elites, and the inspiring resistance of the Palestinians.

As far as his plans for the future, he hopes to take Palestinians on a permanent trip back to Haifa and Jerusalem.

Palestine from Below

They say in Islam, it is forbidden to draw the human form so as to not contribute to idolatry. I am nervous about leading an art class. All I've ever known to draw is the human form. All I've mostly drawn is Tupac Shakur. At the entrance of Aida Camp's Lajee Center, there's a life-size charcoal sketch of Palestinian poet Mahmoud Darwish, who makes me feel it will be alright. I consult with Mohammed about my limitations and he nods about the human form and Islamic art, but says it's not a problem, there's nothing I can't teach the kids.

This was nice to hear, and my first day went well, and it's true about little kids eager to help me with my Arabic. There were a couple of the older girls who misbehaved and reminded me of myself when I was their age and misbehaved with my mother. My Palestinian *cholitas*, the homegirls of the group, who I'm pretty sure were making fun of me for not knowing Arabic.

Todo se paga en esta vida, I heard my mother say. Everything is paid back in this life.

Tupac Amaru Shakur
(1971–1996)
Presente

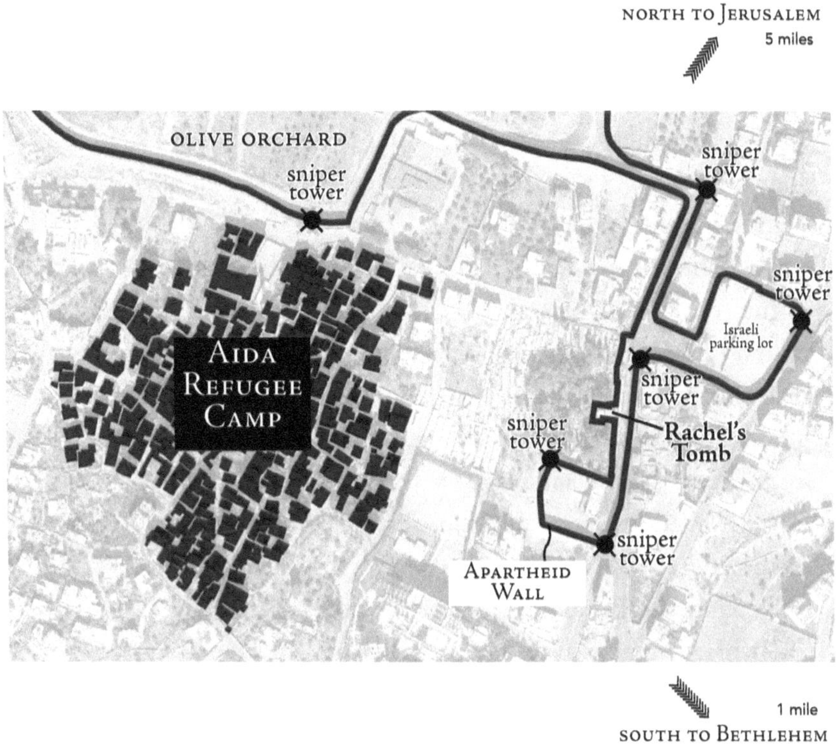

Mohammed suggests that I not mention to anyone that I'm working at the Camp. He knows of instances where the *jaysh*, the IDF, has come into the camps and deported the foreigners, taking them straight to Ben Gurion Airport and out of the country.

Rich is less worried. He says if the *jaysh* comes, to just go about my business. Tell them I'm helping in a class, that I'm American. *Khalas.* That's it.

When I had first asked Rich what to do if the soldiers came, he had exclaimed, "RUN FOR YOUR LIFE!" We laughed, but there are bullet holes on Lajee's front door and on the wall of the balcony where we were sitting, one right above Rich's head. There are sniper towers surrounding the Camp; the Apartheid Wall is adjacent on two sides. Rich says they haven't shot from there in a couple of years. Now they just come in on night raids and arrest people.

Tonight, the *jaysh* are out in Rachel's Tomb, a Biblical site in the cemetery right next to Aida Camp and now an Israeli military base. The *jaysh* are on the roof of what used to be a Palestinian apartment building before Israel took it over. It's the highest building in the area and serves as a lookout point for them. Rich thinks it may be a diplomatic meeting going on.

On Israel's orders, the Palestinian *jaysh*, the Palestinian Authority (PA), are inside the Camp right now. When I first walked into Aida, I almost froze, thinking it was the Israelis.

Rich says that two years ago, people in the Camp started saying "Israeli *jaysh*" instead of just "*jaysh*" because it used to be assumed which *jaysh* everyone was talking about. But not anymore.

Mussa points out the Palestinian *jaysh* will shoot at Palestinians more quickly than the Israeli *jaysh*.

⋮

In Arabic class tonight, Khalil asks if I want to know how to say anything in particular. I have been preparing a list. How do you say, "Black people continue to suffer in America under Barack Obama," and how do you say, "functionary of the white-supremacist society."

The word for functionary is the same as employee: *muwazzaf*, and the supremacist is *al-afdhalia*, which has a shared root with "prefer." Capitalism is *rasmaliya* which is two words: *ras + mali* (head, or chief + money).

Khalil asks who is more racist (*'unsoori*): the USA or France. He argues France, I argue the USA. He knows France. I know the USA. After exchanging notes, we decide in the end it's a tie. From this debate, I learn Khalil likes Malcolm X.

Khalil also teaches me how to talk about maps. The map of historical Palestine is *Falestin al-Tarikhiya*. The maps of just the West Bank and Gaza are *Falestin al-Siyasiya*, political Palestine, but that's not the true Palestine, he says, just the political one.

The true Palestine is the *Falestin al-Tarikhiya* that exists in the hearts and minds of all Palestinians.

⁞

Nellie this morning tells me about her friend living in the USA who feels very lonely. People don't know each other in the USA, her friend has accurately described. Everyone keeps to themselves. Nellie's friend has also been sharing about the foreclosure crisis and how people are losing their homes, often without anyone to take them in.

"Here," Nellie says about Palestine, "If you're hungry, you go to your neighbors for some bread."

I nod. I share with Nellie that some people believe Palestine should become more like the USA.

"*Wala marra!*" she exclaims. It's how I learned and won't ever forget how to say "Never!" in Arabic. Literally, "Not even once!"

Nellie shares more about her mother's family in the 1967 invasion. She says the bomb dropped on Bethlehem University was the first bomb of the war. She also had a cousin killed in the First Intifada by a sniper while leaving mass at the Nativity

Church. He was holding a two-year-old and dropped the baby, falling as if he was drunk. One bullet. She wants to show me where he was shot from, and I'm not going to believe it. It was from a hilltop, really far away.

Nellie's friends often ask why she doesn't leave Palestine, as life is so difficult here. She scoffs at the thought. "*Wala marra!* I will die in Palestine," she exclaims. They can't understand how Nellie's not interested in making money elsewhere.

Nellie asks about my mom and dad, and I tell her the story. She is curious what my mom did after the divorce. "We moved in with my grandmother," I reply.

"You are like Arab," she says. She gets up to wash her coffee cup in the sink, then turns to me to say, "It warms my heart, the story of your mother."

I have just learned that Mahmoud, who is getting to know me as a regular at the Square Café in Manger Square, where they have the good Wi-Fi, also likes Malcolm X. When he was imprisoned in Israel's dungeons for two-and-a-half years, he read the *Autobiography* in Arabic and cried, he says. Other Palestinian men share with me about times when they've cried. They share it without shame, just as a matter of fact. They make me believe it's true what they say about revolution, that love is its defining characteristic.

Mahmoud is Muslim, and Khalil is Muslim, and Malcolm X was Muslim, el-Hajj Malik el-Shabazz. Wondering if Christians also know of him, I ask Nellie. She doesn't know. But she does know who Che Guevara is. Everybody knows who Che Guevara is. His face and name are graffitied everywhere in

Palestine. Here there are even children named Guevara.

Nellie chuckled when I first mentioned Che. She said that Lucy used to have a picture of him in her bedroom in a frame. One day during the First Intifada, Mary flew into a rage, took it down, and slammed it to break it. "Her husband had just been killed, her two sons were in jail…" Nellie explained. Revolution may be defined by love, but revolution is not romantic.

Incredibly, that same night on the *musalsal* before bed, the character of a young man whose rich father had abandoned him was wearing a Che Guevara sweater and had a Che Guevara picture on the wall. I cautiously asked Mary, "Does everyone here like Che Guevara?" She replied right away, "*Na'am, na'am!*" Yes, yes! laughing and nodding. And that was all she had to say about that.

Older Palestinian Gentleman, OPG, walks straight into the Square Café to ask one of the servers, Khalil, something about Arafat and Ramallah. OPG then turns my way and asks in fluent English, "You know Arafat died today?" The day is November 11, 2010. Yasser Arafat was the President of the Palestinian Authority.

"How many years ago," I ask. "Five? Six?"

"I don't know, I don't care, I never liked him." He looks over his shoulder and whispers, "I don't like any authority. None!"

He then peers into the kitchen searching for Khader, who everybody knows likes Arafat. The coast is clear.

OPG pulls up a seat at my table, lights a cigarette, and smoothly we move into shit-talking authoritarian regimes together, and not just some of them but about all of them, and how they need to go.

"It's a dream!" he exclaims. He then reveals that when he was younger in the 1970s, he and his friends had pulled out a world map. They were going to move to an island and build themselves a country, inviting people from everywhere, a couple from France, a couple from here, a couple from there, very Noah's Ark. But as they looked at the map for an island to move to, it occurred to them it was impossible.

"No island is truly an island?" I ask, recently defeated.

"Exactly," he says. Not even Cuba is an island, we agree. No place will the empire leave you alone. Might as well fight where you are, where you know best, and with your people.

I ask OPG why he and his friend didn't pick just Palestinians for their island home. He frowns, almost dropping his cigarette. He opens both hands, signaling the obvious. "Because we are all human." Now he gets up to leave. He says he has said too much, there are too many spies, and I might turn him into the Palestinian Authority.

Yalla bye!

Some of the mothers in Aida Camp have put together a Palestinian cooking class to help raise some money for expenses. Everyone in the group has a family member with a disability, and before each class they collectively decide what to do with the money.

One time, they used it to take the children to a swimming pool in *al-Khalil*, a city pronounced Hebron in English, which means "friend of God," so named after Abraham who is believed to be entombed there alongside his family at the *al-Haram al-Ibrahimi*, site of the Ibrahimi Mosque Massacre of 1994, where a Zionist from Brooklyn opened fire on praying Muslims, killing 29, many as young as 12 years old.

Abraham is the shared ancestor of all three Abrahamic faiths: Judaism, Christianity, and Islam. The empires of the West often like to leave out the Islam. The empires of the West used to also like to leave out the Judaism part in this shared kinship for a long time until the Zionist project made Judaism useful for empire, rather than fight against it. When the wretched of the earth become the wretched of the empire.

On this occasion, the mothers in Aida Refugee Camp will use the money to buy the children some clothes.

The class costs 60 shekels (about USD$20) each person, and includes a cooking lesson, the food, nice conversation, and a tour of the Camp. There are seven of us foreigners, plus a translator. Four have come down to Bethlehem from Ramallah. I don't ask if they took Wadi al-Nar.

On this occasion, we are not getting to learn much cooking, but we are getting to eat well. They showed us the beginnings of things, but then shooed us into the living room and out of the kitchen. It was probably for the best. The food is delicious. The dessert is sweet semolina cake called basbussa, *"bas"* and *"bossa"* meaning "just" and "a kiss," just a kiss. They serve us rice with thin pasta, a soup of spinach and chickpeas, and fried chicken.

One of the couples in our class is from Barcelona. I ask the husband, who is wearing a Barcelona soccer jersey, if his shirt gets him a lot of love in Palestine. "Yes!" he exclaims. Our translator, Mustafa, guesses that about 80% of Palestinians are Barcelona fans and thinks it has something to do with Barcelona being occupied, too. This upsets a woman from Brazil who says, "We have a great soccer team, and we were colonized too! All

the Native people were killed…"

While at the table, we keep being asked if any of us have children. "*Fil mustaqbal*," in the future, I answer, "*inshallah.*" One couple's response is that they just got married and it's too soon. Another couple says that maybe they will never have children. One woman announces she doesn't want any children because there are too many people in this world and there's not enough food. This almost halts the conversation into awkward silence. Palestinians have a lot of children.

"In Guatemala do they have a lot of children?" Mustafa asks.

"Yes, of course. It's not a problem," I answer.

One of the mothers says something Mustafa is eager to translate. "She says she has a casserole dish that can feed seventy."

The kids in our art class let me know right away they dislike drawing with charcoal. It's not colorful enough. Last week I picked up the colored kind and have brought it to Aida Camp. The kids love it. I am thrilled the kids love it. They remark it is similar to *tabaashir*, chalk, and ask me where I got it and how much it cost. I tell them I got it in al-Quds, where each of the 15 pieces cost 6 shekels (USD$1.50) for a grand total of 90 shekels (over USD$22). They are stunned. "You can get 10 pieces of tabaashir for 1 shekel!" they exclaim. Colored and everything. They do the math together. I could have gotten 900 pieces of tabaashir with 90 shekels. They think maybe I got ripped off because I'm a foreigner.

After class they take me by the hand and walk me to a little store in the Camp that sells the 10 pieces of colored tabaashir for 1 shekel. Ammo Mohammad carries tabaashir in his store. He sits blocking the door and I can't really see inside, but one of the kids squeezes through and brings out the tabaashir.

Ammo Mohammad is blessed to be a very old man with not a lot of teeth who loves to laugh and has energy for a lot of conversation. His English is really good, which I'm curious about but don't ask. He wants to know about me, am I married, kids, why isn't my husband here, to which the kids grab my hand and say, "Let's go QiQi!" And it's *yalla* bye.

The *tabaashir* from Ammo Mohammad is a hit. We are drawing together on one big piece of paper, starting from the center out, all abstract shapes. While in shape-drawing mode I put two triangles together accidentally drawing what looks like a Star of David. Safa' points out that is the *jaysh*'s symbol and shows me how to draw a five-pointed star instead. I apologize and thank her for that correction.

Today is Safa's brother's birthday, whose name is Anis. He is turning nine, and I draw him a birthday cake to celebrate the occasion and embrace it with his name in my best Arabic script.

The kids seem to really like this project and become protective of it when little 3-year-old Rand starts to draw on it like a 3-year-old would want to draw on it. They erase her contributions and ban her from the drawing, giving her a piece of paper to draw on instead. This makes her sad, so I put her on my lap and draw for her a Sponge Bob Square Pants waving the Palestinian flag, but there is no black charcoal around anymore, so I can't color it in fully. I start to gift it to her, and she points out it's not yet finished, the flag needs black on the top. I take my orders, successfully locating a black colored pencil.

Rachelle, a Mennonite from Canada also living in Bethlehem, stops by Lajee. We have become close friends since meeting a few months ago, each suspicious of the other at first. She is not with the Mennonites in the Yucatán deforesting the land. Also, she knows she's a settler in Canada and needs to make right historical wrongs.[1] It's nice to have someone to constantly ask questions about Christianity where I don't feel dumb and she doesn't feel insulted. In my research on the "Political Mapping of Palestine," I am having to read the Bible, which may seem obvious now, but I first learned about Palestine through secular writings, so reading the Book of Joshua hadn't been on my list.

Rachelle has stopped by Aida today to purchase some of Lajee Center's children's books, drawn and photographed by the Camp's children. She's going to send the books home to help with the de-indoctrination of some family and friends.

I head to the sink to wash the chalk and hear Mohammad and Lajee's director, Salah, speaking excitedly in the audio/visual room about Barcelona beating the crap out of Madrid last night, 5-0. Both Mohammed and Salah are big Barcelona fans and have been teasing the Madrid fans on the streets, waving at them with five fingers extended, "Hiiiii."

Mohammad guesses that about 70% of Palestinians love Barcelona, and the other 30% love Madrid. Rachelle says it's what's led her to say she's a Barcelona fan: whenever any kid asks, she has a higher probability of being right. I ask

---

1. See Elaine Enns and Ched Myers, *Healing Haunted Histories: A Settler Discipleship of Decolonization* (Cascade Books, 2021)

Mohammad what explains the love for Barcelona, and he says the same thing Mustafa said the other day. Catalonia, a region between France and Spain, holds Barcelona as its major city. "Catalonia is occupied by Spain and there is no place in the world that loves Palestinians more than Catalonia," Mohammad ensures.

"More than Ireland?" I ask, surprised. He thinks about it and then replies, "They're about even, actually."

•

It is February 2011, and day 12 of the Tahrir Square commune, the Egyptian people's uprising and hopeful overthrow of their Zionist dictator, Hosni Mubarak. I am eager to hear my neighbors' thoughts, but they don't seem to want to talk about it. At least not to me. From these 12 days of scanning news and social media on my computer, my eyes are beginning to hurt.

There were solidarity protests for Egypt in Ramallah, Bethlehem, Jerusalem, and Nazareth. About 2,000 people were in Ramallah. There is a video circulating of a guy getting roughed up and arrested by the Palestinian Authority's thugs. The Palestinian Authority, the PA, is a policing body made up of Palestinians that polices other Palestinians on behalf of Israel.

The PA was established with the badly named "peace process" that took place in Oslo, the capital of Norway. The PA is considered by many on the ground to be a collaborationist regime. The difficulty is the PA is heavily intertwined in the social fabric of the West Bank in terms of salaries and special privileges. The PA is fully allied with the Mubarak regime in Egypt and the surrounding regimes who are also being threatened with uprisings right now since the uprisings in Tunisia two months ago.

The PA has been known to regularly crush the protests in the West Bank supporting the resistance in Gaza, and now they've expanded their efforts to crush the protests supporting the Egyptian uprising.

I haven't heard news of the numbers in solidarity with Egypt coming from Nazareth or Jerusalem. Bethlehem's protest was in Manger Square. About twenty people showed up, almost all men, most with leather jackets and bellies that looked well-fed. The protest was mostly security. The demonstration had some Palestinian flags and later Egyptian flags. It lasted for about five minutes and *khalas*, that was it.

Rich was there photographing and gave up. He hates protests, he says. Most of the time they consist of journalists and Israelis, very few Palestinians. Generally, the protests are very small, but the journalists always get close-up shots making it look like there were a lot of people all around.

I gave up, too. I saw a few men arguing about what was going to be said at the protest, but I couldn't understand. There were several people watching, keeping their distance all around the perimeter of the Square, but they didn't join. Just watched.

I invited Rich for a coffee. He says everyone he's been around is thrilled about the Egyptian revolution, a very different experience than I've been having. I ask how Aida Camp reacted to the Palestine Papers, the leaked meeting notes on the corrupt Oslo "peace process." He says at first they thought they were fake and blamed Al Jazeera for publishing them, but by the third day they accepted they weren't false. Time will tell what comes out of this realization.

Most of the *shabaab* in the camp, most of the youth in

the camp, are Fatah party youth, but they make a distinction between Fatah and Mahmoud Abbas, the PA, and Salam Fayyad, who are part of Fatah. They hate all of them but still love Fatah. Mainly for what it used to be.

-
-

Rachelle phoned this morning about a Unity Tent at Manger Square, the March 15 Movement. Near the Mosque of Omar is standing an olive-green tent with Hebrew writing on it. The tent looks like a refugee tent from old photographs. It has come from Dheisheh Camp, but nobody is sure if it's from Nakba times. It doesn't look old enough. About a dozen Palestinian youth are seated inside speaking to five tourists about the occupation.

A German young lady invites me inside and tells me about the March 15 Movement. The *shabaab*, the youth, have been spending the night in the tent. She and her sister are helping by pairing up with a Palestinian to recruit tourists from the Nativity Church to come inside the tent and listen to the demonstrators. "If it's just a Palestinian who asks, the tourists probably won't come," she says.

There is a woman inside, a Palestinian Citizen of Israel, who just held a teach-in with Palestinian school children, describing the struggles of the Palestinians inside the part of Palestine Israel has been occupying since 1948, describing the struggles of the Palestinians "inside '48." Everyone reports that the children sat listening intently to her the entire time.

They also report that because Palestinians in '48 speak fluent Hebrew in addition to fluent Arabic, she has translated the Hebrew writing on the tent: it is instructions on how to assemble the tent. Everyone laughs with a shared nervousness, with a shared relief. We don't say much beyond that.

The Star of David and the Hebrew language trigger a lot of nervousness, even with me. I have to keep checking in with myself. It is what the soldiers wear, it is what the soldiers speak. I'm still trying to figure out how to talk about it. So far, it helps to learn it wasn't always that way. For centuries, there existed Jewish people in Palestine who spoke Arabic until the creation of the State of Israel in 1948, which demands that no Jew can be a Palestinian and that to be a Jew is to be an Israeli.[2]

Saoud, who speaks perfect English, is conducting a teach-in as I walk in. He shares about ending the division between Hamas and Fatah, and the possibility of a leaderless movement. I ask if he's ever heard of the Zapatistas in Mexico. He says yes, he participated in a workshop a couple of years ago in Dheisheh Camp where American Indians came to connect anti-colonial struggles. From them, he learned about the Zapatistas. I tell him about the Zapatistas' Festival of Dignified Rage during Israel's war on Gaza two years ago, Operation Cast Lead, and how everyone kept bringing up the Palestinian struggle every day, and that the Zapatistas made a strong statement for Gaza. His face lights up. We coordinate for a teach-in on the Zapatistas.

I am curious about the larger March 15 Movement's demands to dissolve the Oslo Accords and the PA. Saoud says he wasn't speaking for everyone, and it's not demanded as a group right now in the Manger Square sit-in, but he personally would like to see Oslo dissolved.

We say goodbye for now, and I head to Lajee Center and find Rich inside. He's working on a new book project on Boycott,

---

2. Ilan Halevi, *A History of the Jews: Ancient and Modern* (Zed Books, 1987)

Divestment, and Sanctions, BDS, and invites me tomorrow to a film screening in the Camp on South Africa's anti-apartheid struggle. They're having the director come and speak.

I report to Rich that I just returned from Egypt to stamp out my passport and stamp back in, and have brought back a gift for Aida Camp, *The Autobiography of Malcolm X* in Arabic. He thinks it's fantastic and we discuss showing the film to the *shabaab* and having discussion on the Black revolutionary movements inside the USA.

Mohammad walks in, upset about the March 15 Movement. It has been co-opted by the PA and Fatah, he reports. Also, why are people demonstrating in Manger Square? What's needed is a demonstration against the occupation, not against God. The real protesters today didn't go to Manger Square but headed to the checkpoint to throw rocks, he says. What's really needed is 20,000 people to storm Qalandiya Checkpoint.

Rich replies that the sit-in is not all that useless. People are there talking about ideas and making their presence known. Even though protests are limited, they are still not a total waste. There is no movement in Palestine right now and it needs to begin somehow. How are we going to get 20,000 to storm Qalandiya overnight? Egypt was 30 years in the making.

As the conversation winds down, I ask Mohammad if we can look at the aerial photograph of Aida we were able to get. He spends some time getting oriented. "I've never looked at Aida like this," he says. "Well, only when I was in jail and the Israelis asked me to point out my house."

He points out the camp's seven different neighborhoods and the small squares kids now play soccer in since the Wall came up and divided the camp from the olive orchard.

The land where the Intercontinental Hotel is today also used to be the camp's as a space of play. The Intercontinental bought the land and built additional wings in the back, as well as a swimming pool, erecting its own wall, also separating itself while also taking land. This took place during 1996 or 1997, when Aida still had the olive orchard until Israel's Apartheid Wall took that, too.

Mohammad likes the idea of mapping the camp's everyday life and stares at the photograph for a while before he has to run. He is being asked to give an impromptu tour of Aida to a bus full of tourists.

I return to the Unity Tent in Manger Square. It is 6PM by now, and the sun is going down. I see OPG right away and ask what he thinks about the sit-in. He says he thinks it's great.

"Any *u'malaa'?*" I ask. Any spies?

"No, it's good!" He laughs.

He introduces me to a young man named N who gives a Palestine for beginners teach-in. I listen quietly, taking note that the most interesting analyses he is keeping to himself. When I think we are more comfortable with each other, I ask what he thinks about the March 15 Movement's demands that Oslo be dissolved.

He replies, "Well, earlier this week in Ramallah a 15-year-old boy said out loud in the protests 'Let's end Oslo!' and the police arrested him for that."

"Ah, I won't ask you anymore what you think then," I smile and he laughs.

He mentions that a couple of people had been on a hunger strike, but that ended today when Mahmoud Abbas visited Ismail Haniyeh in Gaza.

He also reports that Afteem and the other falafel shop in Manger Square are handing out free food to everyone at the sit-in, without even a request from the protesters.

Night falls. As I leave Manger Square and head home, I

notice a man has been following me.

•
• •

There was a bombing in the West Jerusalem Israeli bus station that killed a middle-aged Israeli woman.

The corporate press is reporting it has "destroyed years of relative calm" in Jerusalem, by which they mean "calm" only for the Israelis.

Israel's daily violence in Jerusalem's Palestinian neighborhoods of Sheikh Jarrah, Silwan, and Shuafat Refugee Camp, the dispossession, brutalization, arrests, house demolitions, and assassinations of Palestinians in Jerusalem are not mentioned as destroying the calm.

Salaam Fayyad, Mahmoud Abbas, the United States, the United Nations, and European Union quickly condemned the bombing in Jerusalem.

From Salaam Fayyad, Mahmoud Abbas, the United States, the United Nations, and the European Union, no condemnations had come the day before, when Israel killed eight people in Gaza.

•
• • •

Today, I am accompanying Nidal north to Jenin Refugee Camp. Jenin is interested in learning more about the Aida mapping project and hopes to do a mapping workshop, too.

Nidal goes to Jenin every Saturday to conduct a democracy

workshop with youth at one of the women's organizations called "Not to Forget." He says he's using one of Naji Al-'Ali's cartoons to talk about individualism and community.

Naji Al-'Ali was a political cartoonist and creator of Handala, the 10-year-old refugee boy who keeps his back turned to the world and his arms behind him refusing handouts, demanding nothing less than the return to Palestine.

Al-'Ali's cartoons were critical of the collaborationist Arab regimes in addition to the regimes of Israel and the West, for which he was gunned down in London in 1987 with suspicion falling on Israel, Palestinian agents acting on behalf of Israel, and Palestinian agents acting on behalf of the Arab regimes.

Nidal recently held this workshop at Lajee Center, leading Aida's youth to storm Salah's office, demanding more democracy at Lajee, more participation in the decision-making processes. "Salah wasn't impressed," Nidal smiled about his friend.

I met up with Nidal at 8AM at the main station so we could take a *servis* to Ramallah, a seven-passenger transport van that leaves as soon as all seven seats are filled. From there, we switch to a different *servis* to Jenin. We need to be in Jenin by noon, and the ride is about three hours. We easily make it through Wadi Al-Nar, arrive in Ramallah, and I marvel that my motion sickness never came. Maybe because we were talking the whole time.

Nidal invites me to eat falafel right as we land in Ramallah. He always eats falafel on such trips, he says, it holds the stomach together, so you don't throw up.

On the third floor of the bus station, as we're eating our

falafel, Nidal points down to the vegetable market. I peer over and witness garlic, cucumbers, strawberries, onions, cauliflower arranged neatly in their stands. Most of the vegetables come from Jericho and Jenin, he says, and by noon the market is so packed, you can't see the ground.

The road to Jenin is very green right now. It is Springtime and it's been raining a lot, some parts are even reminding me of Guatemala where it rains a lot.

On the road to Nablus from Ramallah, Nidal points to where there used to be a checkpoint. It's now been removed because a shepherd in the hills of Silwad would shoot at the soldiers, picking them off like a sniper. He killed 11 of them at the checkpoint, one by one, and the official Zionist militia had no idea who was shooting at them the whole time. The shepherd was a great shot, using an old rifle from the Second World War, whose ammunition puzzled the Zionists. They were convinced it had to be a European shooting at them. Each time after he was done taking his shot, the shepherd would hide the rifle in the fields and walk away to tend his flock. His entire operation was, in the end, successful, leading Israel to fully dismantle the checkpoint, and nobody ever found out. Then one day the shepherd told the story to some friends, and one of them turned out to be a collaborator. The shepherd was caught and arrested and has become a legend since. The legend of the Silwad Sniper.

We pass Nablus and arrive in Jenin early and head to the vegetable market. Nidal's mother needs a vegetable called 'akub, expensive in Bethlehem like the price of meat, but cheaper in Jenin since it grows in nearby Nablus. The vegetable market had no 'akub for it was the end of the season. But Nidal asked around and found a man who had some in the back, then he haggled over the price, a lot. People started crowding to see the 'akub. There was still 'akub!

So today I met 'akub, who is quite punk with thorns and stems and leaves that shoot out in different directions, and little heads that look like small artichokes. In the end, Nidal was able to get 7 kilos for 120 shekels.

We arrive at Jenin Camp and Nidal introduces me. I describe to the youth and coordinators the Aida Camp mapping project, and the coordinator, Mostahm Salameh, seems to love it. I show her the aerial photograph of Aida, and Mostahm recognizes it right away, "This is the map the Israelis use to intimidate us when we come in for interrogation."

Mostahm is Belgian and Palestinian and speaks French, Arabic, and English. We brainstorm the different maps that could be made of Jenin Camp. For example, the stories of the massacre, the rebuilding of the camp after the roads were made wide enough for tanks to fit in... She loves the project and wants to learn the software. In the meantime, she's going to find out if the United Nations Relief and Works Agency for Palestine Refugees (UNRWA) or the camp's popular committee have any existing maps or aerial photography we can work from.

On our way back to Bethlehem, Nidal tells me there are secret alleys you can't see from above in the aerial photograph, and he's eager to start mapping it. He also shares the story of when the Israelis shot him from a helicopter, right before Israel's siege on the Church of the Nativity in 2002. Nidal was injured in his leg and had to go through a hellish experience to get to a hospital with curfews and checkpoints. He had to hide out in other peoples' homes in the camp for over 30 days until the Israelis left.

I ask Nidal about his memories of when Israel built the Apartheid Wall. It was also during Israel's siege on the Nativity Church. Everyone thought the Israelis were just plowing land for a road for their tanks, but then they started digging a trench. It was after Israel had already started that Israel officially announced its plans. That's how the Apartheid Wall began, how the olive orchard was taken from Aida Camp, and how restricting Palestinian access to Jerusalem became easier for Israel.

We arrive in Ramallah and jump into a Bethlehem *servis*. As we get close to a big Israeli settlement, Ma'ale Adumim, Nidal points out the pine trees, which Israel plants on top of the destroyed villages. Pine trees grow quickly and cover the crime scene faster than other trees. They are planted where they're not meant to be, like on Mount Carmel where they flared up last year when an Israeli kid's argeela coal sparked the Haifa fire.

"At least they didn't steal the olive tree from you," I say.

"What do you mean they didn't steal the olive tree," he replies, "hold on just a moment."

We pass Ma'ale Adumim at a highway roundabout, and Nidal points to the massive olive tree in the middle. "When they built the Wall, they took that tree from Aida Camp," he says. A tree that used to be part of an orchard now stands alone, encircled on all sides by moving vehicles, in the middle of a circle of colored gravel. It taunts every Palestinian who has to pass it about what Israel is able to get away with.

"Every time I see it," he says as we pass the tree, "I want to burn it."

•
••••

Rachelle calls her friends Shaddi and Jihad to sit with us in Manger Square. Everybody owes a lot of electricity since the

Second Intifada, Shaddi mentions to us as they sit. A lot of people haven't been able to pay their electric bill. It hasn't been a problem but recently they've begun electricity cuts. People are getting desperate and have begun selling their land, Shaddi says. "To other Palestinians," he clarifies.

Shaddi has forgotten we have met before, and Rachelle tries to help him remember. He asks what I am doing in Palestine and we start talking about maps.

Jihad, who has up until now been sitting, smoking, uninterested, becomes interested. He has an old Greek map of Palestine, he says, and would I be able to read it? There is a church on that map called Saint Francis that doesn't exist anymore.

I ask if he can draw it, and he draws a sword pointing down with two snakes, one on each side. He also draws a triangle with the number 20 on each edge. I ask him what that is. He says he has seen it on the ground, that there are thousands all over Palestine.

A survey benchmark, we together realize, where surveyors stick their instruments into ground to survey and map the land. The British colonizers did this to Palestine in the late nineteenth and early twentieth centuries.

Shaddi and Jihad say they can show me where they are, if I want to see. Palestinians find all kinds of things they don't let foreigners know about, unless they trust them. There's gold and buried treasure. They share that Palestinians find relics from the Greek and Ottoman period that they then sell to get money, which they have to do since nobody can find a job. They sell the Greek artifacts to the Greeks, and the Ottoman ones to the Turks. Jihad says, "It's part of their history."

"What's part of Palestinian history?" I ask.

"All of this stuff is not Palestinian history. It's the occupiers' history," says Jihad. "We have been occupied by Israel, then the Romans, then the Greeks, then the Turks, then the British, and then Israel."

"So, what would you consider Palestinian artifacts?" I ask the Palestine from below.

"Well, just little things nobody wants to pay for."

•
—

There is a set of identical triplets on Star Street. I learned about them when I first arrived, thinking they were twins when only two of them came into Mary's store.

"*La*'," Mary had corrected me, held up three fingers, and ticked each one off as she said their names, "Musa, Issa, Mohammed." Each named after a prophet of three sibling worlds: Judaism's Moses, Christianity's Jesus, Islam's Mohammed. Identical triplets, ten years old.

For almost nine months I have lived on Star Street, and I have never once seen all three at the same time. Only two at the same time, sometimes only one.

One of them, when he is by himself, always makes faces and tries to whack me. I fight back though.

But walking home on Star Street tonight, I finally encounter the *nabi*-triplets, the prophet-triplets, heading straight toward me.

We are about to pass each other, and I fully expect the one who hates me to throw something at me, but he instead hands it to me. It is a flower. His name is Mohammad, he says, as we introduce ourselves.

I get to meet Issa, and nod. I meet Musa and tell him *abu jozi* is named Musa, too, making him smile.

There is another little boy there. I introduce myself. He has a name I've never heard of and I forget it right away.

I thank them for the flower and ask where it came from.

"*Al-ezbaala*," they answer, the trash. I can only laugh.

As I say good night and turn to walk home, one of the triplets picks up more flowers from the ground and throws them at me. I now know it is Issa who doesn't like me.

Mohammad picks up one of the flowers Issa threw down and hands it to me, so now I have two flowers, both from Mohammad.

I walk home delighted. I have finally seen the *nabi* triplets, all three prophets, all three identical, all at the same time.

And more than that, Mohammad and Musa have set a better example for Issa now, *inshallah*. Maybe next time we cross each other's paths, Issa and I will greet each other instead of fight.

PALESTINE DIARY (2010–2011)

PALESTINE 1492: A REPORT BACK

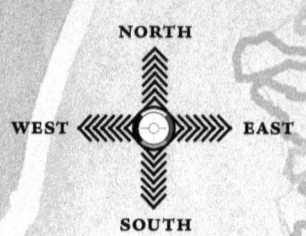

When the Rooftops Are Streets

They started out as tents, as any refugee camp might. A temporary space for people fleeing war. But for many who have never seen a Palestinian refugee camp before, it comes as a surprise that the camps are crowded buildings now. The refugees have been in resistance so long to need all this concrete.

But it took a few years for them to agree to the buildings. The first compromise was walls only, no roofs. Roofs imply permanence. But as families have grown and as the camp's spaces have not, roofs have been added, many roofs, most serving at once as one generation's ceiling and the next generation's floor.

But anyway, these buildings are their houses, not their homes. Their homes are inside '48, the land on which the State of Israel was created after the *Nakba*, after the catastrophe.

While Israel's official maps show borders that express it is impossible for the refugees to return, those same maps communicate that home is only walking distance away. In Bethlehem's Aida Refugee Camp, in the West Bank, I am learning to agree with a common Palestinian refrain: "Here, the map is useless."

The way the map tells the story, distance is space only, not

also time. And not also violence. Checkpoints and borders are mere lines and dots to travelers like me. For Palestinians, those same lines and dots are threats, cruel reminders, traumas of Israel's deadly force.

Outside of Lajee Center in Aida Camp exists a ceramic sign that announces *al-Quds*, Jerusalem, is only 7.34 kilometers away, a distance less than 5 miles. The sign is correct if we assume smooth space: no checkpoints, no walls, no borders, no violence. Nidal remembers when he and his friends could walk from Aida Camp to al-Quds in the evenings to eat *ka'ak*, a sesame-covered ring-shaped bread, and could walk back to the Camp still in time for bed.

That was before Israel closed off the Holy City to most Palestinians years ago. Before the Second Intifada in September 2000. Before Israel's Siege on the Nativity Church in April 2002. Before Israel's Apartheid Wall was officially announced after the Siege that June. Now, al-Quds is too far, a distance impossible for most Palestinians. Most do not qualify for Israel's special privileges called entry permits. It is what the ceramic signs like these, about 80 throughout the West Bank, provide reminders of in claiming the distance to al-Quds: here, the map is useless.

Nidal is a refugee from al-Qabu, five miles away from Aida Camp, and his wife Amahl is a Palestinian Citizen of Israel from the Galilee in the north, close to Lebanon. Israel is the only one who can grant Nidal a special permit to cross into '48 to visit Amahl's family.

Amahl and Nidal share out loud a mental map of what the permit maze has looked like thus far. It has included various visits to different offices over several weeks, each of their movements taking them farther and farther in the opposite direction. Nidal would be denied.

Still, it is from the refugees themselves that I learn the map is not always so useless. Every day, walking past the maps of Palestine on murals and graffiti all over the Camp, letting the world know in English WE WILL RETURN, and like that in all capital letters, I learn to agree. They are all maps of Historic Palestine, of *Falestin al-Tarikhiya* before 1948, before the United Nations' partition, before the Peel Commission, before the British cut up Palestine into smaller pieces of private property to sell on the market, to speculate on the market, to displace Palestinians, today refugees, they say the oldest refugees, or at least among the oldest refugees who still know they're refugees.

The refugees' maps insist on all of Palestine, from the River Jordan at its eastern border to the Mediterranean Sea at its western border. And while the refugees' maps have no authority on the ground, they are still terrifying for the Zionist project. It means the refugees are still refusing their own erasure, refusing their own displacement generations later. It means that maybe it's true what the refugees promise: WE WILL RETURN, in all capital letters just like that.

This is how I can learn to agree with my Palestinian elders: the map is not always so useless.

WE WILL RETURN

Beit-Awa
Deir-Ayob
Al-Ramlah
Khouldah
Abu Gaash
Al-Quds
Jarash
Rafat
Zakariyah
Shirfat
Beer Shebah
Beit-Aylab
Jaliyah
Surief
Al-Emoor
Beit-Jebreen
Ajoor
Al-Walajah
Al-Qabu
Ajar
Dier Aban
Al-Malha
Bait-Nateef
Ras Abu-Amar

AL Qabo

Beit Mahser
Eraq AL Mn shea

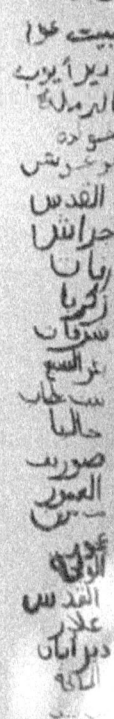

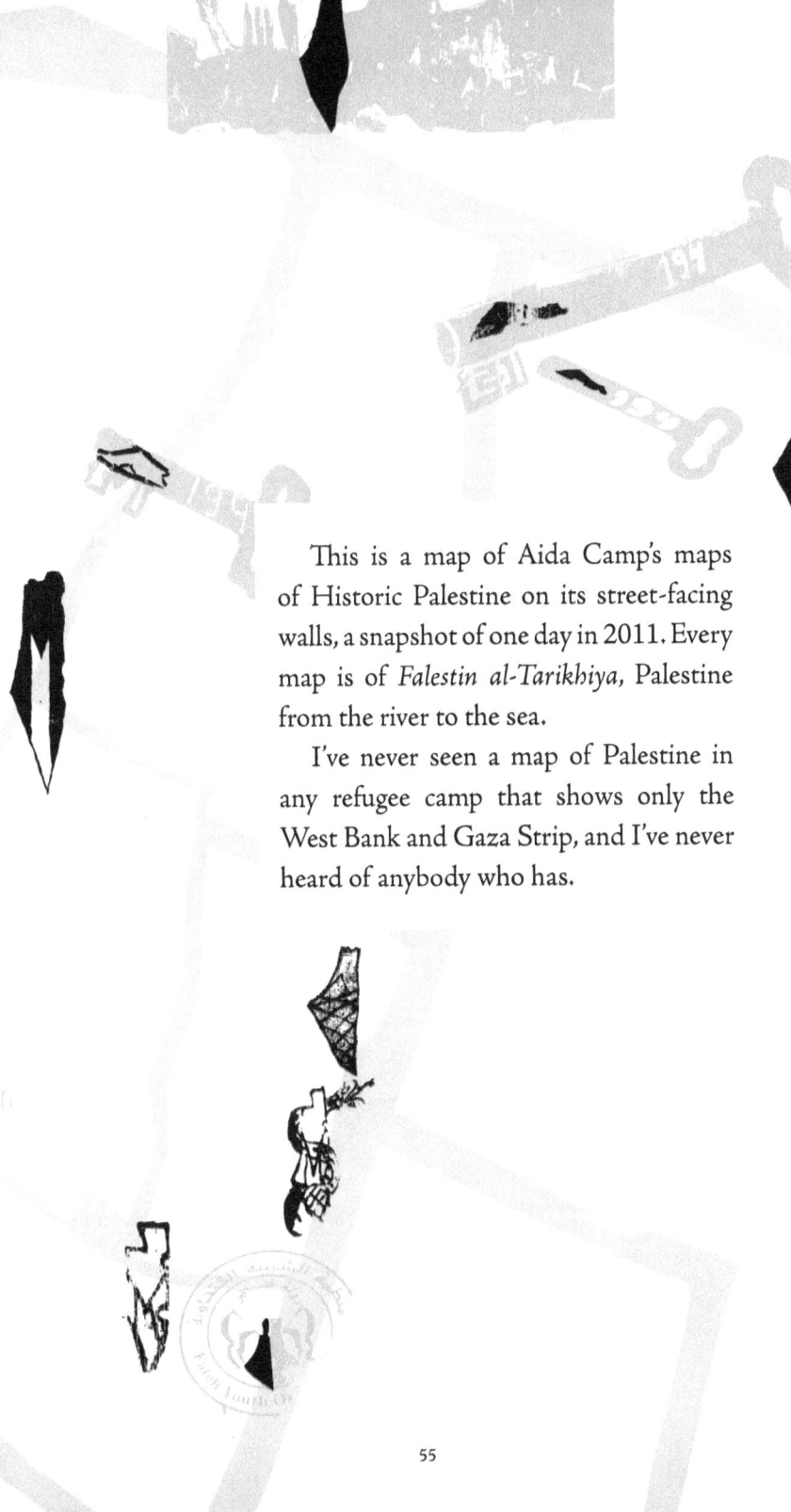

This is a map of Aida Camp's maps of Historic Palestine on its street-facing walls, a snapshot of one day in 2011. Every map is of *Falestin al-Tarikhiya*, Palestine from the river to the sea.

I've never seen a map of Palestine in any refugee camp that shows only the West Bank and Gaza Strip, and I've never heard of anybody who has.

Salah Ajarma, the Director of Lajee Center, learned I was a geographer and asked right away if I could map the camp. I agreed after much hesitation out loud. "What if Israel gets the maps?"

"They already have the maps," Salah replied. "When they arrest us, they even show us the names of our families on the buildings."

Some weeks later, we were able to locate a high-resolution aerial photograph of Aida taken by the Israeli military. They're the only ones allowed to photograph from the air. The photo was shared with us by a Palestinian geographer. I traced it with a Geographic Information System (GIS), and when the final draft was complete, Nidal assigned a young man and a young woman from Aida Camp to walk the camp with me to check my work.

PALESTINE FROM BELOW

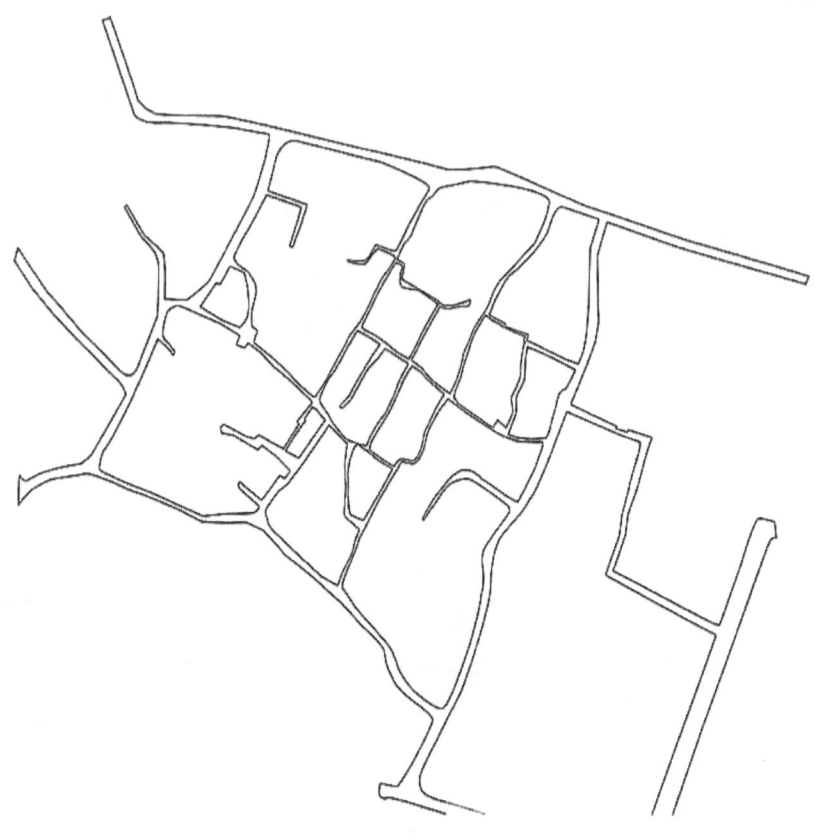

When I asked Nidal if I had accurately traced the streets on the map as shown above, he nodded but remarked, "You know, the rooftops are also streets." He dotted a road network on the roofs as he had maneuvered them while under curfew during the Second Intifada. Nidal's is the map on the next page. Jumping from roof to roof was how he and his friends could check in on everyone and pass medicine, food, news, and supplies.

I soon learned that every Palestinian seemed to have a story like this, especially in times of shaking off the oppressor, especially in times of *intifadas*, with every geography different for everyone yet still the story of everyone, each with their

When the Rooftops Are Streets

own calendars, each with their own ways, each new path out of necessity, each new path impossible to map by anyone else, least by a professional geographer like me.

Israel's predatory geography brings about this necessity. The State of Israel has never defined its borders. The State of Israel is still expanding. For Israel, its border with Palestine is not a line on the map but a life/death confrontation on the ground in everyday life. Israel's border with Palestine is the violence necessary to defend the State, its so-called "iron wall," the apartheid line between the Human/Non-Human legitimized by the United Nations and its institutions, legitimized and created everyday by international law. If this is true, then the problem is bigger than Palestine, bigger than Israel, bigger than Europe, bigger than the United States or the geography called The West and the other geography called The East. Palestine is a problem of the world, the world is the problem of Palestine. What if it's true what they say, that changing the world is difficult, even impossible, and so a new world must be built, a world where all the worlds fit. And what if it's true that resistance comes out of necessity and love, not out of romance.

Palestine's other geographies in the Camp are built and maintained under conditions of death, meaning they are built and maintained under conditions of necessity, out of a love for life in the face of death, a journey possible generations after the Nakba through collectively lived struggle and a social fabric of trust.

Placing my map of Aida Camp's streets next to Nidal's map of Aida Camp's other streets, I was reminded of Amílcar Cabral's appeal to the ones who make their lives at the cost of others. Either they betray the struggle of the below by preserving their privileges, or they can identify directly with the below and commit "suicide" as a class, by going below rather than above, by going below with the below so that the intifadas of the exterminated and displaced becomes an equally shared necessity.[1]

Geographer suicide? *Professional* geographer suicide. The map is not always so useless.

I wonder what it will it look like, what it will feel like, this self-annihilation of the professional class, of the ruling class or of the ruling class in-the-making, of the expert class. What

---

1. Amílcar Cabral, "The Weapon of Theory" (1966)

might it look like, what might it feel like instead to become somebody else, somebody who insists like the Palestinians do that it doesn't have to be this way, with both humility and dignified rage.

What might it look like, what might it feel like to walk with the below, to place yourself under fire with the below so that the need to shake off fascism becomes a shared necessity for you, too?

I do not know, but I hope we will find out together because there's no blueprint. From the Zapatistas I learn to ask questions as we walk, *caminando preguntando*. From Aida Camp I learn sometimes we must ask questions as we jump.

May we learn the answers together.

The trees of Aida Camp, one day in 2011

Salah Ajarma

November 11, 1972 – April 14, 2021

Presente

Palestine 1492: A Report Back

To Die Standing

It has been more than 500 years since Columbus and them first arrived in the Caribbean, or as the elders say, since Columbus and the other cannibals first arrived in the Caribbean spreading the *wétiko* virus, the contagious disease of selfishness.[1] It has been more than 500 years of struggles and still today, worlds exist in their ways from before and in their ways from after, ways that teach the *You are my other me and I am your other you* of the Maya peoples and the *I am because we are* of the Bantu peoples. More than 500 years of death and destruction, and worlds Indigenous to these lands are still in resistance, and not everyone has put down their weapons. The Zapatista Army for National Liberation (EZLN) in Chiapas is an important example of all these facts.

The Zapatistas are a Maya rebel movement in Chiapas, a geography directly north of the border between the State of Mexico and the State of Guatemala. Chiapas has existed far longer than either the State of Mexico or the State of Guatemala and is part of the larger Maya world still called by its many names, including *Iximulew*, where *ixim* means "maize" and *ulew* means "land." (esheem-oo-le-oh)

---

1. Jack D. Forbes (*presente*) *Columbus and Other Cannibals: The Wétiko Disease of Exploitation, Imperialism, and Terrorism* (Seven Stories Press, 1978)

Palestine from Below

I often mention Chiapas whenever I mention Palestine, and I often mention Palestine whenever I mention Chiapas. I encountered the two resistances at around the same time when I was first learning about the global struggles from below and against capital; when I was first learning to listen to the pains and the dignity of the below. There are many similarities between the two; there are many differences. Pains and dignity are constants in both. *I prefer to die on my feet than to live on my knees*, the Zapatistas are famous for saying. *Like trees, we die standing*, the Palestinians are famous for saying. Dying in order to live is a famous saying for both Palestinians and Zapatistas.

Palestinian compas say they don't get to hear too much about the Zapatistas and have asked me to say more about them in this report back. I offer my interpretation of the Zapatistas here in the hope readers will listen directly to them rather than to me. The Zapatistas speak for themselves.[2] Parts of my offering might be more helpfully understood as witness testimony from someone raised by the world of Columbus and Them who can testify that world teaches Palestinians have never existed and that the Maya no longer exist. I can testify that worlds obsessed with "greatness," the very definition of fascism, over-represent the stories of themselves as the stories of all humanity, as if empires, dynasties, kingdoms have ever been our only possibilities.[3]

Thus, when Columbus' world speaks about Palestine, it speaks only of the empires, dynasties, kingdoms that have

---

2. The Zapatistas regularly share their word in communiques that are published, translated, and archived at Enlace Zapatista: https://enlacezapatista.ezln.org.mx

3. For a survey of other possibilities, see *The Dawn of Everything: A New History of Humanity*, by David Graeber and David Wengrow (Allen Lane, 2021). David Graeber, *presente*

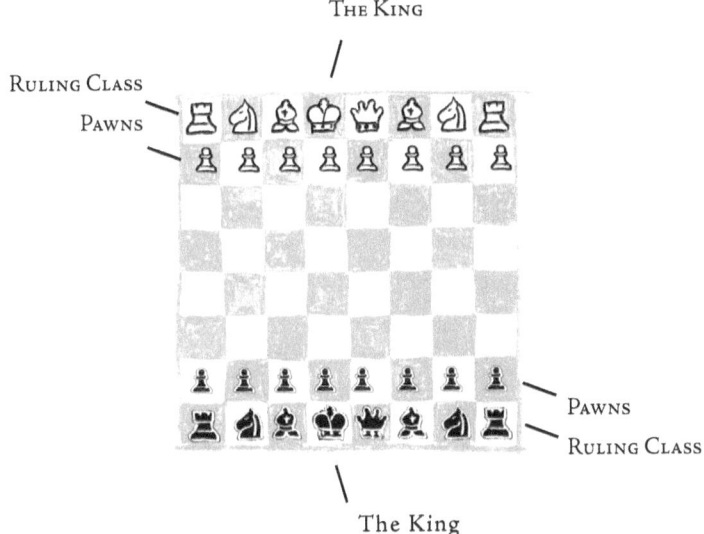

> The goal of chess is to capture the other side's king. So that the king may live, his pawns and the rest of his ruling class are expected to die as necessary.

occupied Palestine. *All of this stuff is not Palestinian history,* Jihad had said. *It's the occupiers' history. We have been occupied by Israel, then the Romans, then the Greeks, then the Turks, then the British, and then Israel.* That is, occupied by the United Kingdom of Israel, then by the Roman Empire, then by the Byzantine Empire, then the Ottoman Empire, then the British Empire, and then the State of Israel on behalf of empire.

For those worlds obsessed with concentrating power as empires do, all relations fall into the logic of the chessboard: the logic of war. Kingdoms vs kingdoms, empires vs empires, states vs states, corporations vs corporations, families vs families, self vs self. Eat or be eaten. Everyone else is ultimately a pawn whether Pawn is their name or they're called another name for disposable.

For worlds like that, where life is a zero-sum game, there is no possibility of peace, of Them *and* Us together, only of

Them or Us. You're either at the table, or you're on the menu, the world of the cannibals likes to say. The small are useful only as discards at the service of the biggest cannibal of all, the master, emperor, dynast, king. It is a world infected by the wétiko disease.

Thus, when Columbus' world speaks about the Maya, it also emphasizes the big: the large city-states, the tallest pyramids and temples, the doings of the rulers and its tax collectors, the size of its armies, the control of trade routes, the comings and goings of the elite. The above writes the history of the above and declares it official; it tends not to listen to the pains and dignity of the below. For the above, the below is wholly unimportant and absolutely necessary at the same time, for structurally there can be no above without a below. *There can be no table if there is no menu.* And nobody wants to be on the menu.

Anyone at the table can become part of the menu; anyone above can fall down below, the predator's greatest fear, becoming the prey. Those above fight hard to maintain their seat and plate. *There's not enough pie,* you often hear them say.

How do we live without becoming the same monsters as Them? When fewer of us can imagine another world is possible and we ourselves struggle for a piece of the pie, we need to know the wétiko has advanced.

In a world where death is abundant and the options are a binary of you against me rather than *You are my other me,* rather than *I am we,* those being crushed feel they have no choice but to crush others on the way to survival, on the way to eat. Cannibalism appears to be the only option when the resistance is weak to the wétiko disease.

Those refusing the binary of predator or prey become the hunted. One cannot opt out without a plan for escape and self-defense. The ones who refuse must self-annihilate as cannibals, if that is what they are, and become somebody else, somebody new with other fugitives and maroons. To build a place where there exists no more above vs below, where there exists no more wétiko. But without land, how does one maroon in place?

There exist some up above who feel bad about injustice but don't see their world as diseased. They seek to keep their privileges, appear to be well meaning, feel bad, and hope to share the table with some of the below, as long as they don't disrupt the status quo. They train them from youth, hence their obsession with the category of *Youth*.[4] They often call themselves "progressive," as if it were progress to create more cannibals today than there were cannibals yesterday.

When the below desires acceptance from the above, the resistance to the wétiko is weak. That's when naked violence is not always necessary. The prey come to defend the predator's world as desirable, mocking other worlds as strange or impossible. The ones who call themselves progressives are key to this advance. Rather than escaping their *dog-eat-dog world*, as they call it, they fight for diversity among the predator class. They don't like it when you point out diverse cannibals are still cannibals.

When the below desires to become the above, when the prey seeks prestige by outperforming the mediocre predators, the wétiko has become most advanced. This has been helpfully diagnosed as advanced fascism by political prisoner, Black Panther, and ancestor George Jackson, *presente*, as the next chapter shows.[5]

Nobody wishes to be on a fascist's menu. In war, how we

---

4. Mayssoun Sukarieh and Stuart Tannock, *Youth Rising? The Politics of Youth in the Global Economy* (Routledge, 2014)

5. George Jackson, *Blood in My Eye* (Random House, 1972)

choose to stay alive is the ethical-political question we have as our task. A most important question before us is, *How do we bring ethics into war?*[6] How do we not eat each other in order to stay alive? How do we keep our resistance strong in the midst of contagion? How do we not become the monsters that we fight?

If warding off an illness is our task, we can learn from the healers. When we are unwell, the Maya healers ask about our mother's life while we gestated in the womb. It is a lesson that the past is also next to us and ahead, not only behind. It is a lesson that time is more a spiral than it is a line. It is a lesson for us to ask about the gestation of worlds, to ask about Columbus and Them's time in the womb.

The world of 1492 carries a deep trauma about happenings from the womb, about things that happened before Columbus. The collapse of its favorite ancestor is a deep womb trauma: the crumbling of the Roman Empire to rival empires and its loss of Jerusalem. A classic story of the above falling down below. The world of Columbus and Them refers to this time as its Dark Ages and doesn't like it when you bring it up.

The world of Columbus is not the only world traumatized. But it is diseased and globally contagious and is everybody's problem now.[7] More than a global problem, the world of Columbus and Them has become a planetary problem. Healers testify it takes a lot of energy to get wounded killers who believe there's no way out to drop their weapons. And still we have to try because it has become everybody's problem now.

---

6. "Notes on Wars: Start of the Epistolary Exchange on Ethics and Politics" Subcomandante Insurgente Marcos and Luis Villoro (2011), reprinted in *La Cuarta Guerra Mundial, The Fourth World War* (Paliacate Press, 2024)

7. Elizabeth Kolbert, *The Sixth Extinction: An Unnatural History* (Henry Holt and Company, 2014)

Knowing this about the world of Columbus and Them helps explain why it laments a so-called "collapse" of Maya civilization, which it marks on its calendar as the time the big structures stopped being built. That is how the world of Columbus and Them marks collapse. That world is unable to imagine that the Maya are still here, at once from before and from after, and that the end of some worlds can sometimes be desirable and even deliberately engineered by those below.

Encountering the below requires attention to things that go erased by the dominant world, most important is attention to the fact that other worlds are still in existence. The Zapatistas say their struggle is for a world where many worlds fit, and by this they don't mean a multi-polar world, they mean a world where *all* worlds can fit, where universalisms are inadequate, where not even a single universe is adequate.[8] A world that begins with *We are equal because we are different*, as the Zapatista women say, is a world where all worlds fit.[9]

Encountering the below requires attention to war, to its predations on life, to the extermination of the ones defending life. To walk with the Zapatistas is to see the reality that there are no honest solutions from empire against domination; empire is the domination. There are no honest solutions from capitalism against extinction; capitalism is the extinction. To walk with the Zapatistas is to see the reality of war and to learn to see it from where you live, too, if you hadn't already been able to see it before.

---

8. See *Pluriverse: A Post-Development Dictionary*, edited by Ashish Kothari, Ariel Salleh, Arturo Escobar, Federico Demaria, and Alberto Acosta (Tulika Books, 2019)

9. See "The Zapatista Women's Revolutionary Law as it is lived today" by Sylvia Marcos in *openDemocracy* (July 2014)

In a context of planetary emergency, the Zapatista struggle is not only for the Maya worlds of Chiapas or the Indigenous worlds of Mexico. Theirs is a struggle for life, and life not just for some, life for all. *Everything for everyone, nothing for ourselves,* as they often say. Thus, to encounter Chiapas requires more than attention to war; it requires attention on how to fight a war so that there will be no more wars; how to have an army so that there will be no more armies. This enormous task requires reflecting on what it means to be human, the deep ancestral work the Maya-Tojolabal are known for living.[10]

> *We are an army, and an army is the most absurd thing there is because it is resorting to the force of a weapon to be right, and a human being who has to resort to a weapon to be right, is not a human being."*[11]

The EZLN is the military, self-defense arm of the Zapatista bases of support. Because it is a military, the EZLN's formation is hierarchical. That the base is organized to exercise authority places the military at the service of the base, not the other way around.[12] The bases are diverse, composed of different Maya communities who speak distinct Mayan languages, including Tojolabal, Tzotzil, Tzeltal, Ch'ol, Zoque, and Mam.

---

10. See Carlos Lenkersdorf's *Los hombres verdaderos: voces y testimonios tojolabales: lengua y sociedad, naturaleza y cultura, artes y comunidad cósmica* [The True Humans: Tojolabal Voices and Testimonies: Language, Society, Nature and Culture, Arts, and Cosmic Community] (Siglo XXI, 1996)

11. EZLN "What Are the Fundamental Characteristics of the Fourth World War?" (1999)

12. See Mara Kaufman's *We Are from Before, Yes, But We Are New: Autonomy, Territory, and the Production of New Subjects of Self-Government in Zapatismo*, a dissertation (Duke University, 2010)

They organize in assemblies in order to build, maintain, and defend themselves from capital's predations. In the land they took back in their 1994 uprising, they have built autonomous schools, clinics, economic cooperatives, banks, communications, media, and government. Power in Zapatista territory flows more dispersed than it does concentrated. Their structure of governing is more horizontal than it is vertical. Their territory is more of a web than it is a container. In terms of size, the Zapatistas are very small, and the Zapatistas are very big, depending. Their reach is local, national, global, and intergalactic, all at the same time.

In the Zapatista Maya world, empire's pyramid is turned upside down. That is, the base is the authority. *Here, the people rule and the government obeys*, the signs throughout Chiapas announce. Their governing structure rotates positions among the base themselves. Positions can be immediately revoked and replaced in case of corruption. The structure of government wards off corruption rather than incentivizes it. There are no politicians in Zapatista territory; there are no salaries. Governing is a community obligation not a career. It is a duty, a burden, a responsibility, and it is everybody's right.

Zapatista governance is guided by a Maya-Tojolabal ethical-political commitment of *mandar obedeciendo* ("to lead by obeying"). To lead by obeying means the people rule and the government obeys. It means the people rule and the military obeys. To lead by obeying guides the flow of power within the community so that it circulates in an everyday dispersed fashion rather than concentrating on any single leader.[13] Its seven guiding principles are based on respectful

---

13. See Mariana Mora's *Kuxlejal Politics: Indigenous Autonomy, Race, and Decolonizing Research in Zapatista Communities* (University of Texas Press, 2017)

power relations that must be followed by anyone in a leadership position, accountable to the assembly, obeying the assembly:

1. To obey, not command
2. To serve, not serve oneself
3. To represent, not supplant
4. To build, not destroy
5. To propose, not impose
6. To convince, not defeat
7. To go below, not go above

Many who walk with the Zapatistas believe their philosophy and practice of *mandar obedeciendo* to be their most important contribution to contemporary politics precisely because it is not a model to be replicated or a blueprint to be followed; it is a strategy to circulate power into harmonious balance. It is an offering, a proposal, a sharing, a lesson, an invitation to not only survive but to thrive, together and side by side.

Without a prescription for revolution, without doctrine to follow, the Zapatista communities encourage us all to struggle for life while *caminando preguntando*, while asking questions as we walk from where we live in our own geographies, in our own calendars, in our own ways.

It was on January 1st of 1994 when the world first heard the shouts of *¡ya basta!* (enough!) of the EZLN in Chiapas. But by the time the world first saw the armed, Maya rebels liberating land in the mountains of the Mexican Southeast that New Year's Day, a decade had already passed since the EZLN first began quietly organizing.[14]

---

14. For histories of the movement during this clandestine decade, see *The Fire and the Word: A History of the Zapatista Movement* by Gloria Muñoz

While the EZLN first formed in 1983, as Maya communities the Zapatistas have been in resistance for much longer, something they made clear in their *First Declaration of the Lacandón Jungle*. Their famous first line, *We are the product of 500 years of struggles*, was amplified globally by journalists and sympathizers with access to the internet back when the internet was still small.[15]

The Zapatistas are sometimes called *neo*-Zapatistas, or "new" Zapatistas, for they take their name from ancestors from an earlier land-back struggle also in Mexico, launched 84 years before in 1910. These "old" Zapatistas were led by Emiliano Zapata who issued his declarations in Nahuatl, his native language. The Mexican Revolution as it became called, began as a demand for regime-change and ended as a struggle for land:

> *Notlac ximomanaca! Nehuatl onacoc; oncuan on ipc tepoztli ihuan nochantlaca niquinhuicatz. Ipampa in Totazin Diaz aihmo ticnequi yehuatl techixotiz. Ticnequi occe altpetl achi cuali. Ilhuan totlac ximomanaca ipampa amo nechpactia tlen telaxtlauhia. Amo conehui ica tlacualo ica netzotzomatiloz. Noihqui nincnequi nochtlacatl quipiaz ital: oncuan on quitocaz ihuan quipixcaz tlaoli, yetzintli ihuan occequi xinachtli. Tlen nanquitoa? Namehan totlac namomanazque?*
>
> *Join me. I rose up. I rose up in arms and I bring my countrymen. We no longer wish that our Father Diaz watch over us. We want a much better president. Rise up with us*

Ramírez (City Lights Publishers, 2008); and *Compañeras: Zapatista Women's Stories* by Hilary Klein (Seven Stories Press, 2015).

15. See "The Zapatista Effect: The Internet and the Rise of an Alternative Political Fabric" by Harry Cleaver (1997)

because we don't like what the rich men pay us. It is not enough for us to eat and dress ourselves. I also want everyone to have his piece of land so that he can plant and harvest maize, beans, and other crops. What do you say? Are you going to join us?[16]

In 1521, after Hernán Cortés and Them took Tenochtitlan, the capital of the Mexica Empire, pronounced "meh-SHEE-ka," or as the anthropologists call it, Aztec, the *conquistadores* right away granted themselves their own slave plantations. They say the King of Spain had ordered Cortés not to. The Spanish Empire had recently entrusted its conquistadores in the Caribbean with a franchise of plantations called *encomiendas*. Becoming an *encomendero*, a soldier-turned-landowner of the Empire's plantations, had been the reward for conquering the Taíno islands in the Caribbean on behalf of the king.

Guanahaní, a Taíno name for an island in the Bahamas meaning "Small Upper-Waters Land," is said to be where Columbus and Them first landed on October 12, 1492 before sailing south and finding out about Cuba, from the Taíno word *cubao*, meaning "Where Fertile Land Is Abundant". After Cuba, they found out about Ayiti to the east, today the island called Haiti, meaning "Land of High Mountains" in Taíno. By the time of Cortés and Them, only a couple decades later, the plantation franchise had nearly exterminated the Taíno communities across the islands.

They say the Spanish Empire had ordered Cortés not to do the same in Anahuac, in the "Lands Close to the Water," the place today called Mexico. Empires aren't known for having a problem with enslavement or extermination. This particular

---

16. See James J. Kelly, *Article 27 and Mexican Land Reform: The Legacy of Zapata's Dream*, 25 Colum. Hum. Rts. L. Rev. 541 (1993–1994)

Empire was concerned with maintaining a steady labor force in its new gold mines and sugar-cane plantations. The Spanish Empire would soon resolve its labor problems by kidnapping and enslaving tens of millions of Afrikans, a human trafficking operation where the empires of the Portuguese, French, Dutch, and British also took part.

It would be three hundred years later, in 1804, when the enslaved Black Afrikans in the Ayiti plantation would rise up against their masters and declare their independence, also on a New Year's Day. As a slave rebellion, the Haitian Revolution was uncommon. Historically, it has been competing masters who have declared independence against other masters. Those are the ones at the United Nations today.

Mexican Independence is an example. After his defeat of the Mexica Empire in 1521, Cortés soon became overseer on behalf of the Spanish Empire of a large plantation called the Viceroyalty of New Spain. Exactly three hundred years later, in 1821, the descendants of Cortés and Them would declare independence from their masters, taking dominion of the land and its people for themselves as the Spanish Empire had previously modeled. The above switched faces and names, but for the below, things remained the same.

During those prior three hundred years as the Viceroyalty of New Spain, not all native communities were enslaved. Many simply paid tribute to the Spanish Empire as they had previously paid tribute to the Mexica Empire. Many were able to maintain their traditions and communal lands, the *calpullalli*, the Indigenous land-tenure system where land-use rights belong to a community as a whole, and the rights and responsibilities to farm the land are granted to the families of that community, similar to the *musha'* in Palestine and neighboring lands. With the common lands preserved, communities outside the plantation system's reach could still grow their *milpa*, their traditional maize field of shifting cultivation where the beans spiral up the maize stalk while feeding the soil, and where the squash spreads widely below while shading the ground. Maintaining a milpa makes it so one does not have to eat other humans to survive. By contrast, the native communities subjected to plantation labor by Cortés and Them had been forced to grown sugar cane for colonial extraction.

After the Mexican ruling class achieved independence from Spain in 1821, that is, after the creation of the United Mexican States, or "Mexico," the descendants of Cortés and Them would divide the communal lands, the calpullalli, into plots of private, individual ownership. This scheme was made constitutional law in 1857, the height of what Mexican historians call the country's "liberal reforms." This was happening in Palestine at about the same time of the Ottoman Empire's modernization reforms, the *Tanzimat*.

The Mexican Revolution would explode fifty years later in 1910 against these reforms and has become described as a struggle against "liberalism," a political philosophy out of Europe that emphasizes individual rights over communal rights. Liberalism shares with other European philosophies the treatment of land as an object of property, profit, and control, deploying a diversity of tactics, using the cover of law and the threat of violence, rather than always resorting to naked violence.[17]

The Mexican Revolution's Emiliano Zapata would become

---

17. For an inventory of land theft through naked violence in Abya Yala (or "the Americas"), see David Stannard's *American Holocaust: Columbus and the Conquest of the New World* (Oxford University Press, 1992)

a beloved ancestor for fighting for land back until his death, dying while standing, dying for refusing to sit on the throne when he was offered it. Zapata would share the fate of others who have similarly refused the disease.[18] Unable to be bought, Zapata would be killed in an ambush by the Mexican ruling class, by the Mexico from above. His assassins would continue to rule over Mexico by co-opting the Revolution and Zapata's image, interpreting the problem of liberalism to mean the problem of foreigners treating land as an object of property, profit, and control; the "nation" was allowed to do with the land between its borders as it wished, extracting, pillaging, destroying it as the so-called "Mexican nation" wished.

This Mexican nation had been designed from the perspective of the descendants of Cortés and Them who added a Mexica aesthetic to designate Mexico as special and unique from the Spanish Empire. Spain's racist categories of blood purity remained. The Mexican nation was designed as *mestizo*, meaning culturally European with Indigenous and Black Afrikan ancestry, but not a lot of discussion about the Indigenous and Black Afrikan ancestry beyond the music, the "Aztec" Empire, and the food. Always the food.

The Mexicanization campaign post-Revolution attempted to impose on everyone the ruling class's conception of Mexico: one language, one religion, one history, one culture, one way. The colonial relation still remained: the above vs the below. The destruction of the Indigenous peoples was successful by some measures. In two generations, most Mexicans would no longer speak their native language and wouldn't even know they were

---

18. On how the assassinations and overthrows of those who refuse has continued worldwide throughout the twentieth and twenty-first centuries, see John Perkins, *Confessions of an Economic Hitman* (Berrett-Koehler Publishers 2004)

Indigenous. New Zapatistas had to emerge to remind them.

The EZLN uprising in 1994 reminded the world of the *Mexico profundo*, the Mexico from below, of the worlds that Columbus and Them for 500 years have tried to erase.[19] The neo-Zapatista uprising had at first been aimed only at the political party of the ruling class: the Institutional Revolutionary Party (PRI). The PRI had long ago co-opted the Revolution in name and brutally clung to power by any means necessary, famously opening fire on university students in protest in a Mexico City borough called Tlatelolco, meaning "In the Little Hill of Land" in Nahuatl. Even after massacring 25 people on October 2, 1968, Mexico City hosted the Olympics on October 12th to celebrate the Mexico of Columbus and Them. Ruling through fear of further massacres, Mexico's PRI would hold uninterrupted government power for most of the twentieth century. New Zapatistas had to emerge to pull off the mask.

Before his assassination in 1919, Emiliano Zapata had lived to witness the drafting of a new constitution that included a form of land back: the *ejido*, a state-protected category of communal lands inspired by the calpullalli. With the new protections, landless communities had been granted the land they required through the ejido, even if it meant expropriating the large private holdings. Private plots could still operate, and their ownership title transferred freely, but the ejido was protected from theft, sale, and real-estate speculation. The land now belonged to "the nation," as Article 27 of the Mexican Constitution of 1917 put it during Zapata's time,

---

19. See Guillermo Bonfil Batalla, *Mexico Profundo: Reclaiming a Civilization* (University of Texas Press, 1996)

> *The lands, waters, and natural resources understood to be within the borders of national territory, belong to the nation, whether they be above or below the land. The nation regulates the management of these lands and resources.*

But what the ruling class is allowed to grant, the ruling class is allowed to take away. Decades later in 1992, the PRI removed the ejido from constitutional protection, doing away with the Mexican Revolution's greatest legacy. The constitutional revision paved the way for mass transfer of rural land from Indigenous communities to transnational corporations through both legal means and illegal means. The lands fought for by the older Zapatistas earlier that century were now an object of property, profit, and control again, a liberalism again, a new liberalism, a *neo*-liberalism.

The ejido's destruction had been made a prerequisite for Mexico's entry into the North American Free Trade Agreement (NAFTA) of 1994, a treaty between Mexico, the United States, and Canada that allowed for the free-flow of capital and commodities while hindering the free-flow of people who NAFTA promised to displace. Factories in the United States and Canada shut down and moved to Mexico, where the government ensured labor was cheaper and environmental restrictions almost non-existent. At the same time, the common lands could now be bought and sold and controlled by transnational corporations.

Thirty years after NAFTA, which now goes by USMCA, the United States–Mexico–Canada Agreement, the destruction of the ejido has led to an emptying of Indigenous peoples from the land for profit at a scale Cortés maybe only dreamed of. Thirty years on, tens of millions are caught in a wandering nightmare of displacement through legal means: they mortgage the land to a bank for credit and are unable to pay back the loan. It is also displacement through illegal means, refusing to sign with mining corporations, kicked off the land through a narco-terror response the politicians pretend to have nothing to do with.[20] A wandering nightmare of displacement through legal means and illegal means, whichever one can be most efficient for capital, whichever one is most pragmatic.

The wandering nightmare of displacement in a foreign place to sell your labor, which you didn't have to sell so much of before and hopefully someone will buy because now there is no land, and now you need money for food, for shelter, for water, for air, for fire, for your children, for your community, for everything, and not many are buying your labor in your country, so you need to see if you can get to *El Norte*, to The North, and see if you can cross the border and make it to the other side while trying not to get caught and while trying to keep alive.

Thirty years after NAFTA, for the Mexico from below the border has become a graveyard in those places where it's not already a wall. For the Mexico from above, a stark contrast: a place at the table alongside global elites, where today nationalities are less important than one's bank account. NAFTA ushered in the ability for a Mexican capitalist of Lebanese descent to only six years later be ranked the world's richest person, the world's biggest cannibal of them all.

The EZLN rose up on the day NAFTA went into effect on January 1, 1994, hoping the rest of Mexico would join them in Mexico City to overthrow the PRI. Their demands were housing, land, work, food, health, education, justice,

---

20. See *Drug War Capitalism* by Dawn Haley (AK Press, 2014)

independence, liberty, democracy, and peace. Instead of joining the rebellion, the Mexican nation called for a ceasefire, seeking to prevent a bloody war like the one in Guatemala next door and Colombia further south next door. The EZLN listened and declared a unilateral ceasefire after 12 days, deploying their word as their weapon to stay in the fight.[21] Six months later, they issued a *Second Declaration*.

While in the *First Declaration*, the EZLN had called upon the Mexican people to take up arms against who they saw as the main obstacle to democracy in their country: the Party-State, in the *Second Declaration*, they called the Mexican people to a civic and peaceful effort through a national democratic convention, an effort that was met by the PRI and its supporters with lies, fraud, mockery, and assassinations.

Six months later, on the first anniversary of their uprising, the EZLN issued a *Third Declaration* where they called on "all honest Mexicans" to form a national liberation movement, install a transitional government, create a new constitution, and destroy the system of the Party-State.

A year later in the *Fourth Declaration*, issued on the uprising's second anniversary, they announced the creation of five peaceful resistance centers in Zapatista territory as gathering points for Mexican culture and cultures of the world. And they announced they would continue with government peace talks, the San Andres Accords, about the rights and culture of Indigenous peoples for all of Mexico, not only Chiapas.

With the National Indigenous Congress (CNI), a network of Indigenous communities throughout Mexico co-founded by the Zapatistas, the Mexico from below drafted the San

---

21. *Our Word Is Our Weapon: Selected Writings*, by Subcomandante Insurgente Marcos (Seven Stories Press, 2002)

Andres Accords, which the Mexican government would sign but would not fulfill. Maybe some Zapatistas knew this would happen because they refused a handshake photograph. Maybe they had learned from a long line of deceptive "peace" treaties not to trust the oppressor's definition of peace. Maybe they had seen what happened with Palestine and the Oslo Accords in September 1993, only four months before January 1, 1994, and learned not to photograph any handshakes.

After signing the San Andres Accords, the Mexican government sent military and paramilitary groups to infiltrate and attack the Zapatista communities and their supporters, even more than the cannibal government had done before. This exploded in a paramilitary massacre in December 1997 of 45 people praying in a church, all members of a pacifist group sympathetic to the Zapatistas. Acteal, *presente*.

In the *Fifth Declaration*, issued in July 1998, the Zapatistas convoked Indigenous communities across Mexico to mobilize with them to demand the San Andres Accords become national law. The process ended with every political party betraying the Accords by refusing to ratify them, including the progressive party of Andrés Manuel López Obrador, at the time the Party of the Democratic Revolution (PRD) and future "progressive" President of Mexico but not for many years yet.

After this betrayal, the Zapatistas retreated into a silence. In 2005 they began issuing the *Sixth Declaration*, issued in sections throughout the following year. The *Sixth Declaration* announced the Zapatistas would no longer engage with political parties, politicians, bad governments, all of the above. Instead, they would struggle "from below and to the left." The *Sixth Declaration* tells the story of the Zapatista struggle in their own words and illustrates how capitalism functions both globally and locally, and shares the beginnings of their political proposal for all the peoples of the world to struggle together, in their own calendars, their own geographies, their own ways.

Well before the *Sixth Declaration*, the movement had long been sharing its theories on global capital in a historical moment they call the Fourth World War, a war that began as soon as the Third World War ended, as soon as the badly named "Cold" War ended.[22] The Zapatistas theorize that since the expansion of global capital following the fall of the Soviet Union, capital has become the global sovereign and has subordinated the nation-state to an administrative function that works on its behalf. Capital's predatory logic and practice means the enemy in this Fourth World War is not any one nation or any one state; it is anyone who gets in capital's predatory way. It is a theory difficult to argue against when using reality as the judge. The Zapatistas say out loud what everybody sees but no one likes to talk about, that the ruling class are administrators of capital, its many overseers of a global plantation made up of other plantations, patriots to their wallets, not to any nation. In such a context, the *Sixth Declaration* emphasized that to continue doing the politics of the politicians would be a death sentence for Indigenous peoples, a death sentence for Mexico, a death sentence for the world. The *Sixth Declaration* was issuing warnings about it decades ago.

The *Sixth* was issued as López Obrador was making his first presidential run in the summer of 2006, running a campaign against the eventual winner, Felipe Calderon. In that election, the Zapatistas did not support any politician, including López

---

22. See "The Fourth World War" (Big Noise Films, 2003) and *The Fourth World War, La Cuarta Guerra Mundial, Bilingual Edition* (Paliacate Press, 2024)

Obrador. They had witnessed his role in the betrayal of the San Andres Accords. They did not tell anyone to vote for president; they did not tell anyone not to vote for president. Instead they launched the Other Campaign parallel to that year's presidential campaigns, except traveling throughout Mexico listening to the pains of the below rather than asking for their vote.

For not supporting the progressive presidential candidate, the Zapatistas predicted they would be abandoned by the institutional left and its cannibalistic platforms of "progress". Their predictions were correct. After the *Sixth Declaration*, the institutional left began calling the Zapatistas irrelevant, hardly in existence, even dead. Just like Columbus and Them.

That summer of 2006 it was widely recognized that Felipe Calderon had stolen the election from López Obrador. Soon after his inauguration, Calderon launched a War on Drugs, imitating the one in the United States. Like the one in the United States, Mexico's War on Drugs is not against drugs but a war to manage each state's surplus populations and a war against those who get in capital's way. The United States tends to imprison its surplus population, as it considers people of Black Afrikan and Indigenous descent when it's not letting them die through landlessness, poverty, illness, and disease. Mexico tends to kill or disappear its surplus, also people of Black Afrikan and Indigenous descent, also left to die through landlessness, poverty, illness, and disease.

In Mexico from 2006 to today, hundreds of thousands of lives have perished between the territorial disputes of drug cartels who buy the politicians and kill or disappear the ones they can't buy. The post-Revolution Mexican nation has unraveled, and few dare to speak about it out loud.

In 2018, López Obrador would become president on his

third try. Again the Zapatistas would not support him. Again the institutional left would slander the Zapatistas, calling them agents of empire while in willful ignorance that López Obrador's presidential campaigns had all been financed by the Sinaloa drug cartel, something few have dared speak about out loud.[23]

To be fair, López Obrador and his followers have not been the only politicians on the narco payroll. The Sinaloa Cartel had previously financed all his rivals, including Calderon, who deployed the War on Drugs against Sinaloa's rivals.

With the function of the nation-state now at the service of a global capital that runs legal and illegal, the narco-state of Mexico oversees a social fabric undone and plunged into fear. Landless people in cities are now dependent on capital to live. Many urban hopes are today placed on fascism, on strong men, politicians, drug lords, and politician-drug lords, anyone who will give handouts, food, a sense of security, even a false sense of security. Thirty years ago, the EZLN called upon the Mexican nation to join their uprising for land. The Mexican nation responded they did not want to spiral into bloody war, like Guatemala and Colombia next door. Mexico thirty years later has spiraled into a bloody war, on many occasions surpassing Guatemala and Colombia next door.

The Zapatistas often say that changing the world is difficult and even impossible, and so the world has to be created anew. Every presidential election every six years, the Zapatistas often find themselves alone in Mexico. Their very other calendar speaks not of six years but of seven generations. In the meantime, they continue building and defending their

---

23. Anabel Hernandez, *La Historia Secreta: AMLO y el Cártel de Sinaloa* [*The Secret History: AMLO and the Sinaloa Cartel*] (Grijalbo, 2024)

autonomy, always from below, weaving with those who can see them, speaking with those who can listen. Sometimes not speaking at all.

On December 21, 2012, as some interpreted the end of the Maya long count as an "end of the world" prophecy, more than 40,000 Zapatistas of all ages marched in silence throughout several cities in Chiapas that day. They erected a stage with a ramp on each side for all to ascend and descend, left fists up. Not a single word was said out loud.

Everything they had to say that day, they published in a brief communiqué:

> *Did you listen?*
> *It is the sound of your world crumbling.*
> *It is the sound of our world resurging.*
> *The day that was day was night.*
> *And night shall be the day that will be day.*[24]

On December 21, 2012, while some interpreted a Maya prophecy for the end of the world, the Maya Zapatistas were promising the end of *this* world.[25] The end of this world for the creation of the world anew.

A new world for which if we must die, we die standing.

On our feet, not on our knees.

Dying standing like the trees.

---

24. EZLN (2012) "Communique of the Clandestine Indigenous Revolutionary Committee – General Command of the Zapatista National Liberation Army. Mexico. December 21, 2012"

25. Alvaro Reyes (2015) "Zapatismo: Other Geographies *circa* 'the end of the world'" *Environment and Planning D: Society and Space*, volume 33

PALESTINE 1492: A REPORT BACK

Panthers and Jaguars

> Yes, Marcos is gay.
> Marcos is gay in San Francisco,
> Black in South Africa,
> an Asian in Europe,
> a Chicano in San Ysidro,
> an anarchist in Spain,
> a Palestinian in Israel,
> a Maya Indian in the streets of San Cristóbal,
> a Jew in Germany,
> a Gypsy in Poland,
> a Mohawk in Quebec,
> a pacifist in Bosnia,
> a single woman on the Metro at 10pm,
> a peasant without land,
> a gang member in the slums,
> an unemployed worker,
> an unhappy student,
> and of course, a Zapatista in the mountains...[1]

---

1. Excerpt from Subcomandante Insurgente Marcos, *Old Man Antonio: "Strength is born in the mountain, but it's not seen until it arrives below,"* (May 28, 1994)

Palestine from Below

A *Palestinian in Israel... a Jew in Germany* the words read. Marcos is not just an identity; Marcos is an identity in a context. Not just a Palestinian and not just a Jew, a Palestinian *in Israel* and a Jew *in Germany*. Marcos is the below being crushed by the above, but not only. Marcos is an identity in a context of resistance: not simply gay, gay *in San Francisco*. Marcos is dignity, the strength to be who you are, not who others want you to be.

The "Marcos is gay" excerpt is from a postscript, from a P.S. of a longer communique from 1994 where Subcomandante Insurgente Marcos, the Zapatista spokesperson at the time, recalls visiting the villages in the Lacandon Jungle in 1992 to learn their decision about going to war. While in the village of his mentor *Viejo Antonio*, Old Man Antonio, awaiting the village assembly's decision, Viejo Antonio guided Marcos to a river nearby. He pointed out that the war between the clouds and mountains above brings the rain, creating the river below. "Strength is born in the mountain, but it's not seen until it arrives below," Viejo Antonio had said.[2]

In Maya worlds, appreciation, innocence, peace, happiness, and tranquility in our hearts closes the window that allows the seven shames to invade: ego, pride, envy, lying, ignorance, ingratitude, and crime, words that my Maya-Q'eqchi' teacher, Tata Julio, does not like to repeat out loud too much. He says a five-pointed star serves as a shield above the windows and above the doors. This morning in our lesson I asked Tata Julio how one can be a defender of the people in war while maintaining appreciation, innocence, peace, happiness, and tranquility in one's heart.

---

2. See also "Antonio's Dream and a Prophecy," in *Zapatista Stories for Dreaming An-Other World* (PM Press, 2022)

"Patience," was his answer. "We don't see the results until much later. But they're there."

The first members of the EZLN entered the Lacandon Jungle trained as urban guerrillas, and they had to learn this patience, they had to learn to listen to the below.[3] The figure of Viejo Antonio in Marcos' stories served as a bridge, connecting them with the Maya world through sacred texts like the *Popol Vuh* of the Quiche-speaking Maya people, the Maya-Quiche. Sometimes called the Maya Bible and often translated as the "Book of the Community," or the "Book of Council," the *Popol Vuh* is a Maya creation story of the beings between the earth and the sky, between the east, west, south, and north, a creation story of the hearts of those between the earth and the sky.

The *Popol Vuh* was largely passed down as oral tradition until the 1550s, when it was recorded in writing as Columbus and Them were burning the Maya books, the Maya codecis. A Catholic priest hosting a mass book burning in the Yucatán peninsula wrote, in 1562:

> We found a large number of books in these characters and, as they contained nothing in which were not to be seen as superstition and lies of the devil, we burned them all, which they regretted to an amazing degree, and which caused them much affliction.

The "Marcos is gay" subscript was responding to the Mexico of Columbus and Them, the Mexico from above that sought to delegitimize the EZLN by calling its spokesperson gay. The subscript was published in 1994, but I first encountered it

---

3. See *The Fire and the Word: A History of the Zapatista Movement* by Gloria Muñoz Ramírez (City Lights, 2008)

many years later. Its reference to *a Palestinian in Israel* and *a Jew in Germany* helped resolve something for me as I was learning about Palestine: there is no eternal oppressed identity, there is no eternal oppressor identity; there is a context of domination, identities can shift between above and below; the root of the problem is that there exists an above vs a below; the root of the problem is the context of injustice.[4]

In 2003, still at the height of the Second Intifada, news traveled around the world when Israel killed a White American woman in Gaza, and again the following year when Israel killed a White British man in Gaza. Rachel Corrie had placed her body in front of an Israeli armored bulldozer in Gaza to protect a Palestinian home from demolition. She was a White American woman, and still an Israeli bulldozer crushed her body.[5] Tom Hurndall was a photography student peacefully protesting with Palestinians in Gaza. He was a White British man, and still an Israeli sniper shot him in the head.[6] Rachel Corrie and Tom Hurndall went to Gaza to resist like a Palestinian in Israel. Defenders of the people who didn't get to see the results of their struggle, but it's there. Rachel Corrie and Tom Hurndall, *presentes.*

There exists no eternally oppressed identity, there exists no eternally oppressor identity. There exists context.

The first time I applied for a National Science Foundation

---

4. For more, see "The Limitations and Dangers of Decolonial Philosophies: Lessons from Zapatista Luis Villoro" by Gregory Fernando Pappas in *Radical Philosophy Review* 20.2: 265–295

5. Rachel Corrie, *Let Me Stand Alone: The Journal of Rachel Corrie* (W. W. Norton and Company, 2008)

6. Jocelyn Hurndall, *My Son Tom: The Life and Tragic Death of Tom Hurndall* (Bloomsbury Publishing, 2008)

doctoral dissertation grant to help me argue this about Palestine, the reviewers didn't like that I brought up so much context. Their rejection letter said my research was "a plain threat" "to Eretz Israel adherents." Eretz Israel is the name Zionists use for an Israel whose borders extend well beyond Palestine all the way east to Iraq, meaning Israel's destruction and death promises to continue well beyond Palestine. It already does.[7]

When I was nine years old, a Jew in Germany had already asked me who I would defend in a context like that. Anne Frank, *presente*.[8] I was an adult now, answering her question, accompanying both Jews in Germany and Palestinians in Israel, Palestinians in a land called Palestine occupied on all sides by an genocidal force called the State of Israel.

My university let me know that if I set foot in the Gaza Strip I would not graduate. Whether I visited Gaza on fieldwork or off, they said, it wouldn't matter, my research wouldn't count. The university was following the U.S. State Department travel restrictions. The year was 2010. The Gaza Strip and the West Bank had long been labeled with the highest travel restriction, but the West Bank had just been lowered one notch to facilitate its new economic reforms. I would be allowed to go to the West Bank only if I signed a waiver saying the university would not be responsible if I was killed. It didn't say killed *by whom*. They did make sure to add, "I further agree that I will not travel to Gaza."

Once finished with course work and exams, and with changing my research site from Gaza to the West Bank, I spent

---

7. See Jimmy Johnson and Linda Quiquivix "Israel and Mexico swap notes on abusing rights" *Electronic Intifada* (May 21, 2013)

8. Anne Frank, *The Diary of a Young Girl* (1947)

the summer before moving to Palestine reading books in the Black Radical Tradition prompted by other teachers of mine at the time, a collective inspired by both the Zapatistas and the Black Panthers, mentored by Ashanti Alston, former member of the Black Panther Party and the Black Liberation Army, former political prisoner, abolitionist, and weaver of the Black Panthers and Zapatismo. That summer was dedicated to reading books I kept hearing about from my teachers. *The Autobiography of Malcolm X* (1965), who inspired the Black Panthers; Black Panther Co-Founder Huey Newton's *Revolutionary Suicide* (1973), and imprisoned intellectual George Jackson through his prison letters: *Soledad Brother* (1970) and *Blood in My Eye* (1971).

Blood in My Eye was the last book I read before moving to Palestine. It was August 2010. In the book, George Jackson theorizes fascism, but not simply the fascism restricted to the Italy of Mussolini or to the Germany of Hitler during the Second World War. George Jackson was a theorist of fascism, but not simply of the fascism experienced within the borders of Europe and on the bodies of Europeans. George Jackson analyzed fascism as a practice and logic beyond the Second World War. In broadening out fascism's geography and history, Jackson complimented prior arguments like Aimé Césaire's in the 1950s that analyzed the genocide of Jews and those who were different within Europe as part of the same logic practiced by Europe against non-Europe. Césaire's word for it was colonialism.

The Black Martinican poet agreed that genocide is the greatest crime against humanity, but was more expansive to include *all* humanity, not only Europe's. As Césaire had put it, Europe's violence onto itself with the Nazi Holocaust was a "boomerang" back to Europe, and that before Europeans were

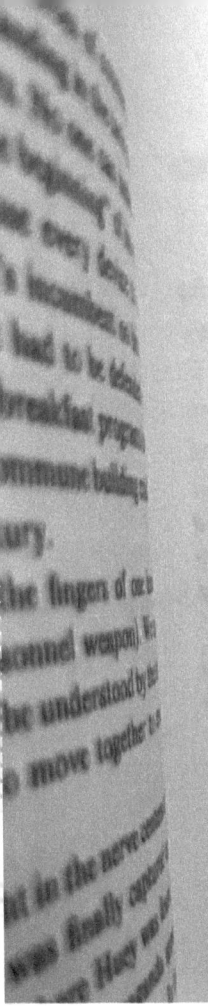

Fascism

Its most advanced form is here in Amerika.

Page 127 of *Blood in My Eye*

its victims, they had tolerated Nazism by another name in non-Europe,

> that they absolved it, shut their eyes to it, legitimized it, because, until then, it had been applied only to non-European peoples.[9]

When *Blood in My Eye* was published in 1971, it had been

---

9. Aimé Césaire, *Discourse on Colonialism* (1950).

a decade since George Jackson began serving a sentence of one year to life. At 19 years old in 1961, he had been convicted of robbing $70 from a gas station. While locked up, Jackson was mentored by other prisoners to study and read about liberation and radical theory, "radical" meaning the *root*. Jackson became an effective teacher and was thrown into solitary confinement because of it. It was in solitary in 1971 where George Jackson had written about fascism that,

> *Its most advanced form is here in Amerika.*

My body had reacted defensively when I turned to page 127 of *Blood in My Eye* that summer and first read those words. *You hadn't known about Israel yet*, I challenged George Jackson. In fact, George Jackson had known about Israel. After they assassinated him, the prison guards found over 99 books in Jackson's cell, including a collection of Palestinian resistance poetry called *Enemy of the Sun*.[10] My instinct had been to argue with him, but the more George Jackson I read, the more I suspected I was going to lose. He was talking about capitalism:

> *We will never have a complete definition of fascism, because it is in constant motion, showing a new face to fit any particular set of problems that arise to threaten the predominance of the traditionalist, capitalist ruling class. But if one were forced for the sake of clarity to define it in a word simple enough for all to understand, that word would be 'reform.' We can make our definition more precise by adding the word 'economic.'*

---

10. Greg Thomas (2016) "Blame It on the Sun: George Jackson and Poetry of Palestinian Resistance," *Comparative American Studies An International Journal*, 13(4), 236–253

> *'Economic reform' comes very close to*
> *a working definition of fascist motive forces.*

Economic reform. I had previously only considered military and police as the faces of fascism. I had only considered naked force. I had not been wrong to, but naked force is not the only force. When fascism doesn't have to be so forced is fascism's advanced form. When the people desire fascism is fascism's most advanced form. George Jackson was in a dungeon serving one year to life for $70, and outside the people were shopping in willful ignorance, distracted from the blood under their feet, desiring captivity not escape.

In Palestine in 2010, I witnessed the beginnings of the West Bank's economic reforms. Palestinians were starting to take out debt, something unheard of before, according to everyone: car loans, house loans, even student loans. It was resembling the consumerist ways of Americans, except in an economy fully dependent on foreign aid, on *Israel-friendly* foreign aid, an economy the Palestinian Authority couldn't even pretend to control, a foreign aid economy of war.[11]

Gaza, in contrast, remained besieged.

As a theorist of fascism, Jackson's greatest concern was the health of the resistance. He argued the resistance is weak when it respects the fascist's accomplishments, when the resistance regards the fascist with prestige. He used that word, prestige:

> *The aura of magic, glamour, luster, and splendid permanence*
> *covers the fascists like a protective layer of fat...*

---

11. See Khalil Nakhleh's *Globalized Palestine: The National Sell-Out of a Homeland* (The Red Sea Press, 2011); and Lisa Bhungalia, *Elastic Empire: Refashioning War through Aid in Palestine* (Stanford University Press, 2023)

> *Prestige bars any serious attack on power. Do people attack a thing they consider with awe, with a sense of its legitimacy?*

Fascism advances when we learn to respect the master, more when we wish the master loved us, and is far gone when it is the master we desire to become. When we regard the fascists with awe, when we wish ourselves to be seen that way too, when we seek a position of prestige alongside them, our resistance to fascism is weak.

It would not be in the West Bank but in West Jerusalem where I would concede the fight to George Jackson. It happened at an Israeli outdoor mall across from East Jerusalem, across from where Palestinians are regularly harassed, assaulted, raided, tortured, imprisoned, displaced, killed by Israel's military and police. At the Mamila Mall in West Jerusalem, by stark contrast, the shoppers looked and acted willfully deluded, just like Americans. Many were probably Americans. It reminded me of the Santa Monica Promenade in Los Angeles, people distracted from the blood beneath their feet, ignoring the displaced dying across the street. There weren't tanks or police in West Jerusalem either. They're not always necessary. Within the people there was plenty of consent, willful ignorance to help cope with the fear, a refusal to escape, a desire for captivity instead.

If we wish to know how advanced the fascism is, ask the resistance if their leaders are their masters.

If we wish to know how advanced the fascism is, ask the resistance who it wishes to be loved by.

If we wish to know how advanced the fascism is, ask the resistance who they desire to become.

Amerika's is certainly most advanced.

George Jackson, *presente*.

Panthers and Jaguars

Palestine 1492: A Report Back

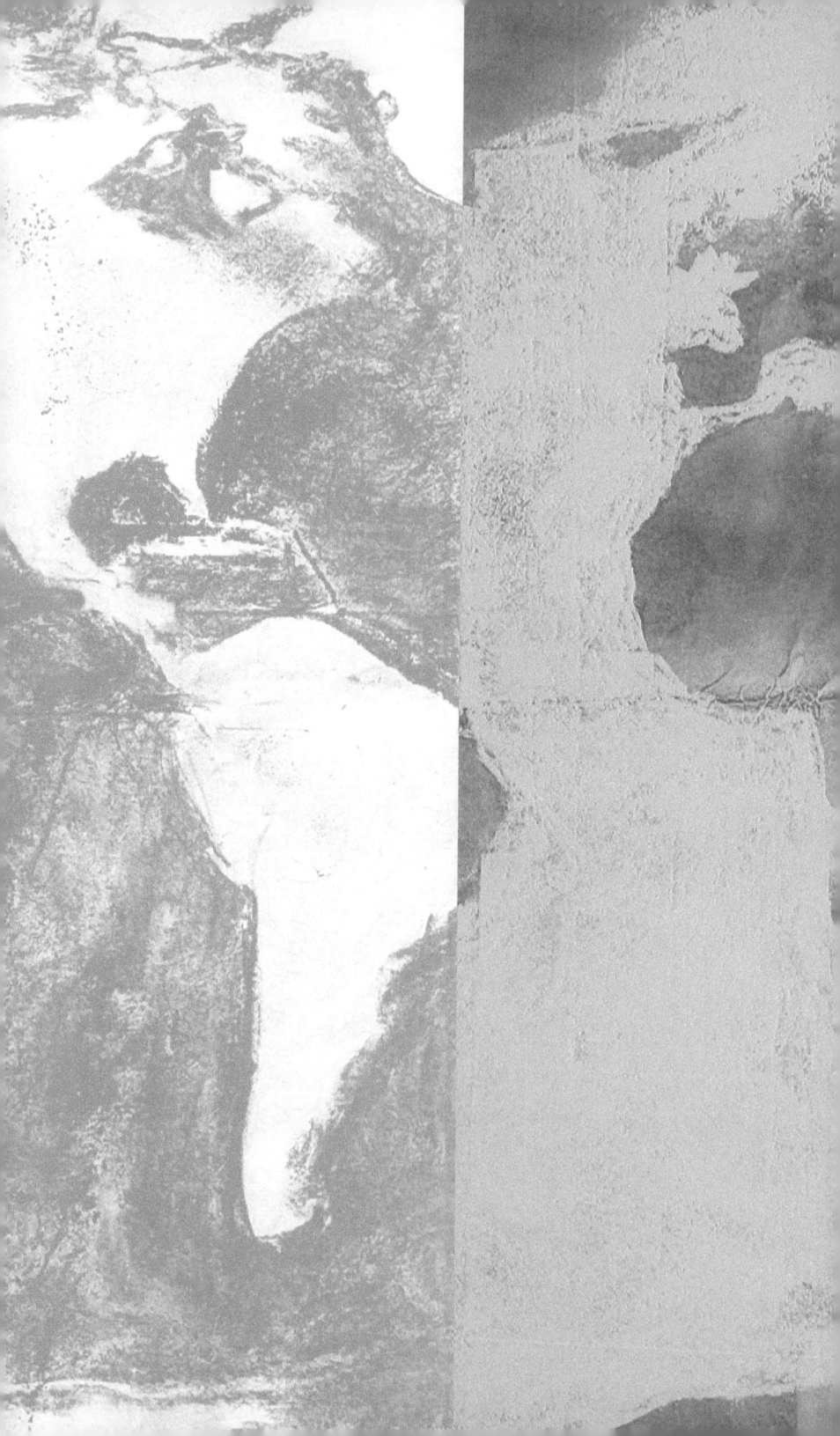

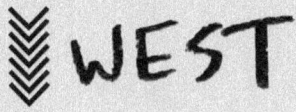

Palestine from Above

"In the history of colonial invasion maps are always first drawn by the victors, since maps are instruments of conquest. Geography is therefore the art of war but can also be the art of resistance if there is a counter-map and a counter-strategy."

—Edward Said, 1994

1

Speak of the Devil

There is a saying in English for when you're speaking about someone who isn't there and they suddenly appear: "Speak of the Devil." This phrase is shortened from the longer "Speak of the Devil and he shall appear." That second part is usually left out, as if too much has already been spoken.

In Spanish, the phrase is, "Speaking of the King of Rome, he'll appear by the door." *Hablando del Rey de Roma por la puerta asoma.* I can't help but to interpret this to mean that across worlds it was previously agreed that the King of Rome was the Devil, or that the Devil was the King of Rome.

In Palestine, depending on who you ask, the Devil's origins were far humbler than that. According to tradition, before he became known as the cosmic enemy of God, a figure called "the satan" appears in the Bible as God's obedient servant whose job it is to check in on people unannounced, making them pass cruel tests to confirm their devotion to God.

When the Jewish people of Jesus of Nazareth organized their rebellion against the Roman Empire two thousand years ago, they were neither the first nor the last to adopt a good vs evil binary dualism to guide their struggle.[1] They say Christianity

---

1. See Richard A. Horsley, *Jesus and Empire: The Kingdom of God and the New World* (Fortress Press, 2002); and Neil Forsyth, *The Old Enemy: Satan and the Combat Myth* (Princeton University Press, 1989)

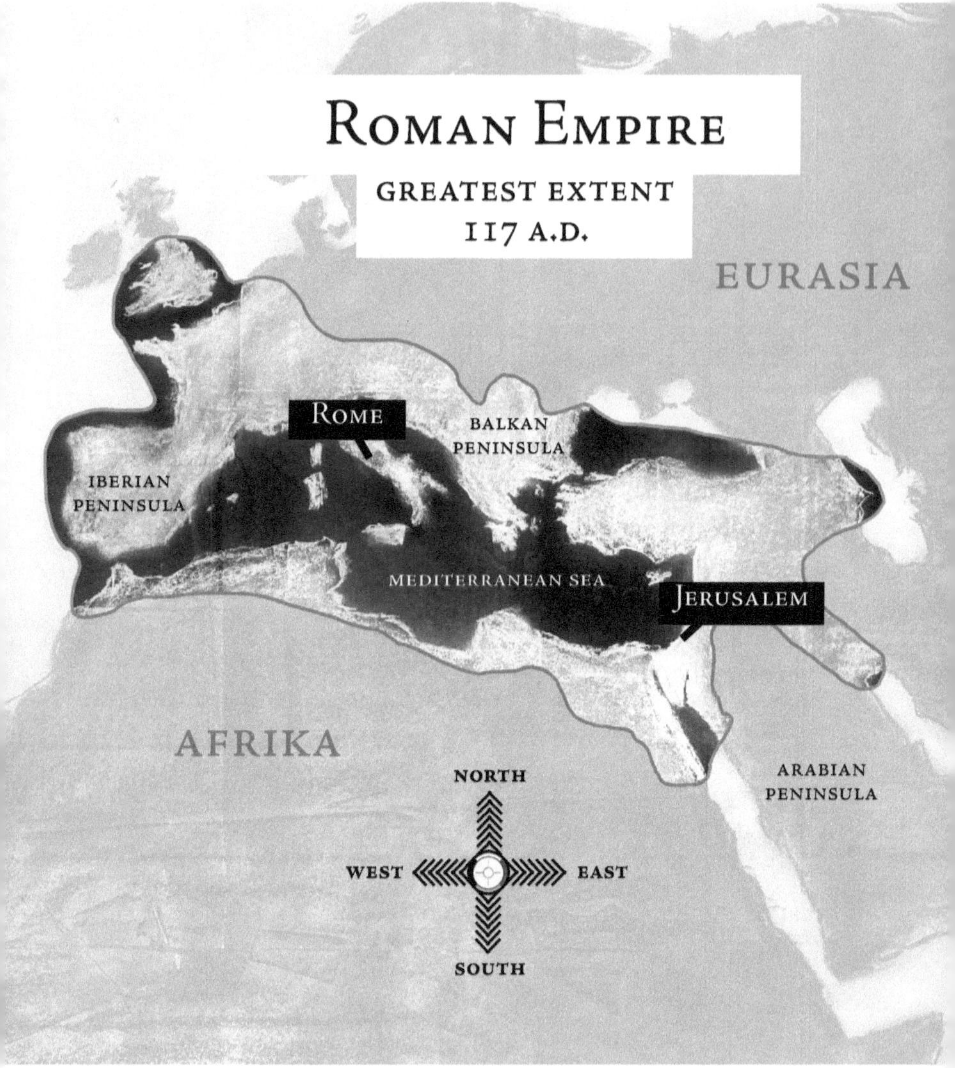

Palestine from Above

Roman Empire
Greatest Extent
117 A.D.

borrowed the binary from Manicheanism in Persia some centuries back, but still Christianity is credited with inventing the Devil in Palestine. I wonder: is this Christianity's main difference from Judaism? That Judaism interprets God as doer of both good and evil, and in Christianity God is only doer of good and the Devil is doer of evil?

Speaking of the Devil, he has appeared. He is on the map on the opposite page. They say the Roman Empire reached its greatest territorial extent in the year 117 A.D. This is another way of saying the Roman Empire went into decline the day after. This was almost one hundred years after Rome assassinated Palestine's rebel Jesus. As the map shows, the Devil used to surround all the Mediterranean Sea and its adjacent lands, including North Afrika, the Iberian Peninsula, and the Balkan Peninsula, all the way to Jerusalem.

It would still be two hundred years before the Devil would be baptized as Christian, his second-greatest trick, crucial for his first. By then the Roman Emperor almost had no choice but to co-opt the resistance. The word of the rebel Jesus was spreading widely along the Mediterranean's peninsulas and ports all the way from Jerusalem.

Rome's capture of Christianity granted it legitimacy to determine who was the Devil now, and it wasn't going to be the King of Rome. Not in official History. The Emperor could now label his enemies the Devil to deflect attention from himself: Black Afrikans, Indigenous peoples, women, Jews, Muslims, pagans, other Christians against the empire were called the Devil by Rome, a baptism that transformed Christianity from a religion of the earth into a religion of the empire.[2]

---

2. Wes Howard-Brook, *Empire Baptized: How the Church Embraced What Jesus Rejected* (Orbis Books, 2016)

There still exist today many Christianities from below, both from before and from after. But the health of their resistances to the capture has been weak.

Christianity has not been the only world captured. The Kingdom of Israel captured Judaism in the past and the State of Israel has captured Judaism again in the present.³ Caliphs, kings, sultans, and ayatollahs have captured Islam in the past and continue holding Islam captive in the present.

Christianity's capture has an official date and event: 312 A.D., the day Roman Emperor Constantine was baptized in the city he would soon name after himself, Constantinople.

The acronym A.D. in all this means *anno Domini nostri Jesu Christi*, meaning after the birth of "the Year of our Lord Jesus Christ". This notation is used today by a global empire that calls itself "secular," meaning not religious. Secular is a word that helps the Devil pull off his greatest trick, getting everyone to believe he does not exist where he actually exists.

For the years before the birth of Christ, the traditional notation is Before Christ (B.C.). Its secularized notation is Before Common Era (B.C.E.), and A.D. is secularized as C.E. (Common Era). Not everybody uses the secularized notation. There is no secularizing that the birth of Christ remains the empire's Year Zero. That's not every world's Year Zero.

In the Jewish calendar, Year Zero is "From the Creation of the World" according to Jewish tradition, almost 4,000 years before Europe's Year Zero. Islam's Year Zero comes 622 years after Europe's, that is, 622 A.D., the year of the *hijrah*, the journey the prophet Muhammad and his followers took from

---

3. Marc H. Ellis, *Beyond Innocence and Redemption: Confronting the Holocaust and Israeli Power: Creating a Moral Future for the Jewish People* (Harper Collins, 1991)

Mecca to Medina. Year Zero for the Maya is the domestication of maize in one of the calendars, while events millions of years from before and after are counted in the other Maya calendars.

Empires, secular or not, regularly capture the resistance from below to co-opt it, to neutralize it. Too often they succeed; death and destruction are not easy to resist. Neither are the Devil's seductions.

Three hundred years after Christianity's capture, Islam would be born in the Arabian Peninsula, spreading quickly up to Jerusalem and throughout Rome's territories. Understandably, this upset the Roman Empire, less because it was Christian, more because it was an empire, one challenged by other empires similarly familiar with the power of capture.

Notice Granada on the map.

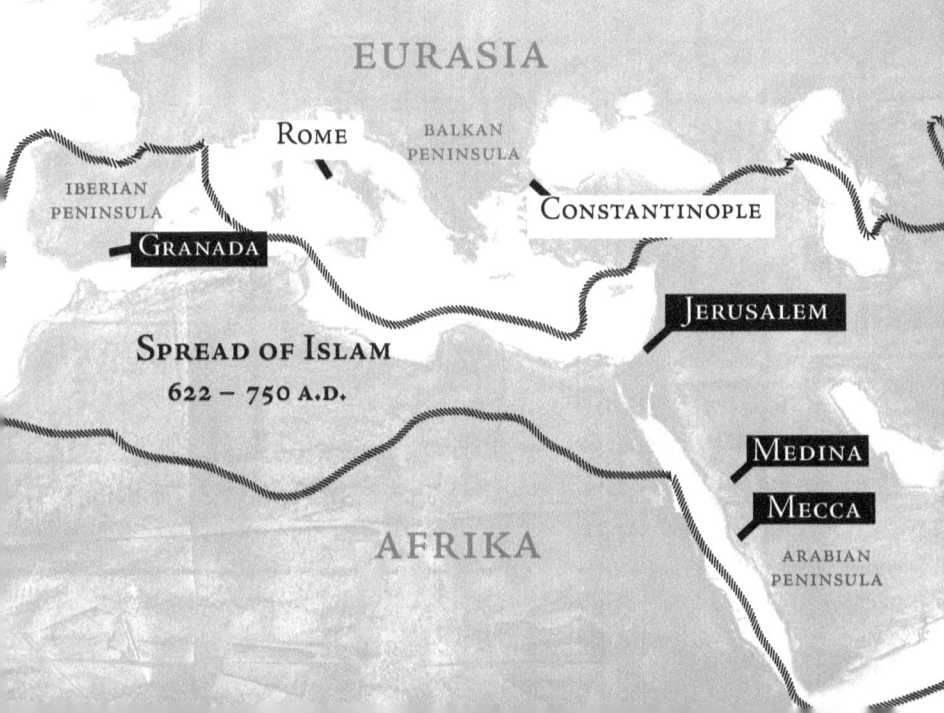

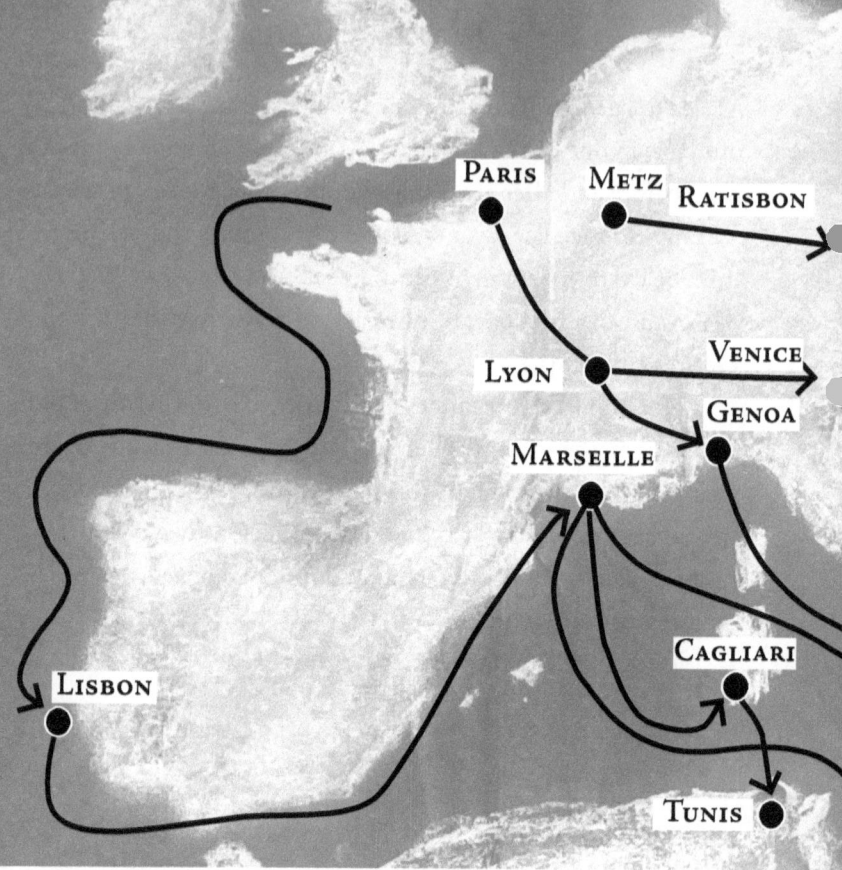

After losing Jerusalem, a wounded and dangerous Rome launched Holy Wars to reconquer the Holy City. Known as the Crusades, the best known of these took place between 1095–1291 A.D., resulting in the brief retaking of Jerusalem.

Crusading is said to mark the early unification of modern Europe, a geography usually at war with itself absent an external enemy, absent an external "Devil."

Many Crusaders were recruited to do Europe's fighting with promises of God's salvation. Others were motivated by economic and political temptations. All were told by Rome that the Devil was Islam, continuing to pull off its greatest trick, getting everyone to believe the Devil does not exist where he actually exists.

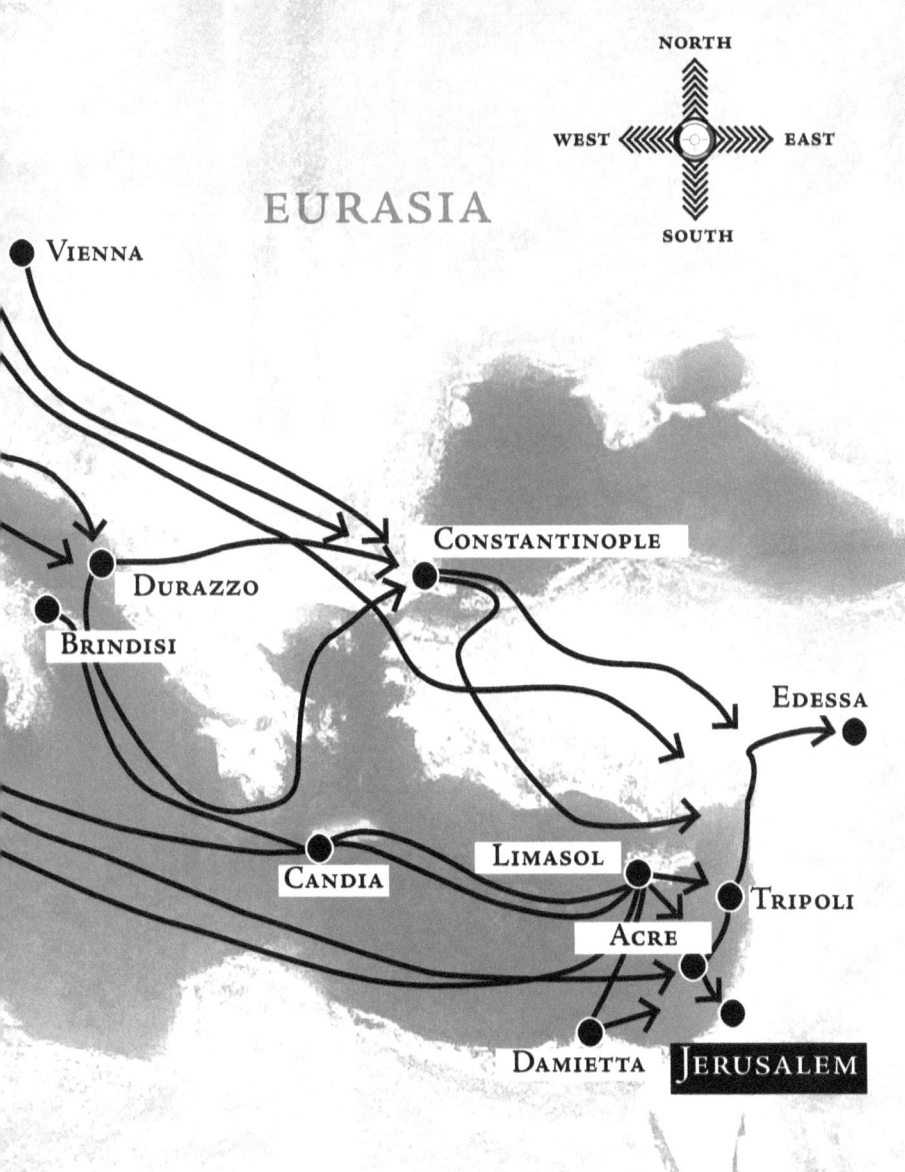

ruffen

SIRIA

Noschaw

Antiochia 70.

Türckey

Damascus

AR

IERVSALEM

Das

Alexandria 72.

Egypten

yrenez 4.

·

Wounded Europe

I begin this chapter by clarifying right away that there exists a Europe that isn't an asshole. I met that land briefly some years back. It has a different name though, *Slumil K'ajxemk'op* in Mayan-Tzotzil, meaning *Tierra Insumisa* in Spanish, Rebellious Land in English.[1]

This chapter is not about Slumil K'ajxemk'op, those lands from below in the struggle for life. This chapter is about the Europe from above, a wounded and dangerous Europe of great physical, spiritual, emotional, and mental imbalance.

Not everyone who sees Europe as extremely dangerous also sees it as wounded. But we can hear the wound if we know where to listen. When Europe talks about its calendar, for example, it describes what happened before its year 1492 A.D. as "dark." For centuries, it was "the Dark Ages," Europe says about a time when it was wasn't an empire anymore, a time it doesn't like to talk about. The rest of the earth, Europe alleges, was also in the Dark Ages, capitalizing it like that to declare it

---

1. See *Asking Questions with the Zapatistas: Reflections from Greece on Our Civilizational Impasse*, by Theodoros Karyotis, Ioanna-Maria Maravelidi & Yavor Tarinskicover (Transnational Institute of Social Ecology, 2022); and "Building alliances in pandemic times: the Zapatista journey through Europe" by R. Aída Hernández Castillo in *Debates Indígenas* (August 1, 2021)

official. It was only after 1492 A.D. when Europe says it found Enlightenment, also capitalized.

We can also locate Europe's wound if we learn to listen to how Europe speaks in everyday life. It often talks about light and dark in binaries of light *vs* dark, not in fluid dualities of light *and* dark. It maps this a binary onto a morality of good vs evil, which it translates as Europe = always good, non-Europe = always evil. Binaries have a hard time allowing any fluidity between opposites. It's like Europe is stuck.

We can feel Europe's wound if we pay attention to how we feel when we try to be next to Europe. It feels as if on reflex Europe always wants to fight, a type of paranoia that the stranger is an enemy rather than the stranger is a mystery. Wounded Europe's basic relation tends to be war with only two options: kill or be killed, eat or be eaten, rise above or be crushed below. Europe's war forces lightness and darkness into a cosmic imbalance where lightness is always good and darkness is always evil, not mattering to Europe that's not how the cosmos work. But you learn pretty fast when you encounter Wounded Europe that it maps this binary war onto almost everything, even onto colors, even human skin color. That's how fast you learn when you encounter Europe, or when Europe encounters you.

That time when Europe wasn't an empire that it doesn't like to talk about signals a wound. You can tell because when you bring it up, Europe always interrupts, preferring to jump back further in time to when Europe says it was Great, to when Europe says it was the Roman Empire, whose geography back then extended much farther than what is today known as the Continent of Europe, capitalized like that so you won't look it up and learn Europe isn't even a continent.

That Europe claims to be a separate continent is a fact of

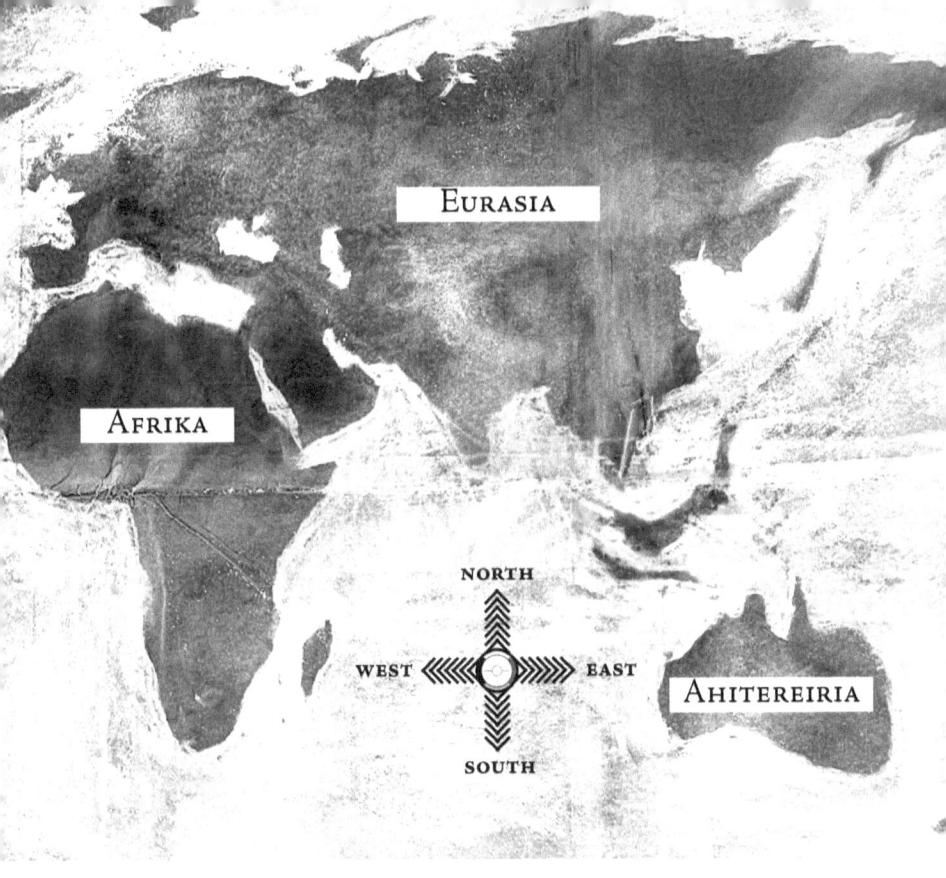

great confusion for those who value accuracy and consistency, for there exists no separate landmass called Europe. Which body of water separates Europe from Asia on that great landmass called Eurasia, nobody has been able to convincingly show. On the map above, Europe exists on the western edge of the large continent called Eurasia and directly north of Afrika, another continent.

A third continent appearing on this map is Ahitereiria, an Indigenous name for the lands that have been called Australia by the Europeans since that land's misfortune of having been found out by the Europeans.

For Ahitereiria it happened in 1606 by the world's first corporation, the Dutch East India Company, a formation that allowed regular rich Europeans to collectively finance

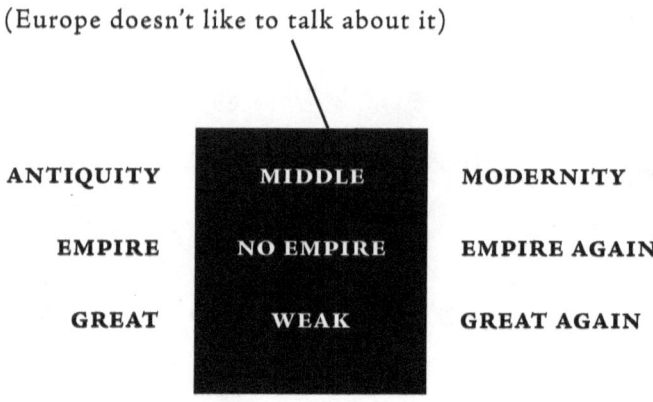

Wounded Europe doesn't like to talk about the life that happened in the middle between Antiquity and Modernity, an era it often refers to as "Dark".

and profit from colonialism without having to appeal to the monarchs for resources or permission. Just like today.

That time when Europe says it was weak spanned over one-thousand-and-one years, but Wounded Europe smothers it in between its beginning, which it calls Antiquity, and its end, which it calls Modernity, eras it understands as Great and Great Again, respectively. The time in between, Europe calls the Middle Ages when it's not calling it the Dark Ages, which it doesn't like to talk about. Its calendrical arc thus goes from Great to Weak and back to Great Again. There is no more calendar after that.

The absolute End of Time is central to Europe's calendar, an era with astonishing finality that it calls the End Times or

Israel, a child of Wounded Europe is just as dangerous. Wounded Israel maps its calendar with the same linear arc that returns to an imperial era, ignoring the 1800 years of Jewish life that happened in the middle, a time Israel doesn't like to talk about.

the End of History, depending. Maybe Europe's obsession with the End is rational if you listen to how it describes itself: a world filled with "continual fear and danger of violent death, and the life of man, solitary, poor, nasty, brutish, and short."[2]

Wounded Europe has a hard time thinking in allegories and metaphor about the end of the world. It speaks about ending it all literally, meaning the end of life on Planet Earth, meaning extinction, which is why it's not mad at the current extinction, it is part of the plan. Wounded Europe fully expects to be rescued from a dying Earth in a literal sense. It is right now working on the spaceships.

---

2. Thomas Hobbes, *Leviathan* (1651)

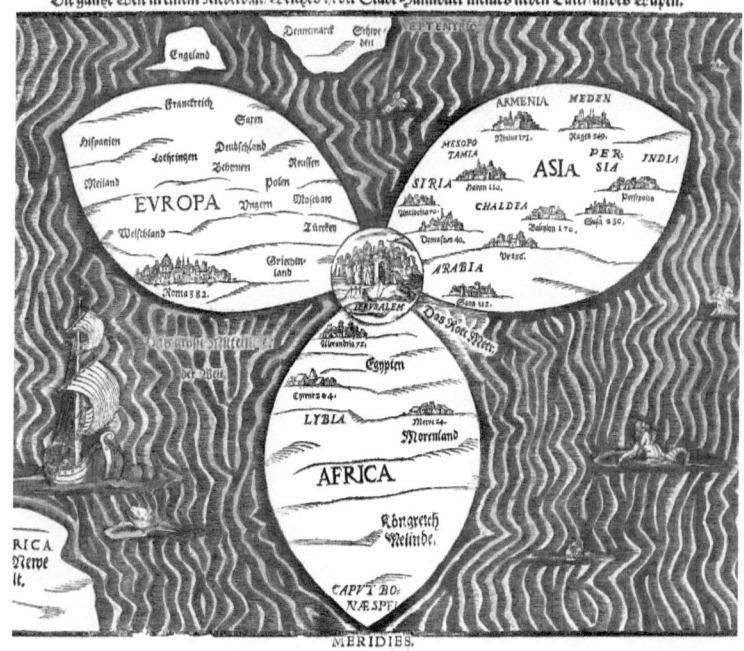

Europe's precise End Times calendar is accompanied by a geography of equally astonishing certainty: Jerusalem.

Christendom's loss of Jerusalem to the Islamic empires appears to have slipped Europe into its Dark Age, and its obsession with Jerusalem appears only to have gained strength during this time. Europe's world maps used to place Jerusalem not just anywhere on the map but at the center of the world.

The Bünting Cloverleaf Map, on the opposite page and on the next pages, was published in 1581 by a Protestant pastor of the so-called Holy Roman Empire. The map placed Jerusalem in the center of the world surrounded by Europe, Asia, and Afrika, following the world geography that believes Europe is its own continent.

This map was published almost one hundred years after 1492. The existence of Abya Yala, a very other continent, was still a recent disruption to this Biblical world geography. Thus, rather than appearing as another clover leaf among the other continents, Abya Yala appeared as an out-of-place a blob in the bottom left corner labeled "America."

Palestine from Above

IIII Die gantze Welt in einem Kleberblat/Welches ist der St

Dennemarck
Schweden
Engeland
Franckreich
Saxen
Hispanien
Deudschland
Lothringen
Behemen
Reussen
Meiland
Polen
Moschaw
EVROPA
Vngern
Welschland
Türckey
Griechenland
Roma 382.

OCCIDENS.

Das grosse Mittelmeer der Welt.

Alexandria 72.
Cyrene 84.
LYBIA
AFRIC

AMERICA
Die Newe
Welt.

CAPVT
NÆ
MERI

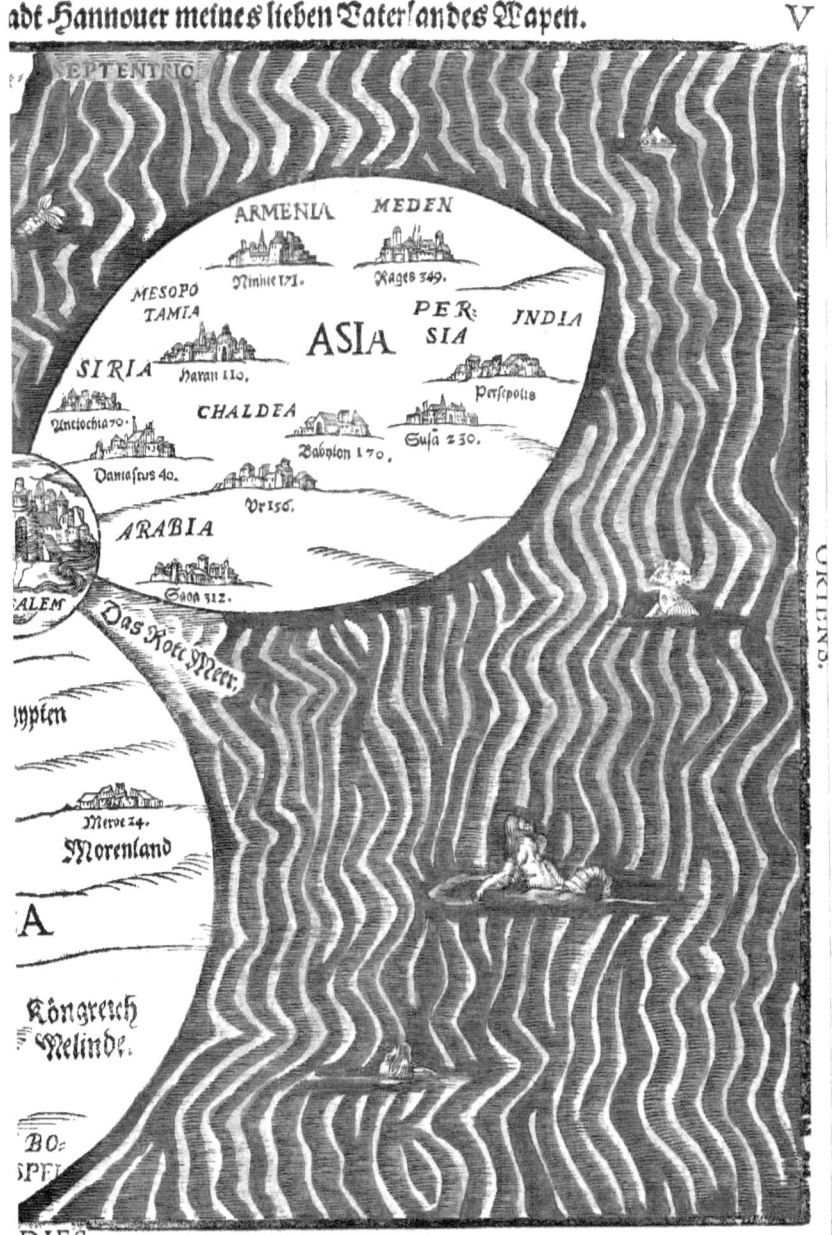

Oriens
MARE OCEANVM
ASIA
Sem
Mare magnum siue
mediter
raneum
EVROPA
Iafeth
AFRICA
Cham
Septentrio
Meridies
Occidens

EAST
NORTH
SOUTH
WEST

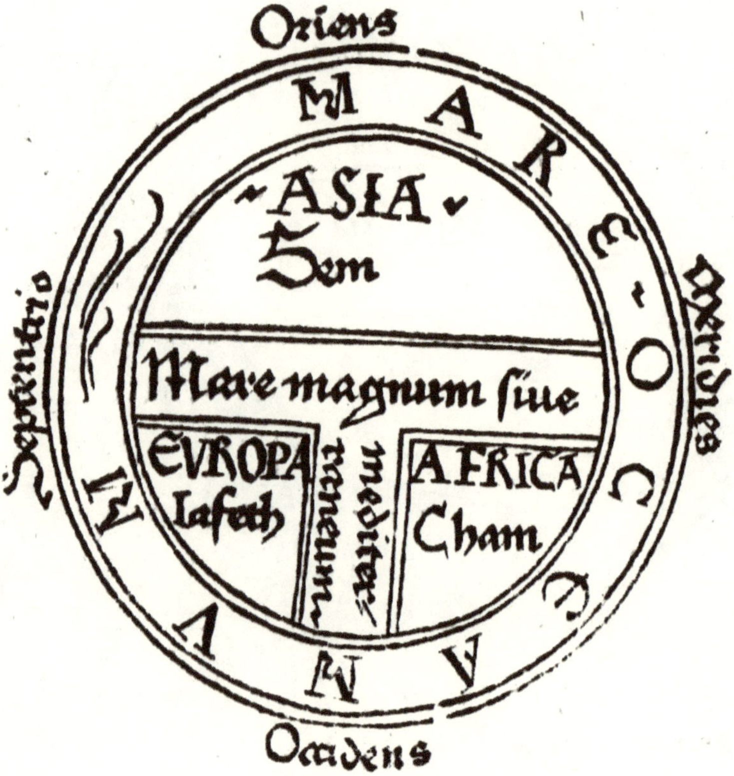

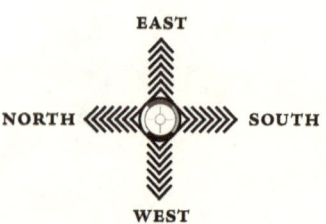

On the opposite page is an example of Europe's earlier world maps during its Dark Ages, known as T and O maps. The known landmasses on these maps were surrounded in a circle O of ocean, and a T in the center separating Asia, Afrika, and Europe. Notice how Europe depicted itself as a continent equal in size to Afrika and placed itself directly as Afrika's opposite. Also notice the top of the map is oriented with east at top toward Asia, the direction of the Garden of Eden, the beginning of the Christian creation story.

Europe's creation story tells that Europeans are the direct descendants of Noah, the Flood hero of the Hebrew Bible. Noah is said to have had three sons: Sem, Iafeth, and Cham, and each was sent to populate the world after the Flood: Sem to Asia, Iafeth to Europe, Cham to Africa. According to Wounded Europe, Noah cursed Cham and his descendants in Africa with Darkness and blessed Iafeth and his descendants with Lightness.

This map was published in 625 A.D., but originally did not have the labels shown here for Noah's sons: Sem in Asia, Iafeth in Europe, and Cham in Africa. Those labels would be added by Europeans during the wave of race science in the nineteenth century, when they deployed science to prove their racism and anti-Blackness as a directive from God.

According to this map, Jews are descendants of Sem not of Iafeth and should be living in Asia not in Europe. This map helped me better understand the label Europe created for the Jewish people: *Semites* and the label Europe created for itself: *anti-Semite*.

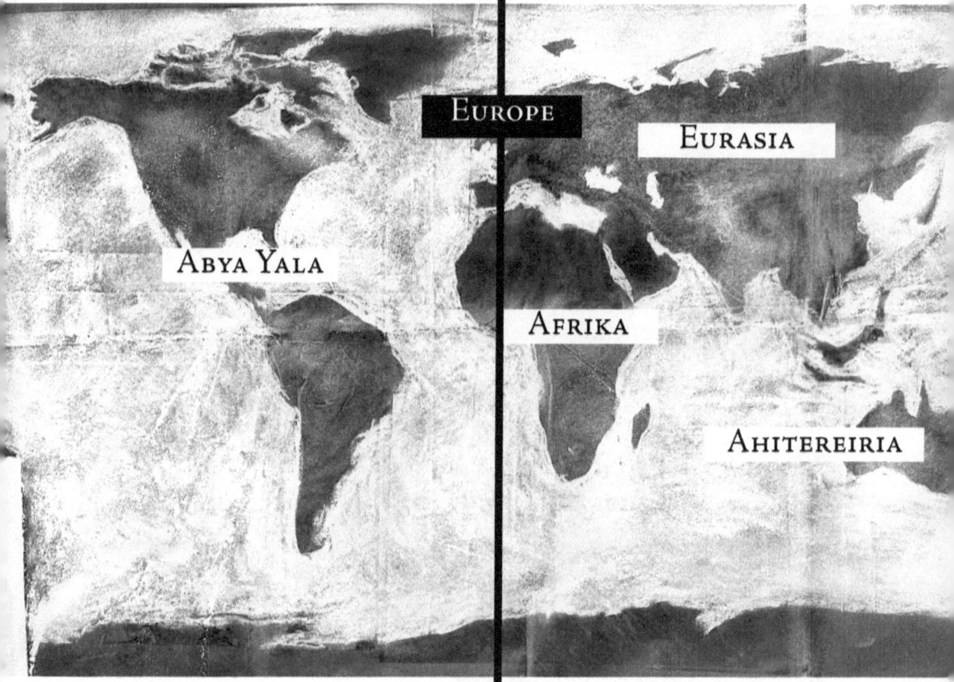

Palestine from Above

ABYA YALA

EUROPE

EURASIA

AFRIKA

AHITEREIRIA

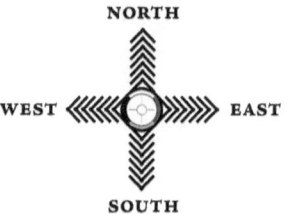

NORTH
WEST — EAST
SOUTH

Wounded Europe

Today, Wounded Europe's world maps place Europe at the top of the map and as the center of the world.

And not content with placing itself at the center of Space, Europe also places itself at the center of Time. The vertical black line on the map goes right through the Royal Observatory in Greenwich, London, a place that marks London's midnight hour as the beginning of the day for the rest of the globe.

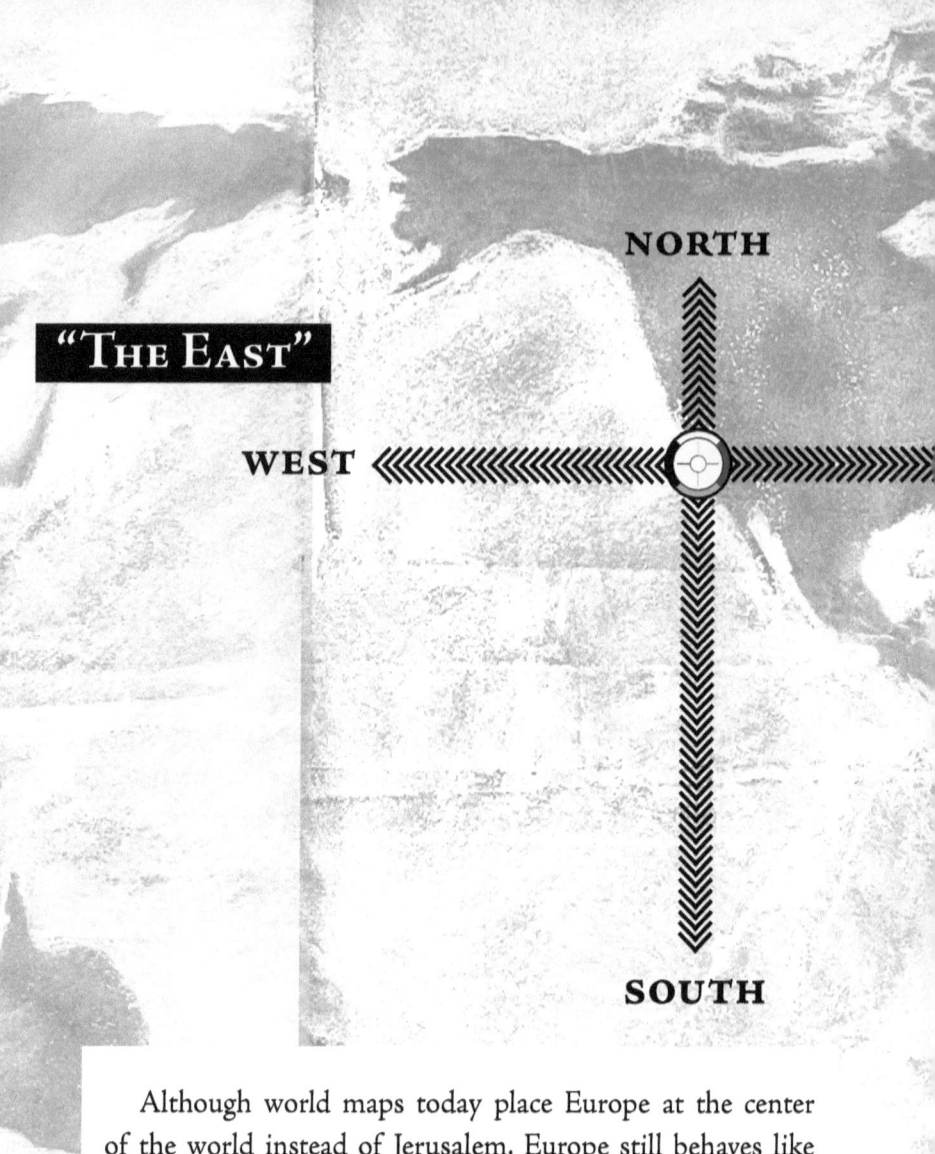

"The East"

Although world maps today place Europe at the center of the world instead of Jerusalem, Europe still behaves like Jerusalem is at the center of the world, no matter how non-religious or "secular" Europe pretends to be.

Europe still expects everyone to call Europe "The West" even when Europe is not to everybody's west, and expects everyone to call Asia "The East" even when Asia is not to everybody's east. Europe's world remains a geography still centered on Jerusalem.

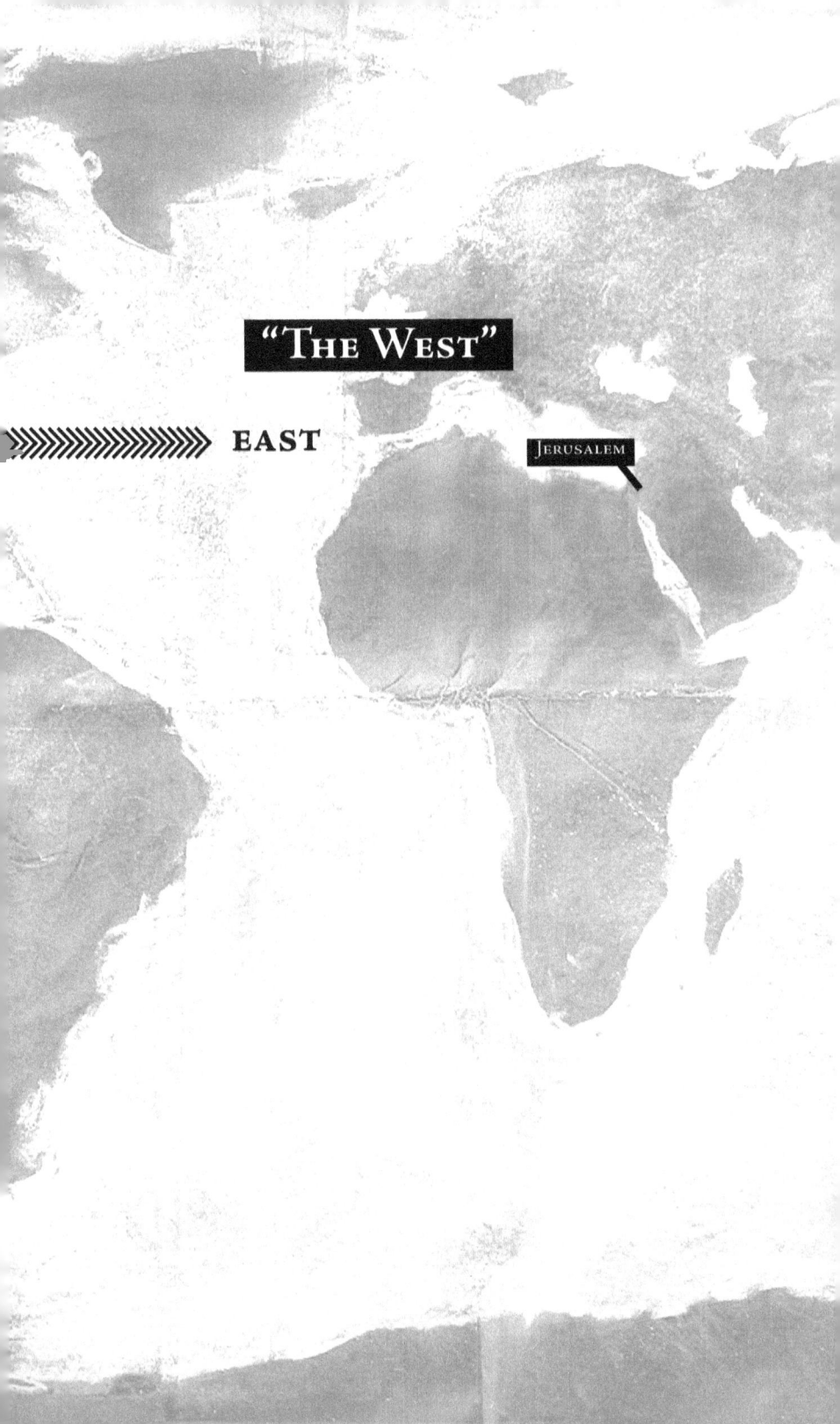

Palestine from Above

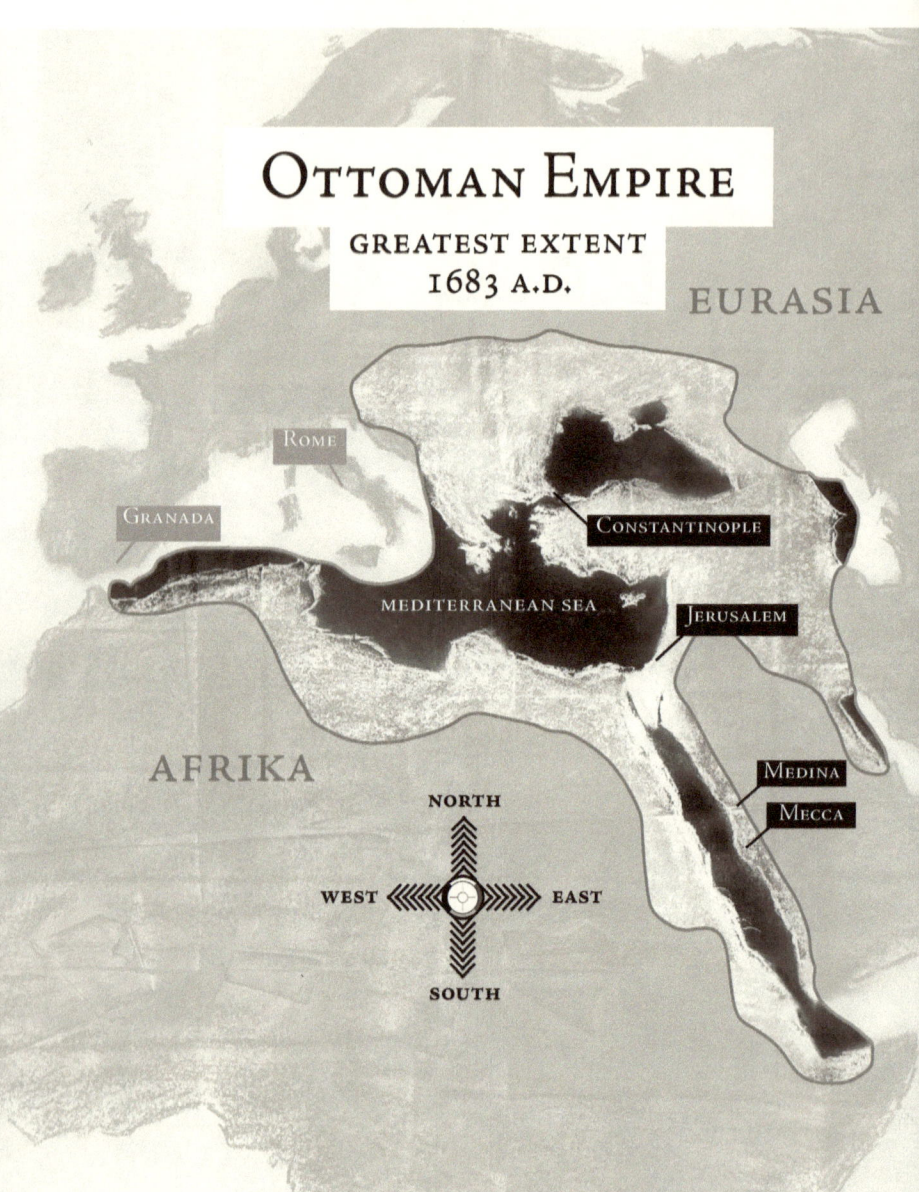

In 1453 A.D., the Ottoman Empire captured Constantinople, marking the final death of the Roman Empire until its rebirth later that century by another name.

Constantinople, the City of Constantine, had been the seat of the Eastern Roman Empire, holding on much longer than the ancient Western Roman Empire had held on, which some historians argue had fallen almost one thousand years before in the year 476 A.D., an event many mark as the West's transition from Antiquity to the Middle Ages.

Historians today debate whether the capture of Constantinople by the Ottoman Empire in 1453 marked the birth of Modern Europe, or whether Modern Europe was birthed later that century in 1492.

When time is more of a spiral than it is a line, everything is at once future, present, and past. Still, dates can be helpful bookmarks, and maybe it's more helpful to mark 1453 as a year of death and 1492 as a year of resurrection.

Because they say the Devil also knows about resurrection.

FRANCE

NAVARRE

ARAGON

PORTUGAL

CASTILE

MEDITERRANEAN
SEA

GRANADA

AFRIKA

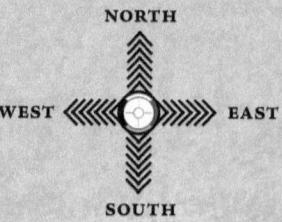

Jerusalem Next

Christopher Columbus had been convinced the End of the World would arrive in exactly 155 years.[1] By the "End of the World" Columbus meant the return of Jesus to Earth, and he didn't mean it metaphorically. He also didn't mean Jesus would return just anywhere, he meant specifically to Jerusalem.

According to his *El Libro de las Profecías*, his Book of Prophecies (1502–1504), in order for Jesus to return to Jerusalem, certain events must first be enacted. These included imposing Christianity throughout the world and launching a final Crusade against Islam to reconquer Jerusalem.

Columbus' genocidal imposition of his world in Abya Yala was far more religious than it is today given credit. Settler-colonial genocides are far more religious than they are today given credit.[2] Before Columbus declared his Holy War in Abya Yala on October 12, 1492, he had already taken part in a Holy War some months before. Columbus had been in Granada on January 2, 1492 witnessing the Black Afrikan

---

1. Pauline Moffitt Watts, "Prophecy and Discovery: On the Spiritual Origins of Christopher Columbus's 'Enterprise of the Indies,'" *The American Historical Review*, 90(1), 73

2. For an important corrective, see Steven Salaita, *Holy Land in Transit: Colonialism and the Quest for Canaan* (Syracuse University Press, 2006)

Muslims surrender their last palace on the Iberian Peninsula to the Catholic Monarchs, imposing Christianity as universal throughout the Peninsula, and solidifying the Mediterranean Sea as Europe's border with Afrika.

Columbus the Crusader had known the Earth is round. After the taking of Granada from the Muslims, he was convinced he could reach the east by sailing west to help take from the Muslims Jerusalem next.

Throughout Columbus' lifetime and for many centuries before, the Roman Empire had been re-establishing itself in the West by a Crusade against Islam of another name, the *Reconquista*, Rome's Reconquering of the Iberian Peninsula from the Black Afrikan Muslims sometimes called the Moors. It had taken the Catholics centuries to "reconquer" the whole Peninsula by 1492. Granada had been the final battle won by Queen Isabella of Castile and her husband, King Ferdinand of Aragon. On January 2nd, when Isabella's forces accepted the surrender of the palace in Granada, many historians say Modern Europe could be born.

That's another way to say that Modern Europe was birthed by the blood of Black Afrikans, Muslims, Jews, and anybody different, anyone the empire considered the Devil. The Catholic Queen decreed right away that Jews could remain on the Peninsula but would have to convert to Christianity or leave. Jews could assimilate or go. Back when there were still places to go.

Today in Granada, on the other side of the street where tourists wait to enter the infamous palace, a very other palace beckons, *el Palacio de los Olvidados*, the Palace of the Forgotten. A sign points to one of its permanent exhibitions: the Spanish Inquisition Museum of Torture, where exhibited are the various torture instruments Isabella used on Jews suspected of

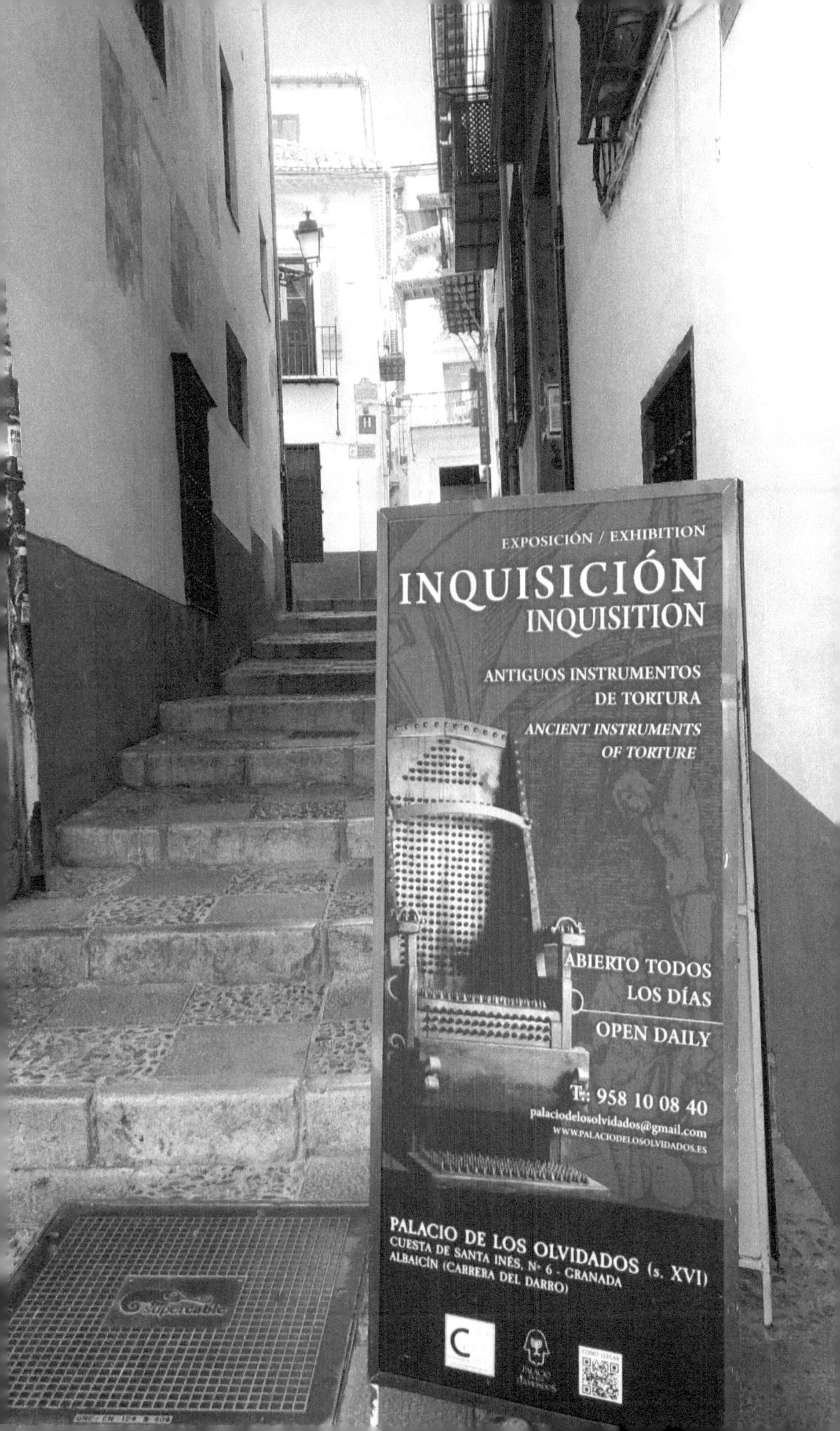

EXPOSICIÓN / EXHIBITION

INQUISICIÓN
INQUISITION

ANTIGUOS INSTRUMENTOS
DE TORTURA
ANCIENT INSTRUMENTS
OF TORTURE

ABIERTO TODOS
LOS DÍAS
OPEN DAILY

T: 958 10 08 40
palaciodelosolvidados@gmail.com
WWW.PALACIODELOSOLVIDADOS.ES

PALACIO DE LOS OLVIDADOS (s. XVI)
CUESTA DE SANTA INÉS, Nº 6 - GRANADA
ALBAICÍN (CARRERA DEL DARRO)

lying about their conversion to her world.

Conquest, assimilation, torture, extermination. Holy War was already under way within Europe before it was declared on Abya Yala by Columbus and Them. Columbus called the weapons of the Taíno people *alfanjes*, a Spanish word derived from Arabic for a curved metal scimitar inscribed with Quranic verses, commonly used by Muslim soldiers in battle. Hernán Cortés who followed Columbus wrote that the Mexica women looked "Moorish" and claimed to see more than 400 mosques in Anahuac, referring to the emperor as a "sultan."[3]

Everywhere Columbus and Them looked in Abya Yala, there was Islam, there was a Muslim, there was the Devil according to the Empire. This was Abya Yala's great misfortune: that Columbus was a Crusader.

Today, in the middle of a busy intersection in Granada, three banks and a department store guard a statue called the *Monument to Isabella the Catholic and Columbus*. The two of them are up there making a deal. Their statue's foundation has two dates:

January 2, 1492

October 12, 1492

Down the street from their statue, there exists a big church you can tell was built to make you feel small. Not like you should be quiet, but like you should shut up. I hate it. I tell it I hate it. I don't even know what it is yet. The next morning I learn it's called the Royal Chapel of Granada. I learn it's there where the corpses of Isabella and Ferdinand have been rotting for only 500 years.

---

3. Alan Mikhail, *God's Shadow: Sultan Selim, His Ottoman Empire, and the Making of the Modern World* (Liveright, 2020)

Jerusalem Next

Palestine 1492: A Report Back

A World Cut In Two

In 1493 Columbus and Them returned to Europe from their first pillage in Abya Yala, landing in Portugal first instead of Castile. The King of Portugal was the first Catholic Monarch to hear the news. When Isabella learned Columbus failed to inform her first, a fight ensued between the Catholic Monarchs over who had the right to invade the new lands. To keep the peace, the Bishop of Rome stepped in.

The Pope, the Bishop of Rome, issued a Doctrine of Discovery proclaiming the right of Christians who "discovered" the lands of non-Christians to take the lands as property. To keep the peace between invaders, the Pope cut the world in two with a line dividing the globe between Portugal and Castile. It was the first global border, a line between the invaders so they don't fight each other and can keep fighting everybody else.

The primary global border assumed that day was not the line for peace but the line between Same/Different, between Superior/Inferior, between Christian/non-Christian, Europe/non-Europe, Human/non-Human. Today, the Christian/non-Christian split is less spoken out loud but remains in practice. As decolonization institutionalized in the twentieth century, the Europe/non-Europe split became less explicit but also today remains in practice. The Human/non-Human split remains openly explicit and in practice, paradoxically strengthened by the institutionalization of Human Rights.

Palestine from Above

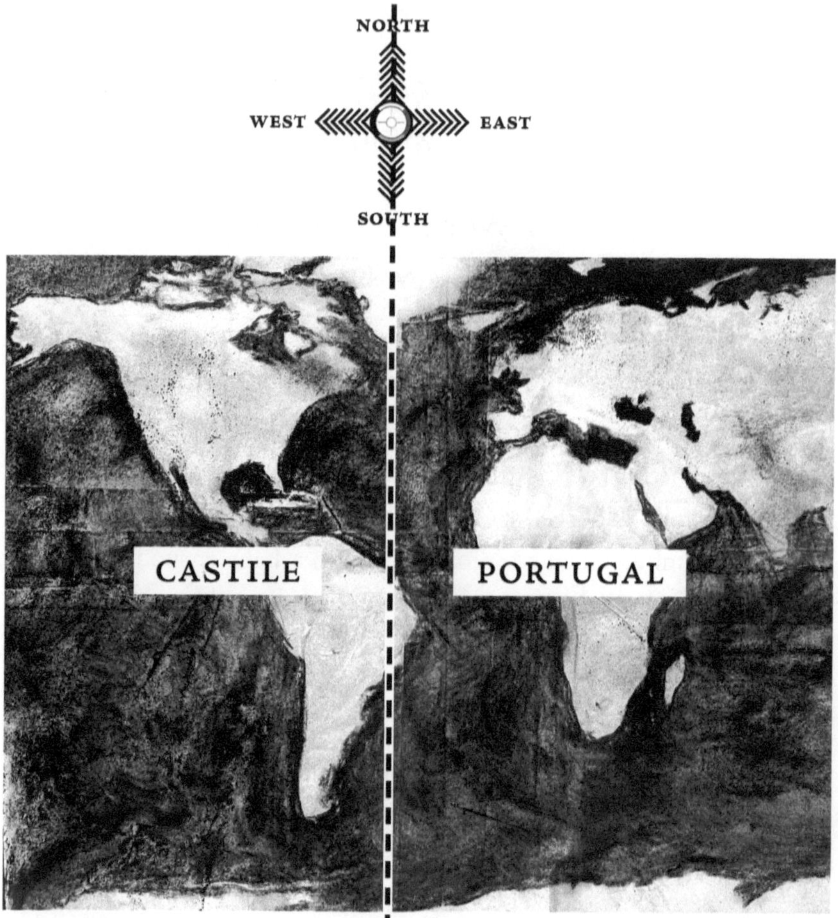

Following the Doctrine of Discovery, the Bishop of Rome's Treaty of Tordesillas in 1494 cut a line from North to South at the Atlantic, right at portion of Abya Yala today called Brazil.

The Portuguese Empire was granted by Rome the right to invade everything east of the line, including all of Afrika. Castile was granted everything west.

The Doctrine of Discovery became the basis of all claims to non-Europe by Christian Europeans, including by the United States who pointed to it in 1823 as the legal foundation for its westward expansion. It remains on the law books today.

A World Cut in Two

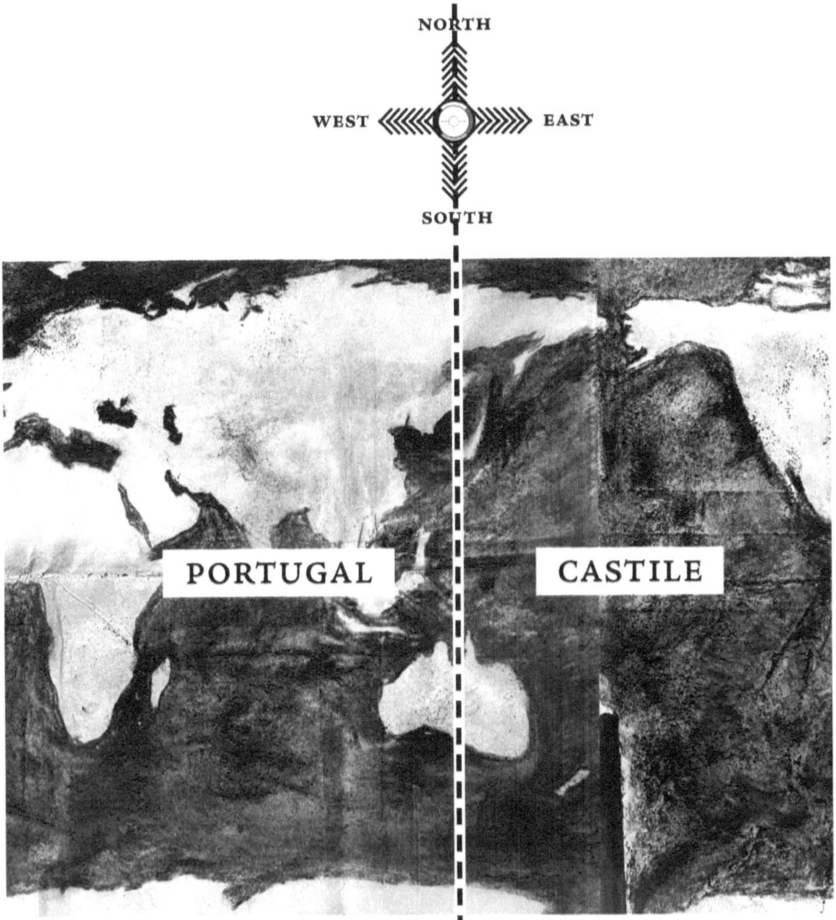

PORTUGAL CASTILE

In 1521, Portuguese explorer Ferdinand Magellan sailed west of Abya Yala and landed in Asia on an island archipelago where he would be killed by the native people in an uprising.

On this other side of the globe, where the east could indeed be reached by sailing west, invasion rights between the Europeans were still unclear. In 1529, Portugal and Castile signed the Treaty of Zaragoza in order to keep their peace. Still, the Spanish would later transgress the line and colonize the islands where Magellan died, naming them the Philippines after a Spanish King named Philip.

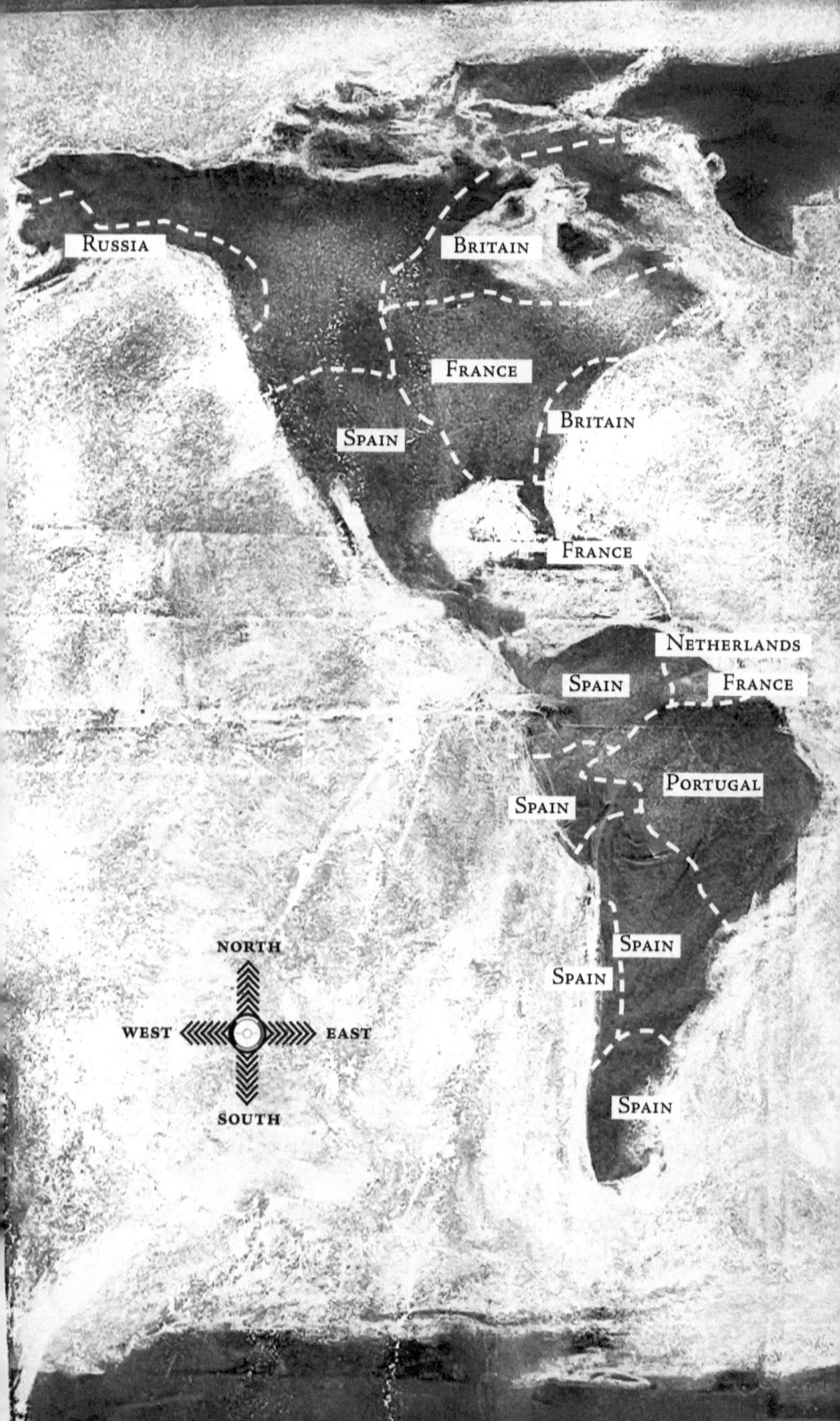

Those who followed Columbus and Them to Abya Yala continued cutting up the land into borders between them as plantations called Viceroyalties. These lines eventually informed the footprints of today's nation-state borders, agreements between the overseers so they don't fight.

Abya Yala was not consulted.

The establishment of clear lines between European invaders in Abya Yala and a clear distinction between Europe/non-Europe were foundational to International Law, originally designed to produce Europe as the place of lawfulness, even under conditions of war, and non-Europe as the place of lawlessness and under conditions of perpetual war.

Following the global decolonization movements and the implosion of Europe after the Second World War, Europe created the United Nations and adopted a new doctrine of a Universal Human Equality. It de-emphasized the split between Europe/non-Europe and instead emphasized the split between Human/non-Human, different words for the logic and practice of Superior/Inferior, of Haves/Have-Nots. The United Nations has since granted the overseers the legitimacy on the monopoly of violence and has labeled as "terrorists" those who disagree.

Lamenting the the doctrine of Universal Human Equality, a Nazi philosopher argued that with the dissolution of Europe/non-Europe, the neat geography between Peace/War was also dissolved, meaning violence between Europeans could not easily be exported to non-Europe, transforming Europe back into a space of perpetual war and all of the globe into a space of perpetual war.[1]

---

1. Carl Schmitt, *The Nomos of the Earth in the International Law of Jus Publicum Europaeum* (Telos Press Publishing, 2006)

Previously in 1618, with Europe out warring with non-Europe outside of Europe, a bloody 30-year war had erupted inside Europe's so-called Holy Roman Empire, a regime many argued even was neither holy, Roman, nor an empire.

As the favorite ancestor of today's State of Germany, the Holy Roman Empire had been baptized that way by the Bishop of Rome in the year 800 A.D. He had been seeking to revive the title in Western Europe more than three centuries after the fall of the Western Roman Empire in 476 A.D.

Kingdom of Sweden

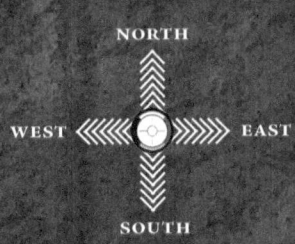

Tsardom *of* Russia

Poland-Lithuania

Ottoman Empire

The 1648 Peace of Westphalia ended the 30-Year War and established a secular order. This set in motion the internal cutting up of Europe into borders so its tyrants wouldn't fight each other inside of Europe. The lines didn't look as neat as they do even on this map. For a long time, this "colonial reflection" of bordered territory inside Europe remained administered through lists of place names; not until much later did it reference scientific maps.[2]

2. Jordan Branch, "'Colonial reflection' and territoriality: The peripheral origins of sovereign statehood," *European Journal of International Relations* 18(2): 277–297

The so-called Holy Roman Empire continued its decline until Napoleon fully destroyed it in 1806. In 1871 it resurrected as the nation-state of Germany, the Second Reich to the Nazis' future Third Reich.

During the Second Reich, during the so-called "unification" of Germany in 1871, difference within Germany's borders was annihilated in the name of unity, in the name of creating a nation-state. The Third Reich would later seek to annihilate difference within all of Europe, also in the name of unity.

The Second Reich had been a late comer to the imperial conquests of its European peers. Wishing to join, the new State of Germany hosted the Berlin Conference between 1884–1886 to peacefully cut up Afrika between it the other European powers, placing a map of Afrika on the wall.

Also known as the Congo Conference, the border around the Congo River was decided and granted to King Leopold II of Belgium as his personal property.

The Congo River was not consulted.

The "Scramble for Africa," as the Europeans called it, continued until 1914. Throughout this time, the invaders refined the rules between them to reduce the possibility of conflict erupting among them. It was during this decades-long process when Europe's Zionist movement tried negotiating for a Jewish State in East Afrika before it settled on a Jewish State in Palestine.

As in Abya Yala and as in Europe before it, the lines the Europeans cut over Afrika eventually informed the footprints of today's nation-state borders and are central to the story of the genocides in Afrika that have not ceased to this day.

Neither Afrika nor its people nor its waters nor its trees were consulted in the political process. As in Abya Yala and as in Europe before it, the borders of Afrika were and continue to be peace agreements between the overseers, between the administrators above so they don't fight each other and can instead focus on fighting everybody else.

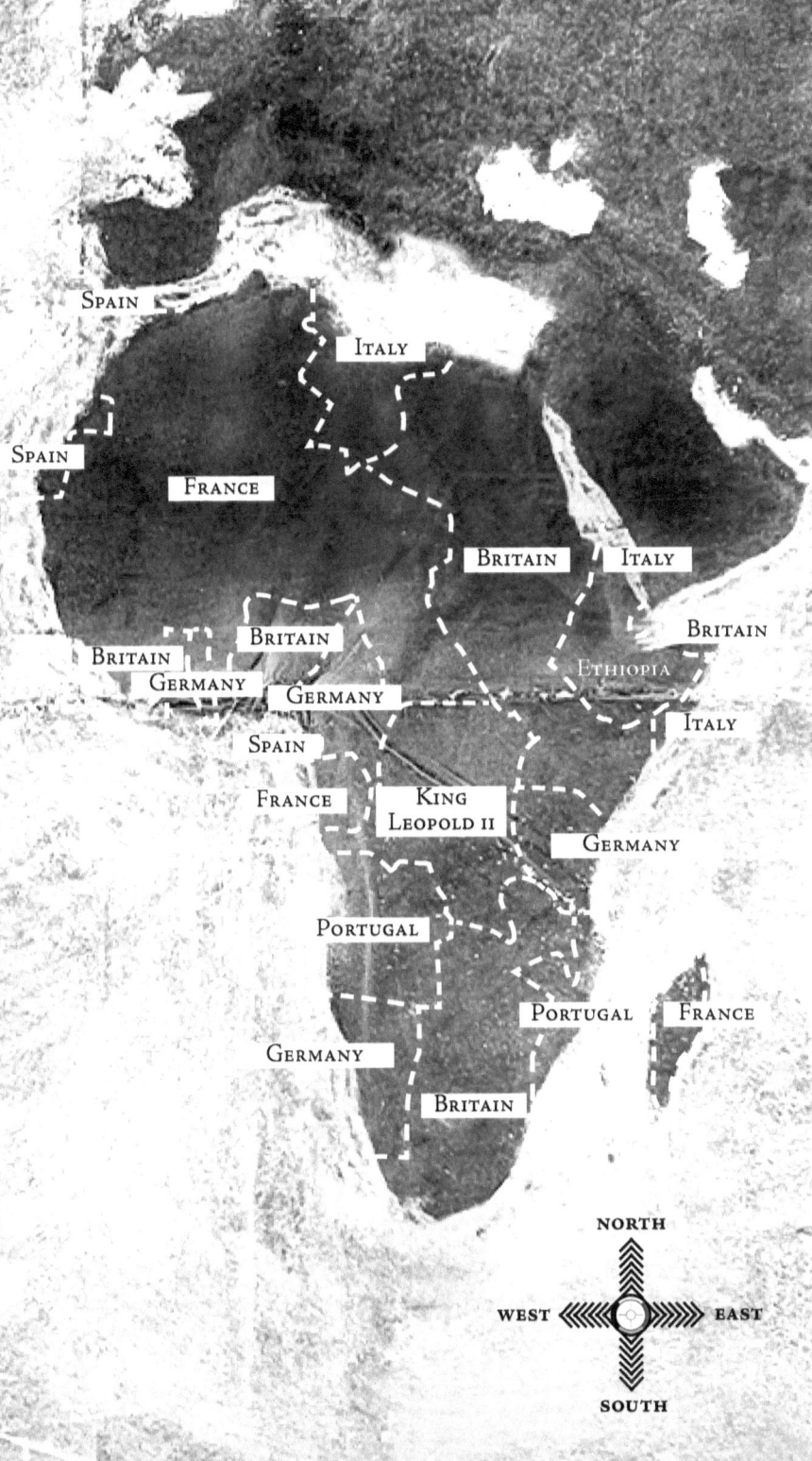

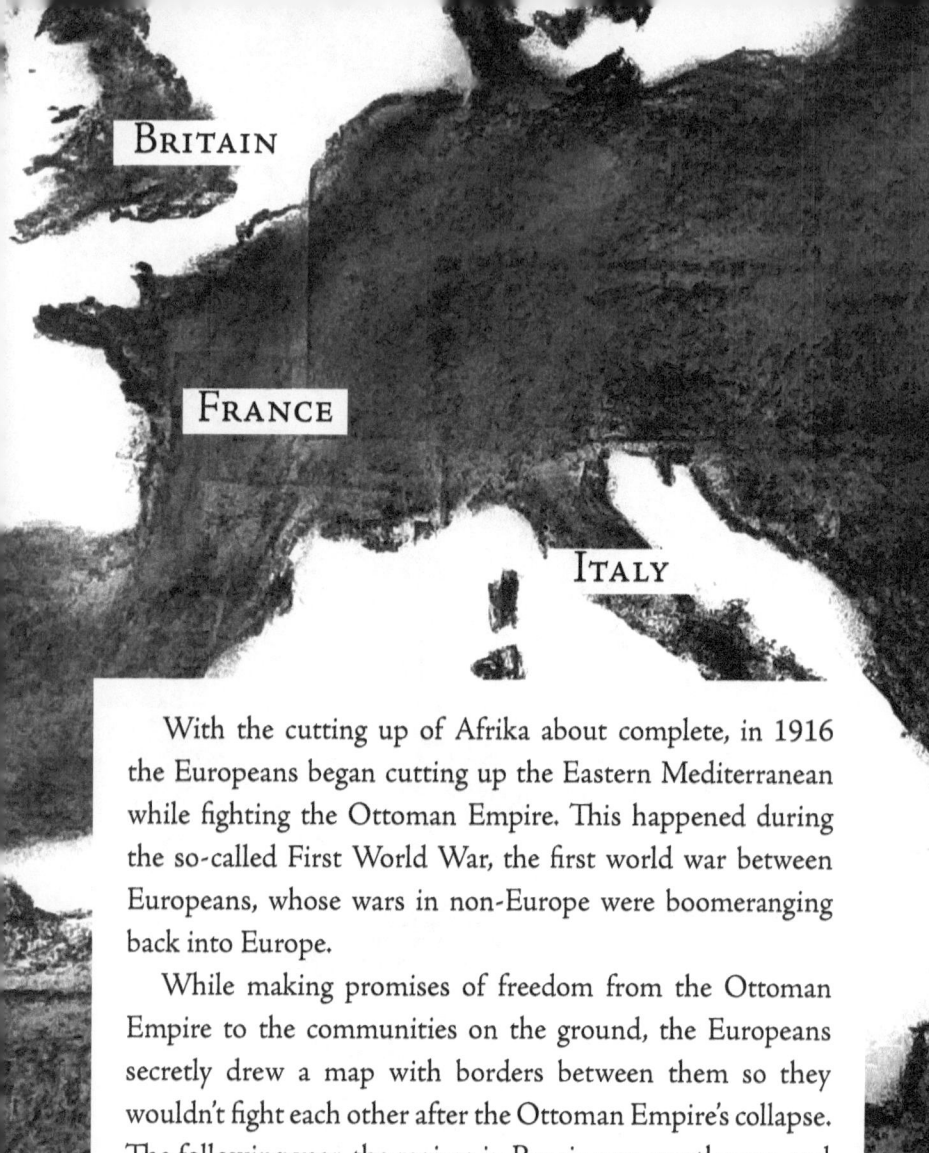

BRITAIN

FRANCE

ITALY

With the cutting up of Afrika about complete, in 1916 the Europeans began cutting up the Eastern Mediterranean while fighting the Ottoman Empire. This happened during the so-called First World War, the first world war between Europeans, whose wars in non-Europe were boomeranging back into Europe.

While making promises of freedom from the Ottoman Empire to the communities on the ground, the Europeans secretly drew a map with borders between them so they wouldn't fight each other after the Ottoman Empire's collapse. The following year, the regime in Russia was overthrown and the rebels leaked the secretive European agreement, "Sykes-Picot" and its map.

The Sykes-Picot borders between European invaders eventually informed the footprints of today's nation-states, including Turkey, Syria, Lebanon, Palestine, Jordan, and Iraq.

Neither the land nor its people nor its waters nor its trees were consulted.

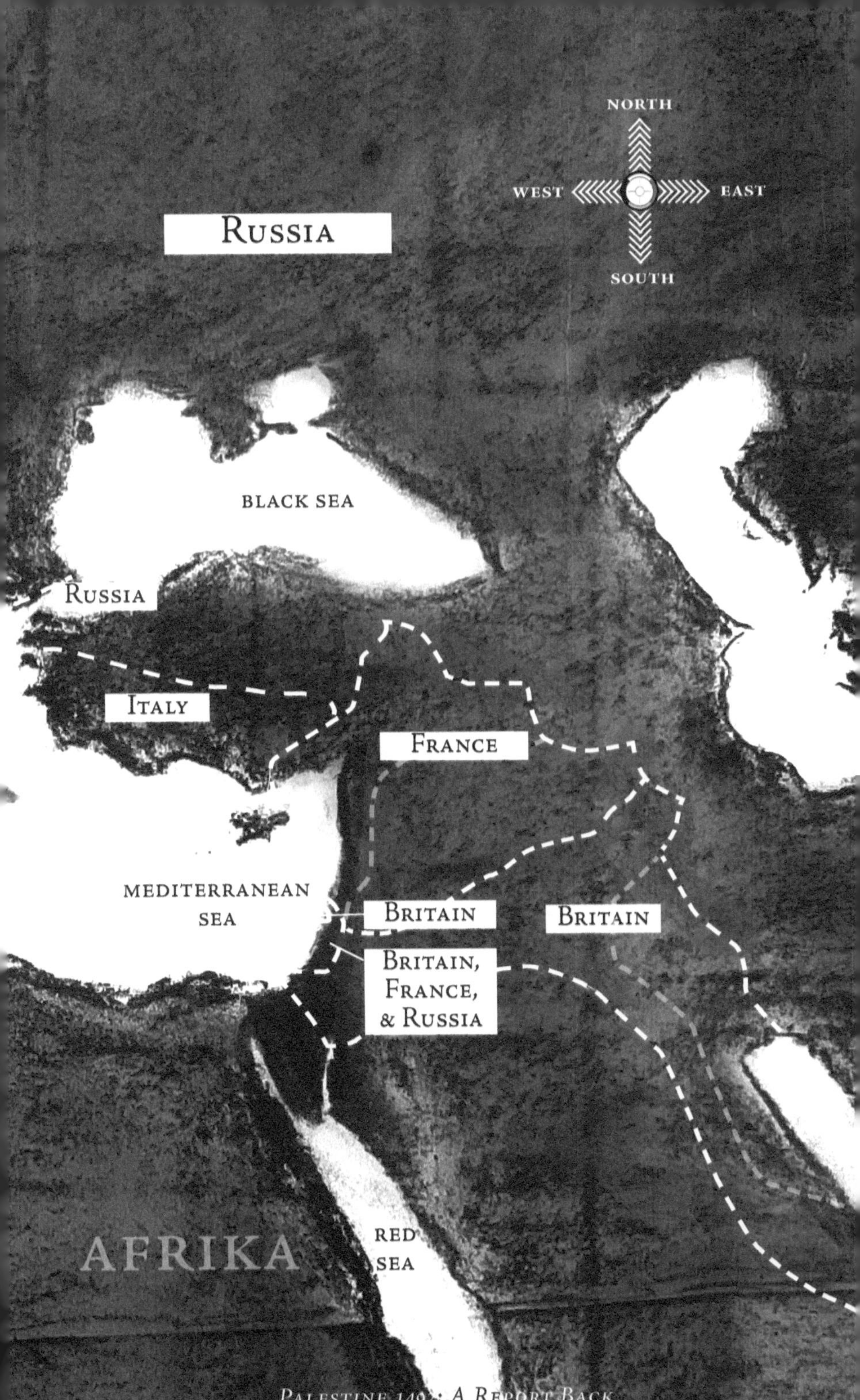

RUSSIA

NORTH · WEST · EAST · SOUTH

BLACK SEA

RUSSIA

ITALY

FRANCE

MEDITERRANEAN SEA

BRITAIN

BRITAIN, FRANCE, & RUSSIA

BRITAIN

AFRIKA

RED SEA

PALESTINE 1492: A REPORT BACK

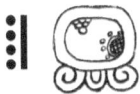

The Last Crusade

By the time the Ottoman Empire completely collapsed in 1922, it had been slowly losing territory for more than two hundred years. The Empire had reached its maximum extent in 1683, on the eve of the Battle of Vienna. It had failed to capture Vienna.

From the perspective of Europe, it became evident that possession of the Ottoman territories would soon be thrown into question and their capture by Europe itself would throw into question the balance of power between Europe's various empires.

The British, French, and Russian empires, all descendants of the Roman Empire, had coveted the Ottoman territories. At the time of the Ottoman's decline, the British were the most militarily powerful of the three. Whoever got those lands would enjoy immense riches, they believed, and not just on earth but in the hereafter.

Jerusalem was there.

BRITISH
EMPIRE

FRENCH
EMPIRE

The Russian Empire in the east wished for a port with warm water year-round. It sought control over the Black Sea and its connection to the Mediterranean Sea right at Constantinople, taken earlier by the Ottomans in 1453.

In 1798, the French Empire was losing Haiti in the Caribbean to a slave revolt. To make up for the loss of its most valuable colony, the French planned to steal Britain's most valuable colony: India in South Asia.

Instead of directly fighting the British, Napoleon turned his warships to non-Europe. He boarded soldiers and scientists alongside him on expedition to Egypt. His strategy was to take India by simply getting to it faster than Britain. At the time, the Europeans were still having to round Southern Afrika to get to Asia. Napoleon planned to cut a canal between the Red Sea and the Mediterranean, the future Suez Canal.

Napoleon would fail, but the idea lived on. In 1859, the British would begin cutting the Suez Canal, displacing many, including the Nubian peoples who wear black clothing today in mourning, demanding their return to their ancestral lands when they will again wear their traditional white clothing.

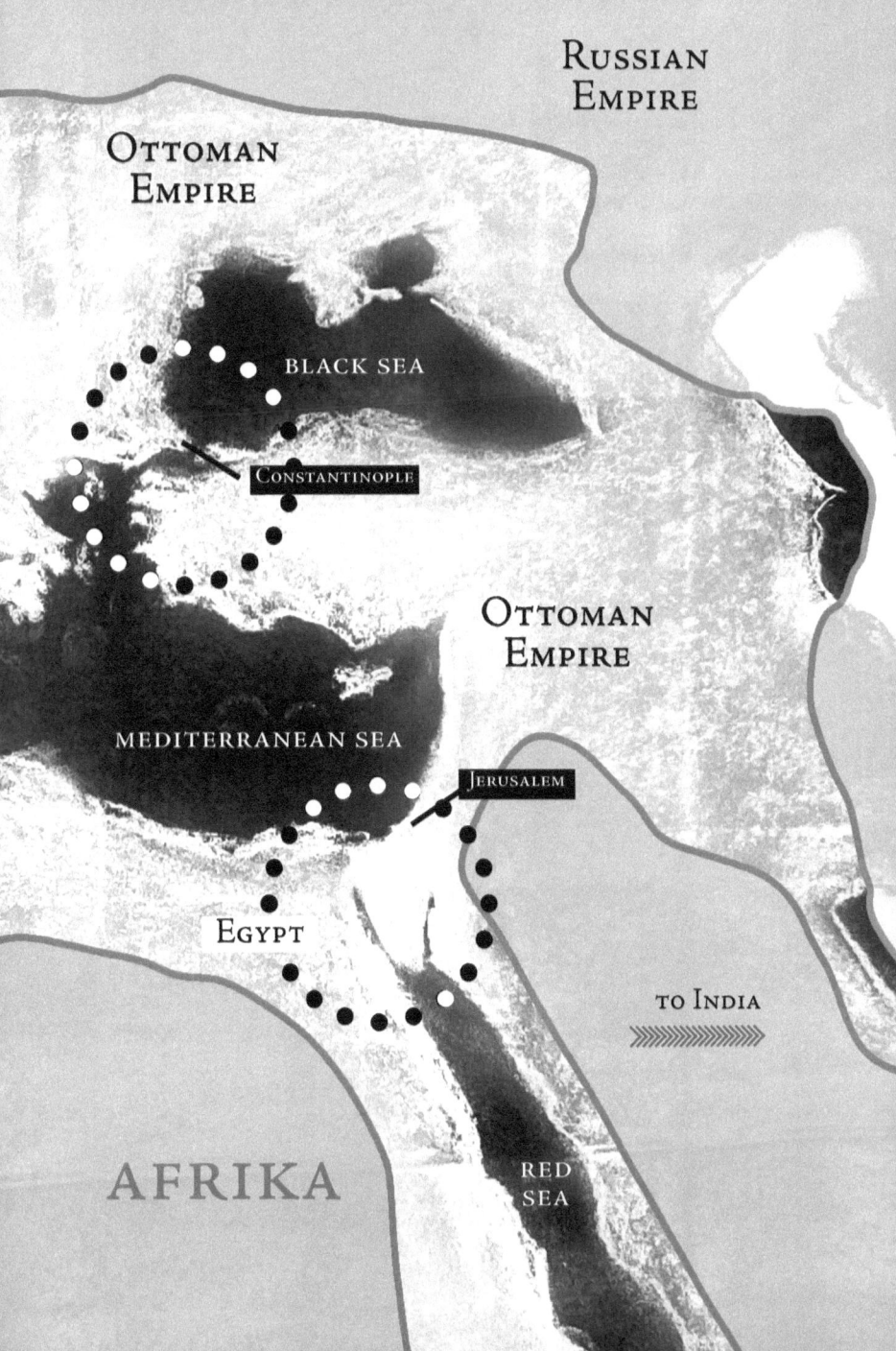

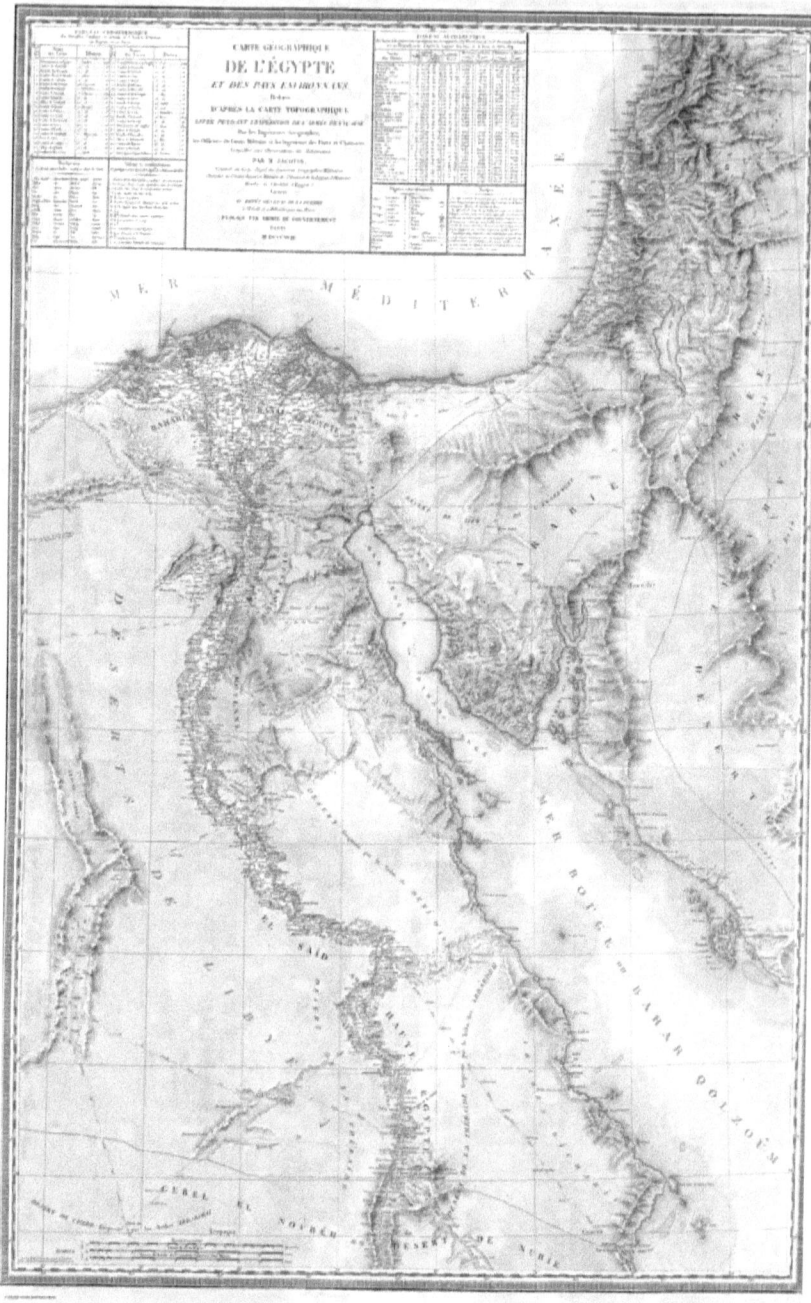

After some early victories in Egypt, Napoleon and his French expedition returned to Europe in defeat. The British had stepped in, allowing the Ottoman Empire to live on so it would not be conquered by France.

Still, that Europeans had managed to stay in the Holy Land as long as Napoleon had stayed was momentous news for Europe, and in that way, the French expedition was a success. It led to the publication of the *Description de l'Égypte* from the findings of Napoleon's scientists. First published in 1809, the encyclopedia would travel across the Atlantic and inspire a type of "Holy Land mania" from Europe to America.[1]

The map on the opposite page consists of 47 sheets and starts at the south end of Egypt, follows the Nile, and then up to the Delta in the north. Palestine appears on the eastern banks of the Mediterranean Sea.

The map is considered the first triangulation-based survey of Egypt and Palestine, the area's first scientific map, meaning its results could be replicated by others using the same measurement techniques.

---

1. Hilton Obenzinger, *American Palestine: Melville, Twain, and the Holy Land Mania* (Princeton University Press, 1999)

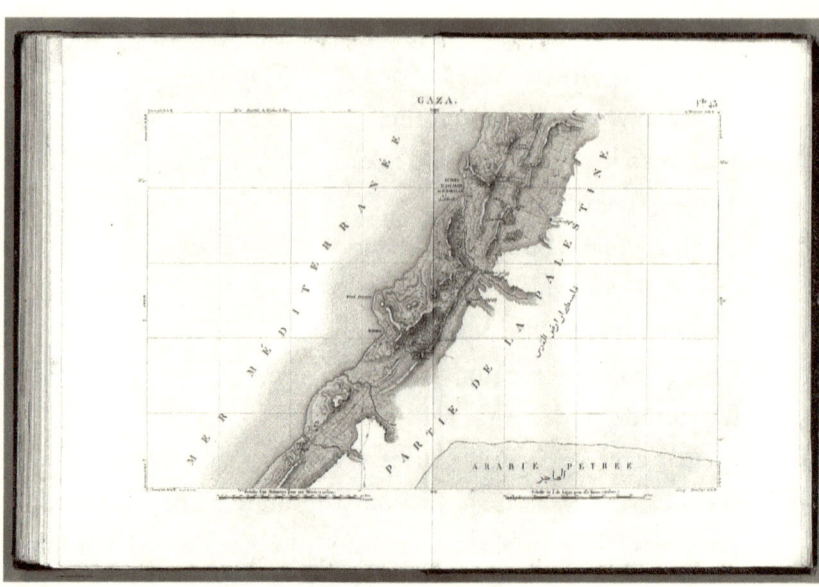

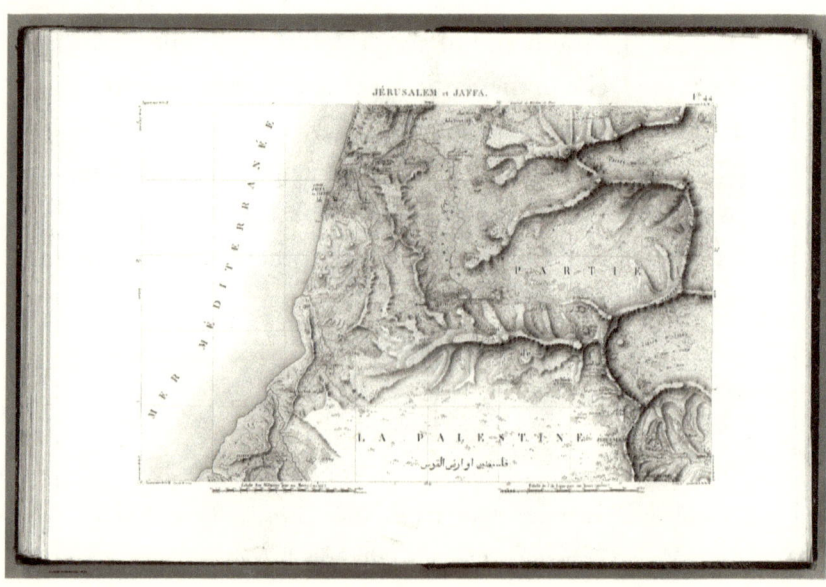

The frontispiece to the first edition of the *Description de l'Égypte* shows an obelisk, the inspiration for the Washington Monument built later in 1848.

On the opposite page is *Sheet 43, Gaza* and *Sheet 44, Jerusalem and Jaffa*. While the coast is mapped relatively accurate, the French expedition did not survey Jerusalem but included it for its great significance to readers of the encyclopedia.

Palestine from Above

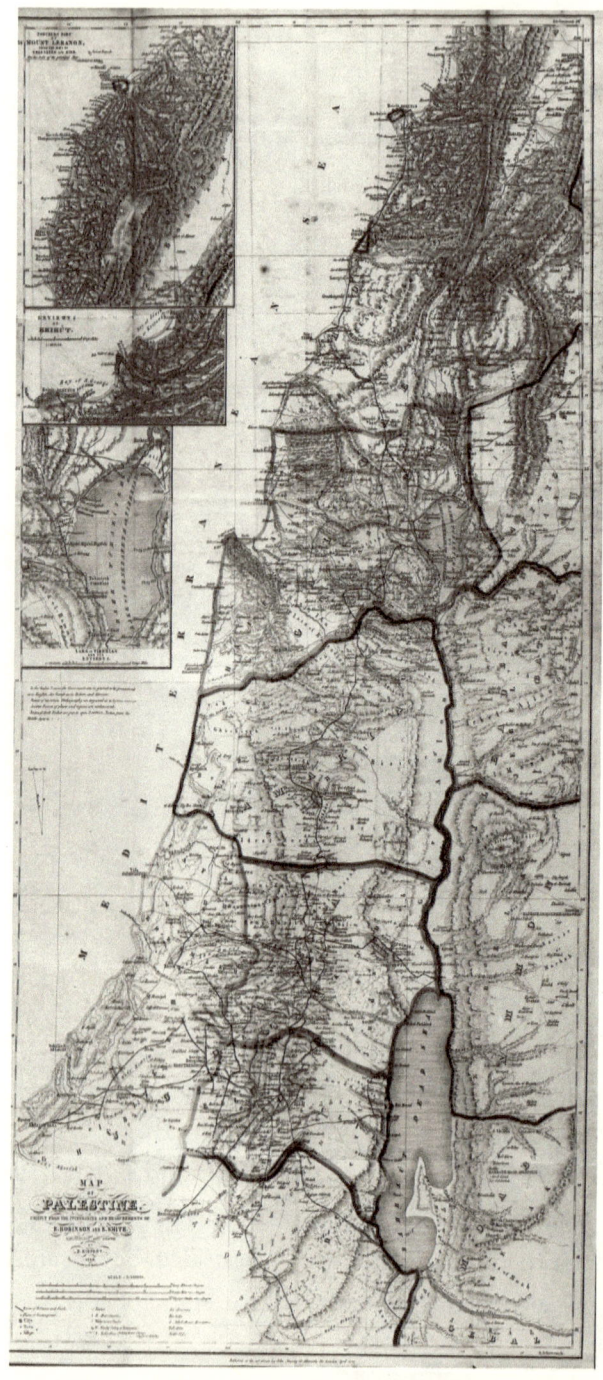

Napoleon and Them's encyclopedia inspired many Christian Evangelicals who interpret the Bible literally instead of metaphorically. This included Edward Robinson, a professor of Biblical literature at Union Theological Seminary in New York.

In 1838 Robinson and a translator traveled to Egypt and Palestine, wishing to use science to prove Robinson's interpretation of Christianity true. With Bible in hand, they traveled the country and encountered the communities living in the land, mapping the region's ancient Biblical place names by listening for echoes of the Hebrew spoken in the Arabic of Palestine.

Robinson's *Biblical Researches in Palestine, Mount Sinai and Arabia Petraea* was published simultaneously in the United States, England, and Germany. It became a cornerstone of nineteenth century Palestine exploration and made Robinson known as the Father of Biblical Geography.

The maps illustrated by his German mapmaker on the opposite page have been described as the beginning of Modern cartography of the Holy Land. Notice how the map extends to the east beyond the River Jordan and Dead Sea.

Palestine from Above

Some thirty years later, the British War Department began producing the first scientific map of Jerusalem, the Ordnance Survey of Jerusalem. Ordnance surveys are maps that cater to military strategy, and Britain's Ordnance Survey had been born out of its need to crush rebellion in Scotland one hundred years before.

The same Biblical archaeologists and clergymen who supported Jerusalem's Ordnance Survey would soon found the Palestine Exploration Fund (PEF) in London. In its first meeting in 1865, the Archbishop of York and first President of the Fund famously announced: "This country of Palestine belongs to you and me, it is essentially ours," making clear Palestine belonged to England, not to Palestinians.

Under the cover of science and religion, British war engineers would survey Palestine between 1872–1877 and complete the Survey of Western Palestine on the opposite page. The PEF's younger counterpart, the American Palestine Exploration Society (APES) had failed to complete the survey east of the Jordan River that it had been assigned by the more established PEF. This accident of history caused Palestine's eastern border to stop at the River Jordan.

Forty years later during the First World War, the PEF Survey of Western Palestine would help British Army soldier Edmund Allenby capture Jerusalem by Christmas in what the British called the Last Crusade. The Survey's shape of Palestine would become the footprint of the borders of Palestine in 1923 from the River to the Sea.

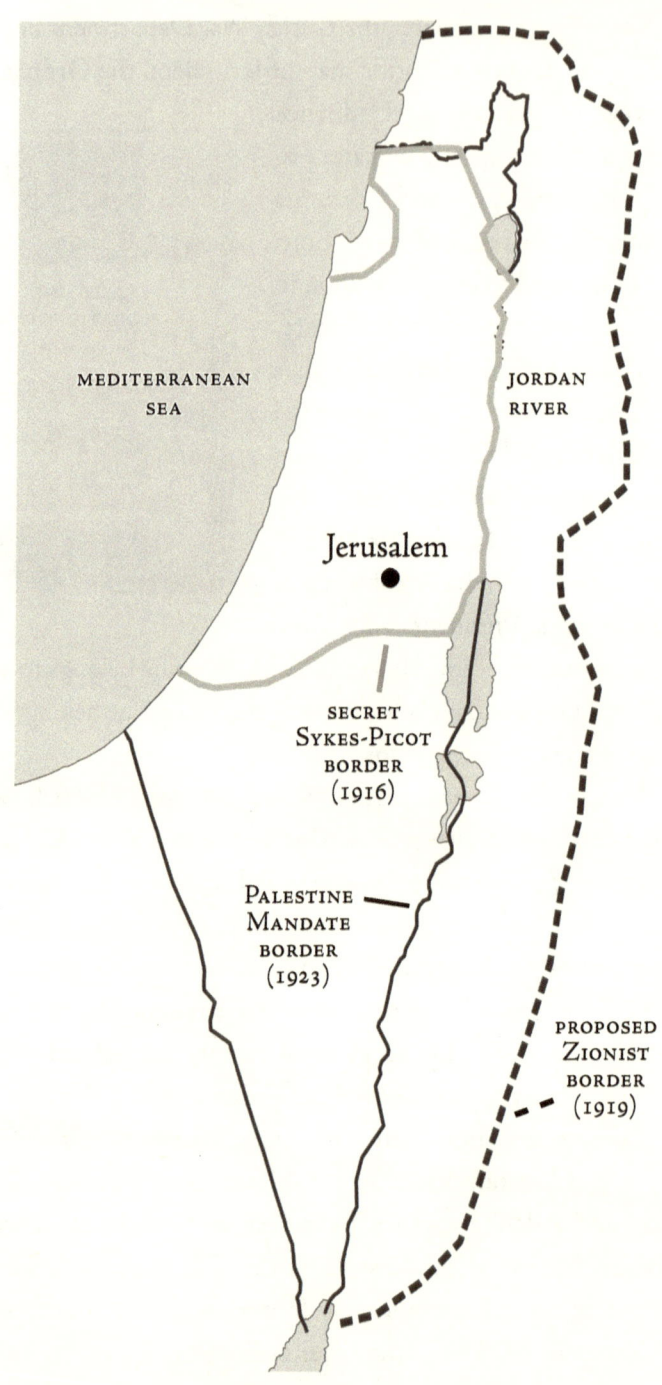

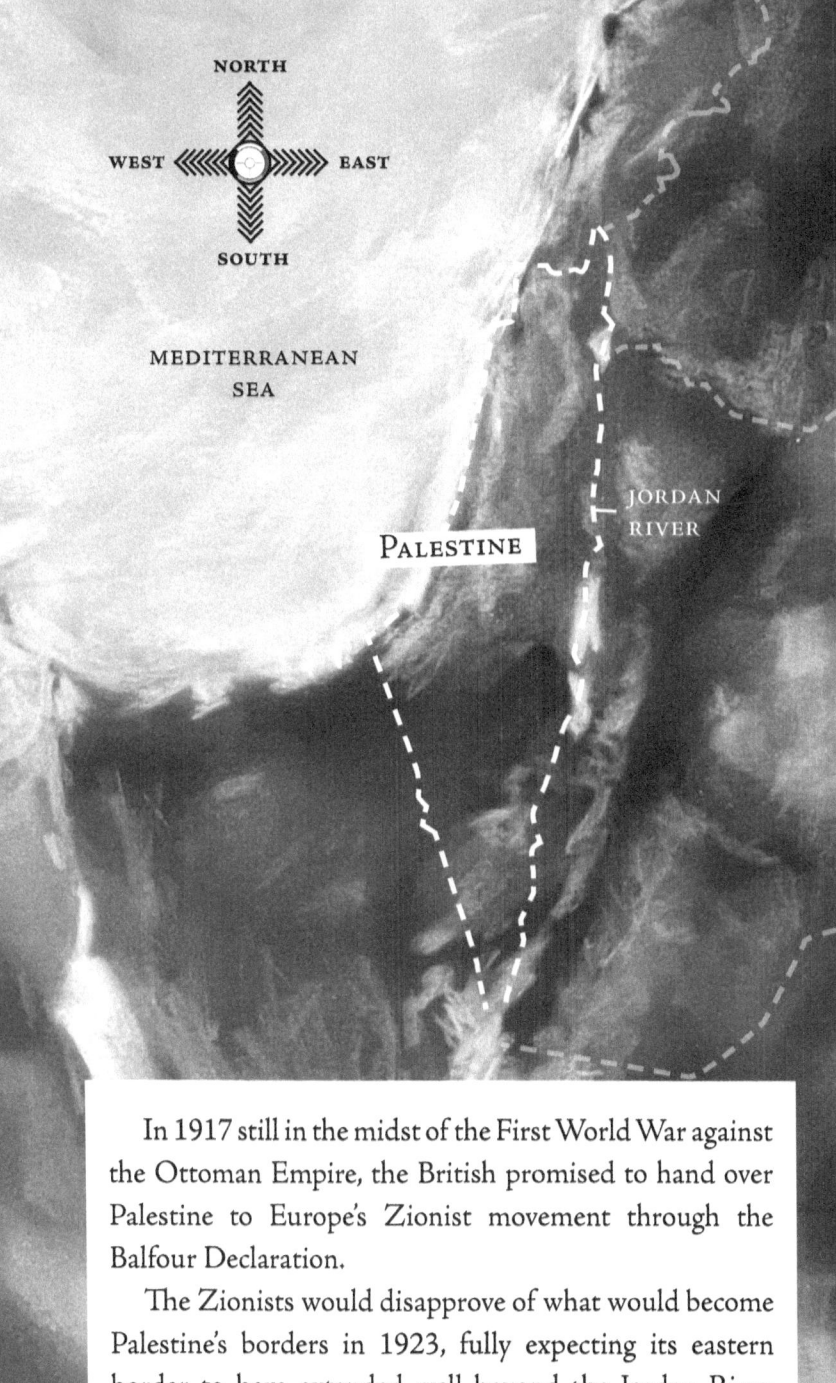

In 1917 still in the midst of the First World War against the Ottoman Empire, the British promised to hand over Palestine to Europe's Zionist movement through the Balfour Declaration.

The Zionists would disapprove of what would become Palestine's borders in 1923, fully expecting its eastern border to have extended well beyond the Jordan River, farther east.

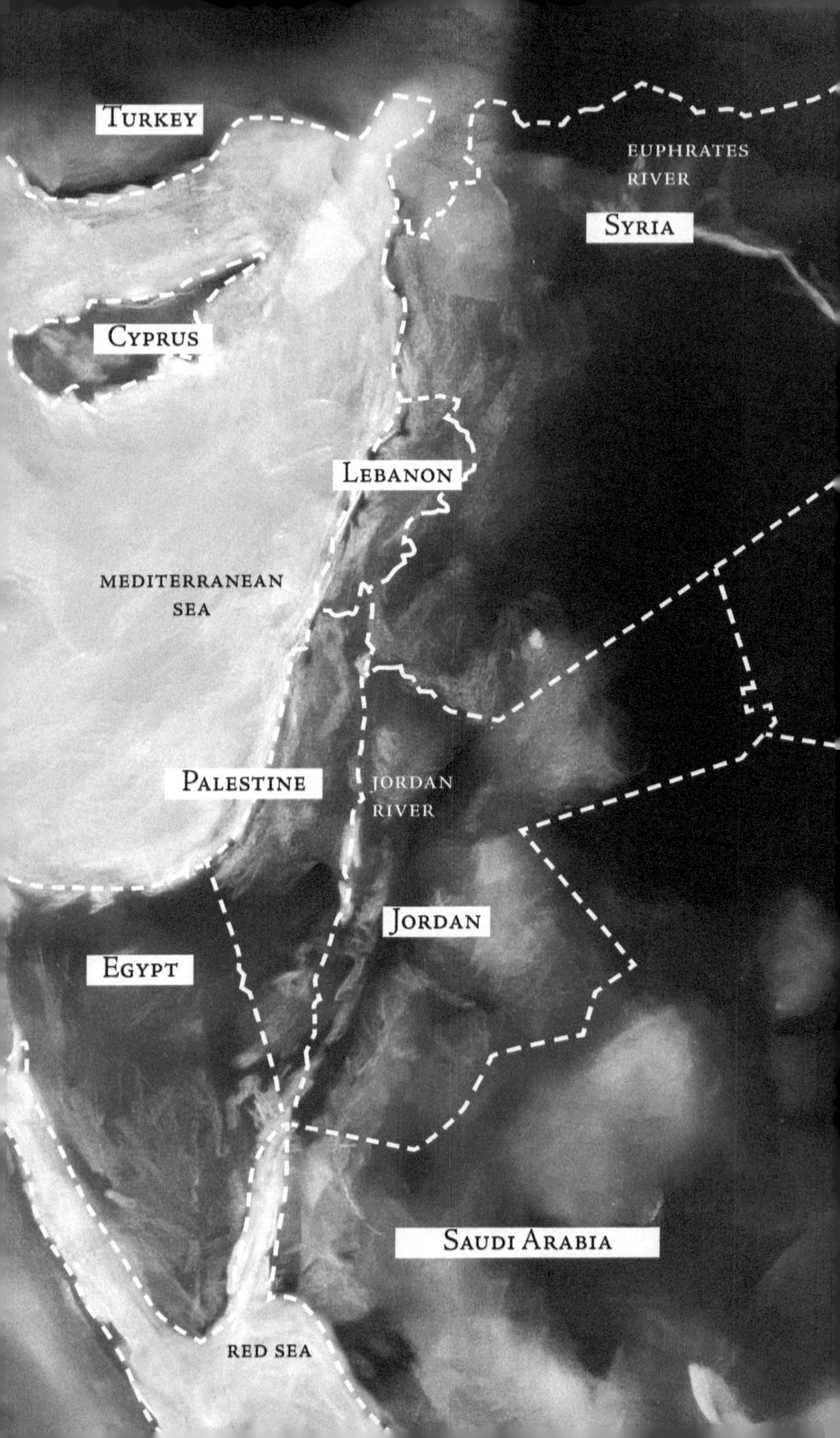

TURKEY

EUPHRATES
RIVER

SYRIA

CYPRUS

LEBANON

MEDITERRANEAN
SEA

PALESTINE

JORDAN
RIVER

JORDAN

EGYPT

SAUDI ARABIA

RED SEA

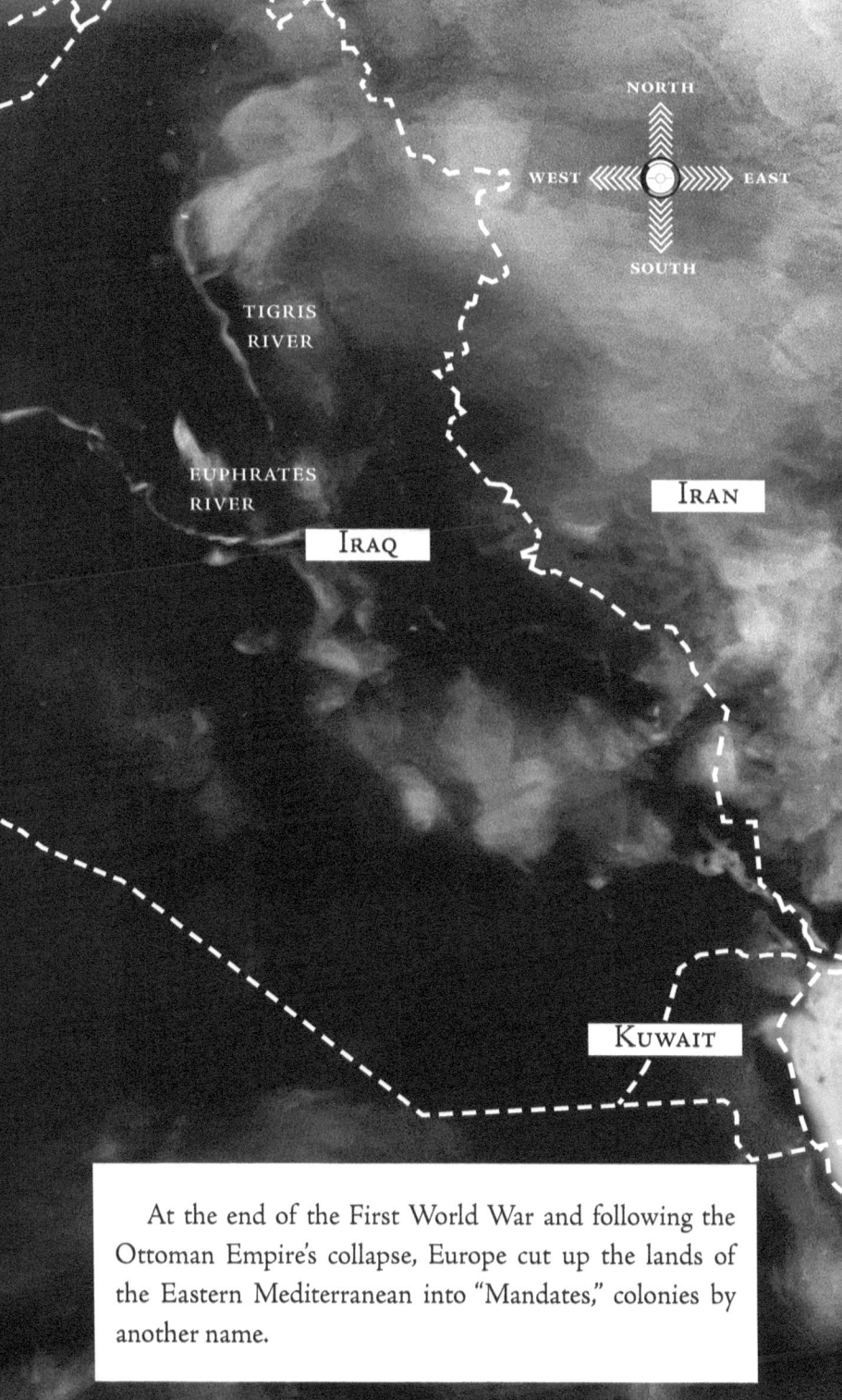

Palestine from Above

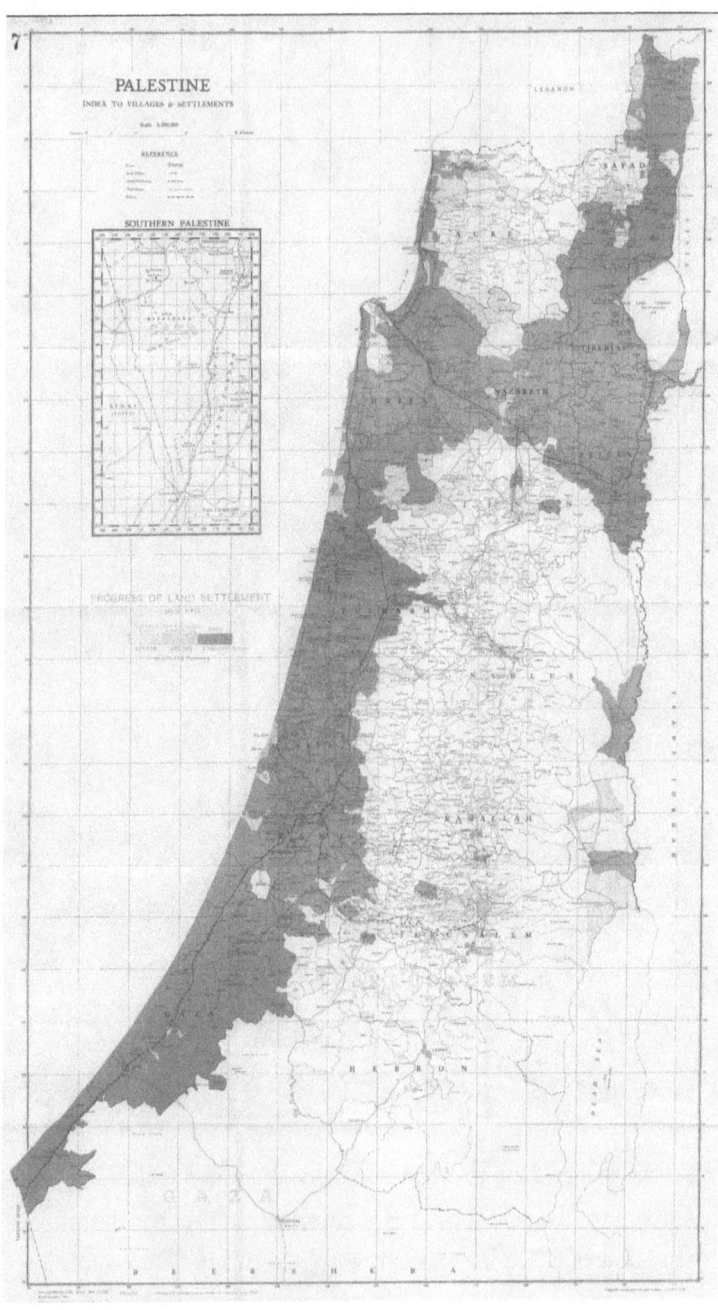

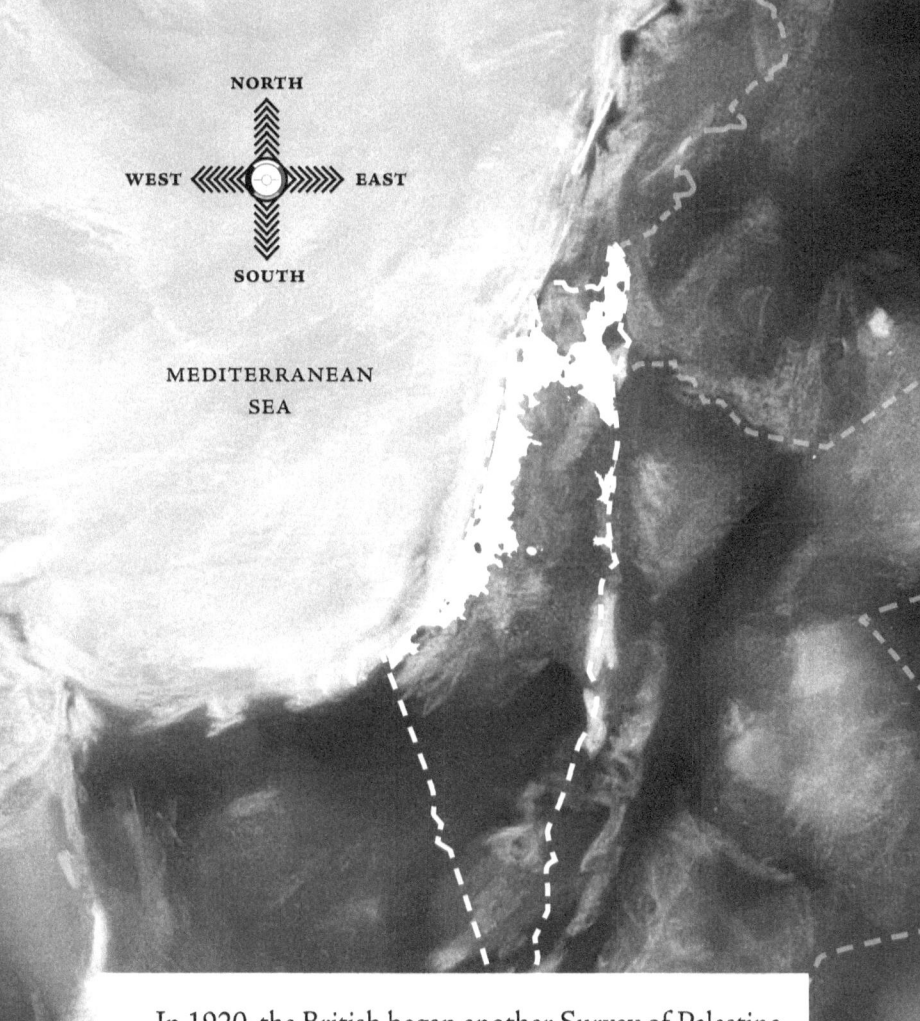

MEDITERRANEAN SEA

In 1920, the British began another Survey of Palestine, this time cutting up the land into private property lots, a cadaster map with each lot titled to an individual owner. Surveying and settling the title of land to an individual facilitated the land's sale to European settlers who readily expelled the Palestinian communities who lived there once they became owners.

The amount and location of Palestine's land surveyed by 1947 would correspond closely to the land the United Nations would allot to the proposed Jewish State in its Partition Plan for Palestine that same year.

Palestine from Above

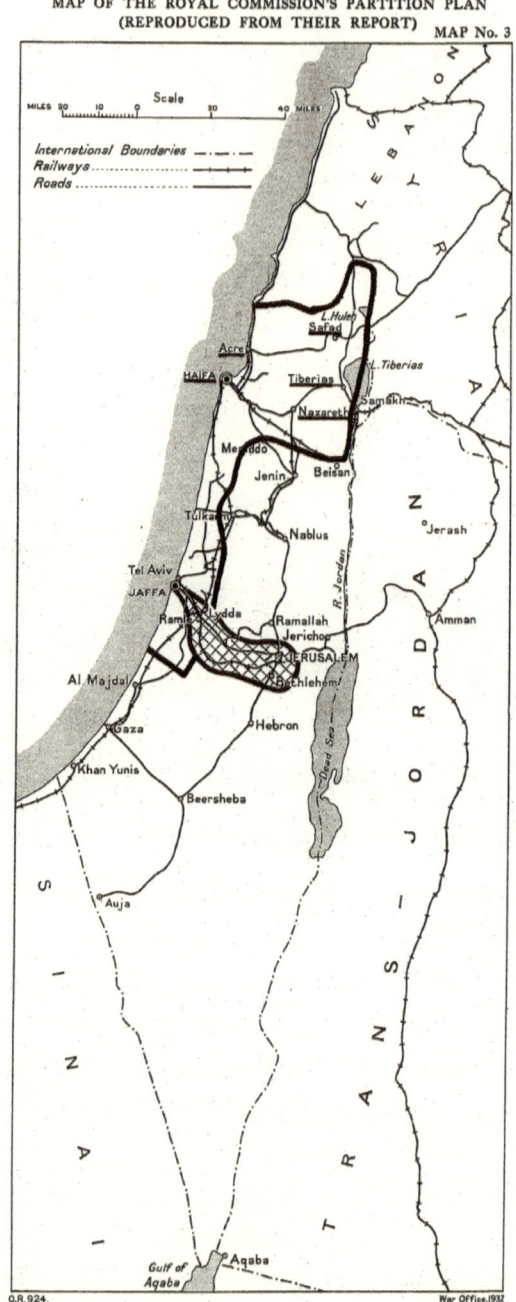

MAP OF THE ROYAL COMMISSION'S PARTITION PLAN
(REPRODUCED FROM THEIR REPORT)

MAP No. 3

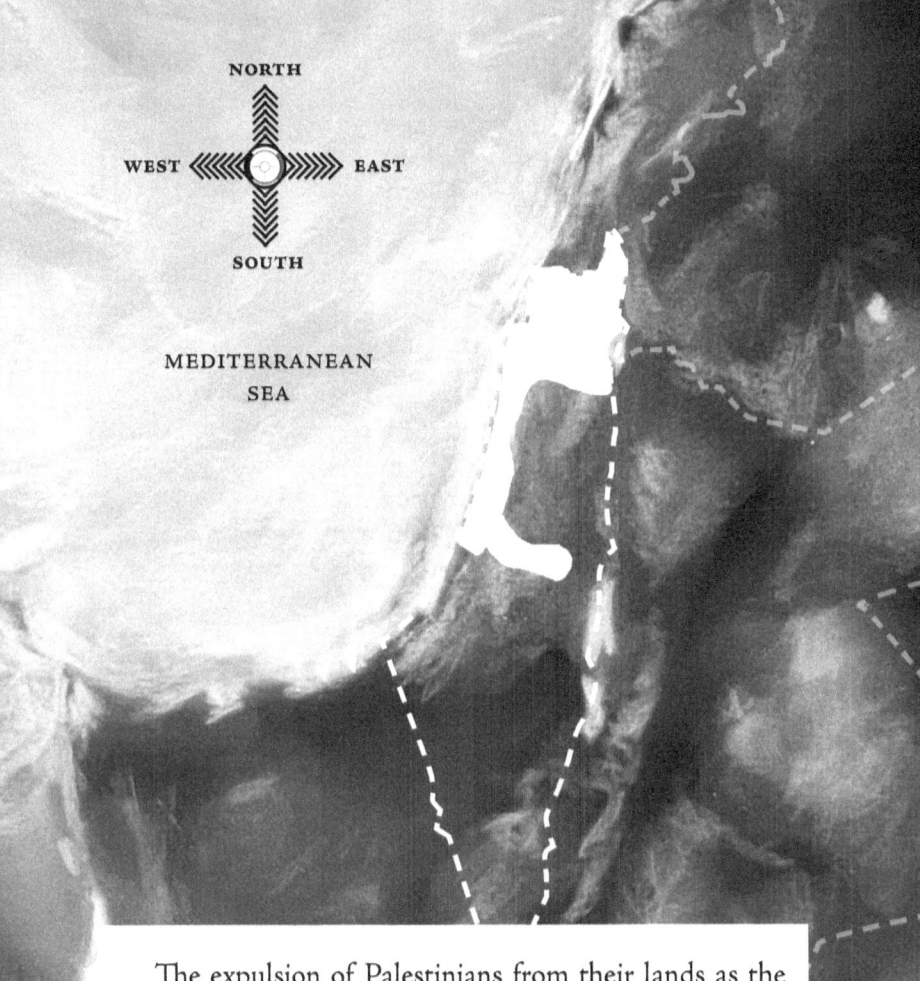

NORTH
WEST EAST
SOUTH

MEDITERRANEAN
SEA

The expulsion of Palestinians from their lands as the Survey progressed led to a much earlier intifada, the Arab Revolt of 1936–1939. In its investigations on the revolt, Britain's Peel Commission reported that throughout the countryside, Palestinian peasants were breaking the surveyor's instruments and halting the Survey's progress.

The Peel Commission proposed a partition of Palestine in 1937 allotting the surveyed lands to a future Jewish State and adding an international corridor to maintain European access to Jerusalem from the Mediterranean at Jaffa, with "international" meaning European.

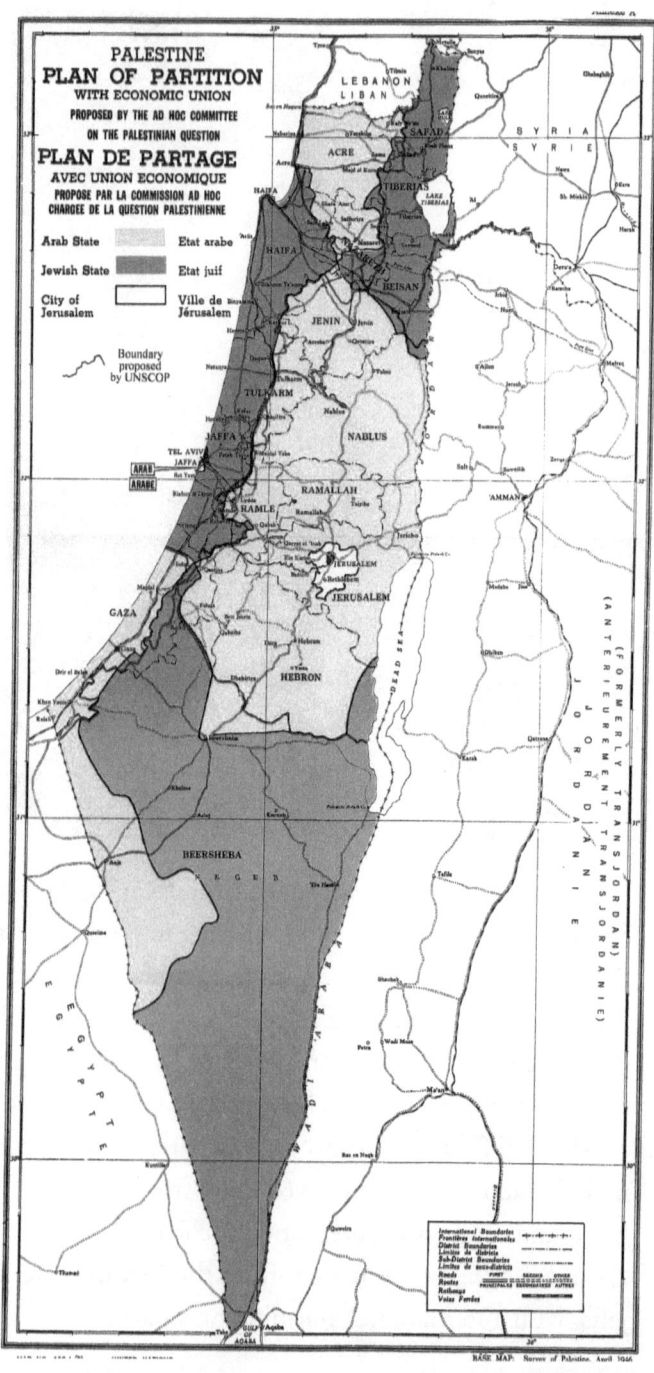

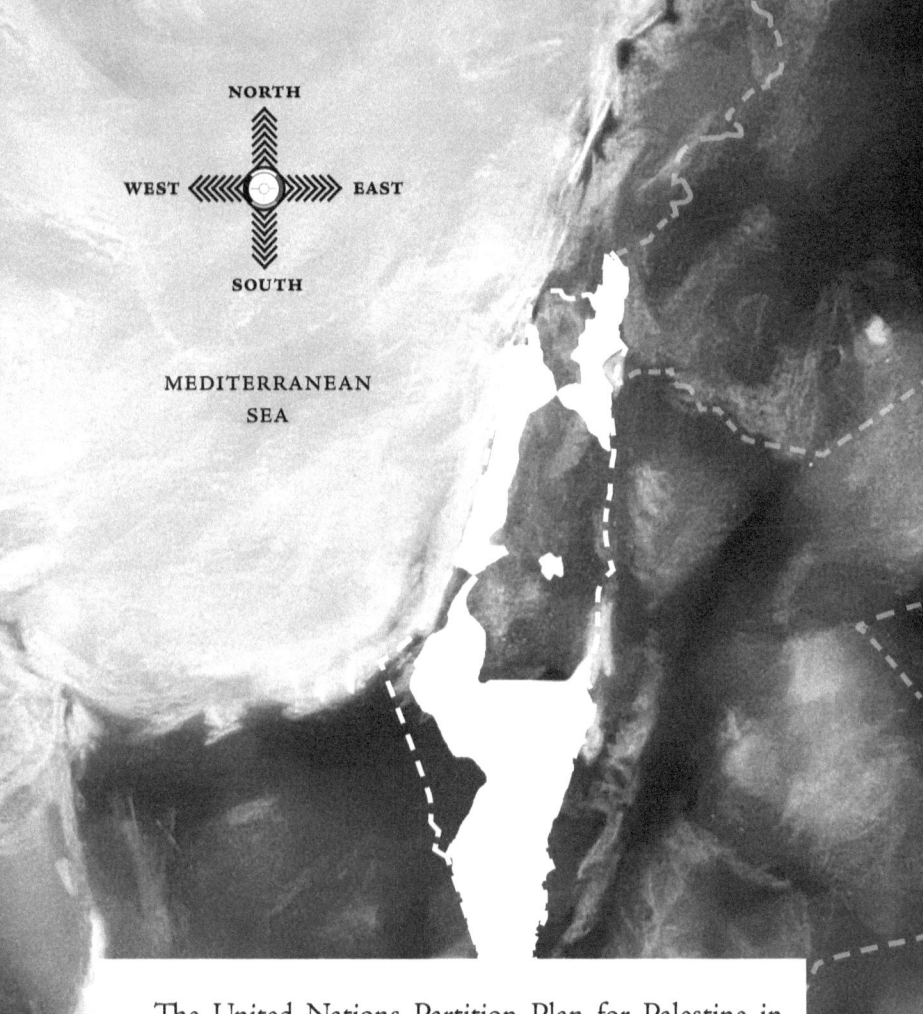

The United Nations Partition Plan for Palestine in 1947 allotted the surveyed lands to a Jewish State along with large swaths of the Negev Desert in the south to accommodate the further transfer of Jews out of Europe.

The newly created United Nations General Assembly had just approved the partition of Palestine into an Arab State and a Jewish State and a special "international" regime for Jerusalem and its surroundings, including Bethlehem. The plan implied the forcible transfer of Palestinians from the area allotted to a Jewish State.

Of course the Palestinians refused.

Palestine from Above

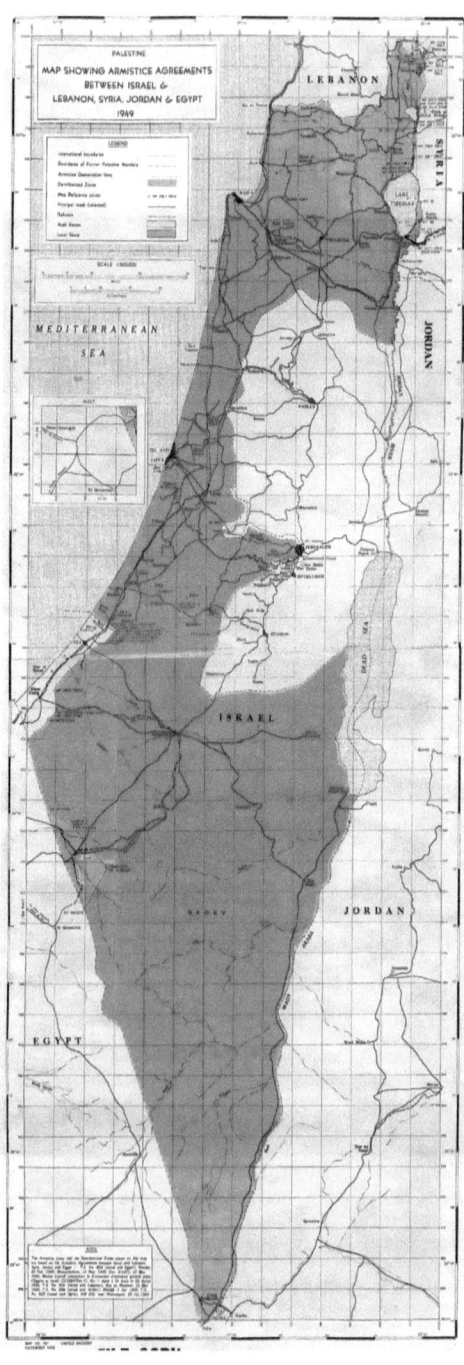

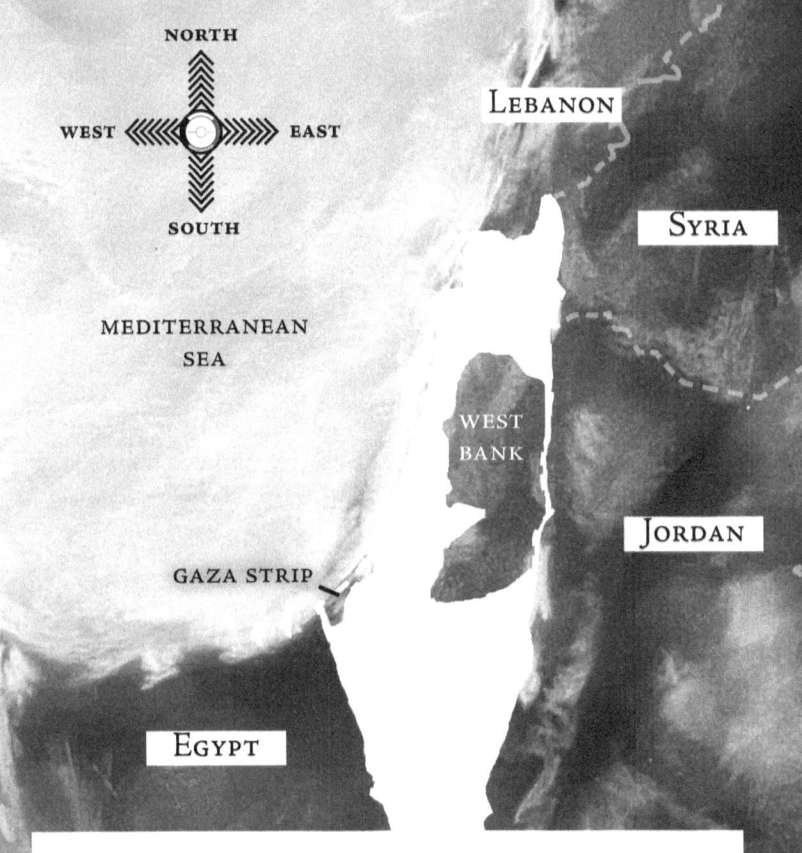

In 1948, Zionist militias armed by Europe successfully went to war against the resistance, which also came from Egypt, Jordan, Iraq, Syria, Lebanon, and Yemen. Approximately 750,000 Palestinians, about half of the Palestinian population at the time, were expelled from their homes or made to flee through various violent means to live in refugee camps in the Gaza Strip, West Bank, Jordan, Syria, and Lebanon.

The Nakba resulted in the establishment of the State of Israel up to the edges of Jerusalem. No Palestinian state was created. Jordan would control Jerusalem and the rest of the West Bank, and Egypt would control the Gaza Strip until 1967 when Israel would take those lands too.

In 1967 through more war, Israel expanded its territory by capturing Jerusalem and the rest of the West Bank, the Gaza Strip, Sinai Peninsula, and the Golan Heights. It immediately began building settlements in them all. In 1979 Israel would eventually return the Sinai Peninsula to Egypt in exchange for peace in a deal brokered by the United States, for which Egypt would become the second-largest recipient of military aid from the United States after Israel, the first-largest recipient.

Israel today still occupies the Golan Heights, originally mapped as part of Syria in the 1920s. Israel's border with Syria had remained quiet for decades until May 15, 2011 during the first months of the Arab uprisings, when thousands pulled up on buses from Syria and marched toward the Golan Heights, Palestinian flags in hand. Their Golani kin on the other side of the fence had cheered at first but shouted in disbelief the closer the protesters approached. *Bikafi!* they pleaded, warning of the landmines near the fence. Enough! Still, the protesters kept on and answered back, "*al-sha'b yurid tahrir Falesteen!*" The people want the liberation of Palestine. About a hundred of them jumped the fence, entered, and dispersed. Stunned Israeli border guards recovered quickly and opened fire, wounding and martyring several. The rest were captured and deported back to Syria, but one Palestinian refugee had slipped through. Hassan Hijazi hopped on a public bus and reached Jaffa, the place of his grandfather's birth. After searching for his family's house with no luck, he contacted an Israeli television correspondent and by evening turned himself in to the police. He was soon deported to Syria but not before his message was relayed to Israelis that Palestine's refugees had returned.[2]

---

2. Ury Avnery, "The Odyssey of Hassan Hijazi" in *The Greanville Post* (June 10, 2011).

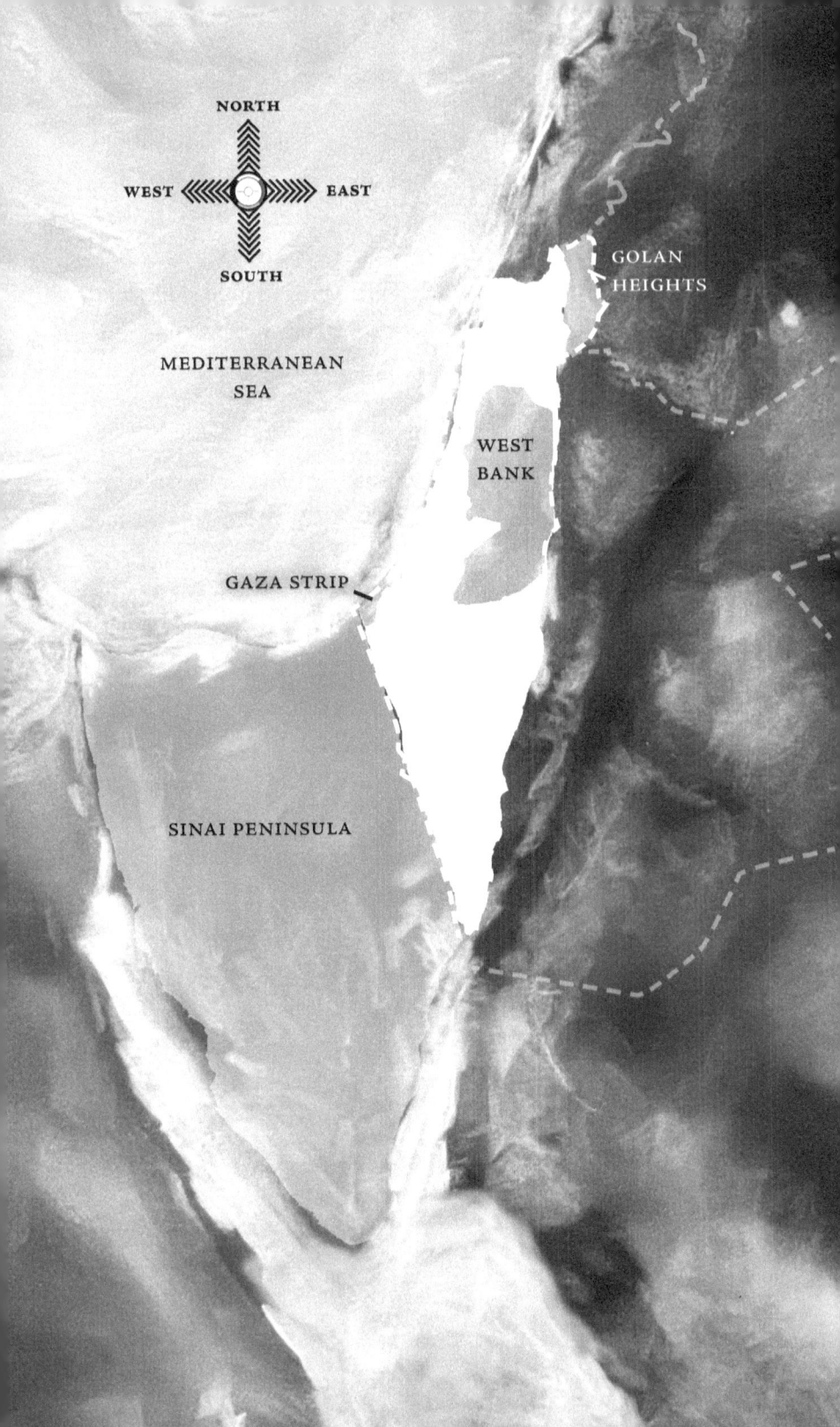

In 1948, when Zionist militias expelled half of Palestine's people from the land, the half that remained were placed under martial law by the State of Israel until 1966. During this time, Palestinians inside '48 were governed by military rule and subjected to travel permits, curfews, and detention. Many continued being expelled from their homes and lands in the Galilee, homes and lands transferred to Jewish settlers or Israeli institutions. Israel has since forced citizenship onto them but continues to treat them like second-class citizens. The '48 Palestinians are often forgotten even by many Palestine awareness maps of Palestine whose focus stays mostly on the Gaza Strip and West Bank.

Also regularly forgotten on awareness maps is the Golan Heights, but the territory is certainly included in the mental maps of what Israelis believe their borders to be. But Israel has never defined its borders for Israel is not done expanding. According to Zionist mental maps, *Eretz Israel*, the Land of Israel, is supposed to expand further east to the Tigris and Euphrates Rivers in modern-day Iraq. On Israeli military uniforms the Eretz Israel map reminds Zionist soldiers of the larger territory they've been conscripted to kill for.

The image below is from a social media post shared in June 2024 by nine-year-old Lama Jamous. In the midst of Israel's escalated genocide in the Gaza Strip, Gaza's youngest journalist had a question for the world about the map under the Israeli flag:

Do you know what is the meaning of this sign?

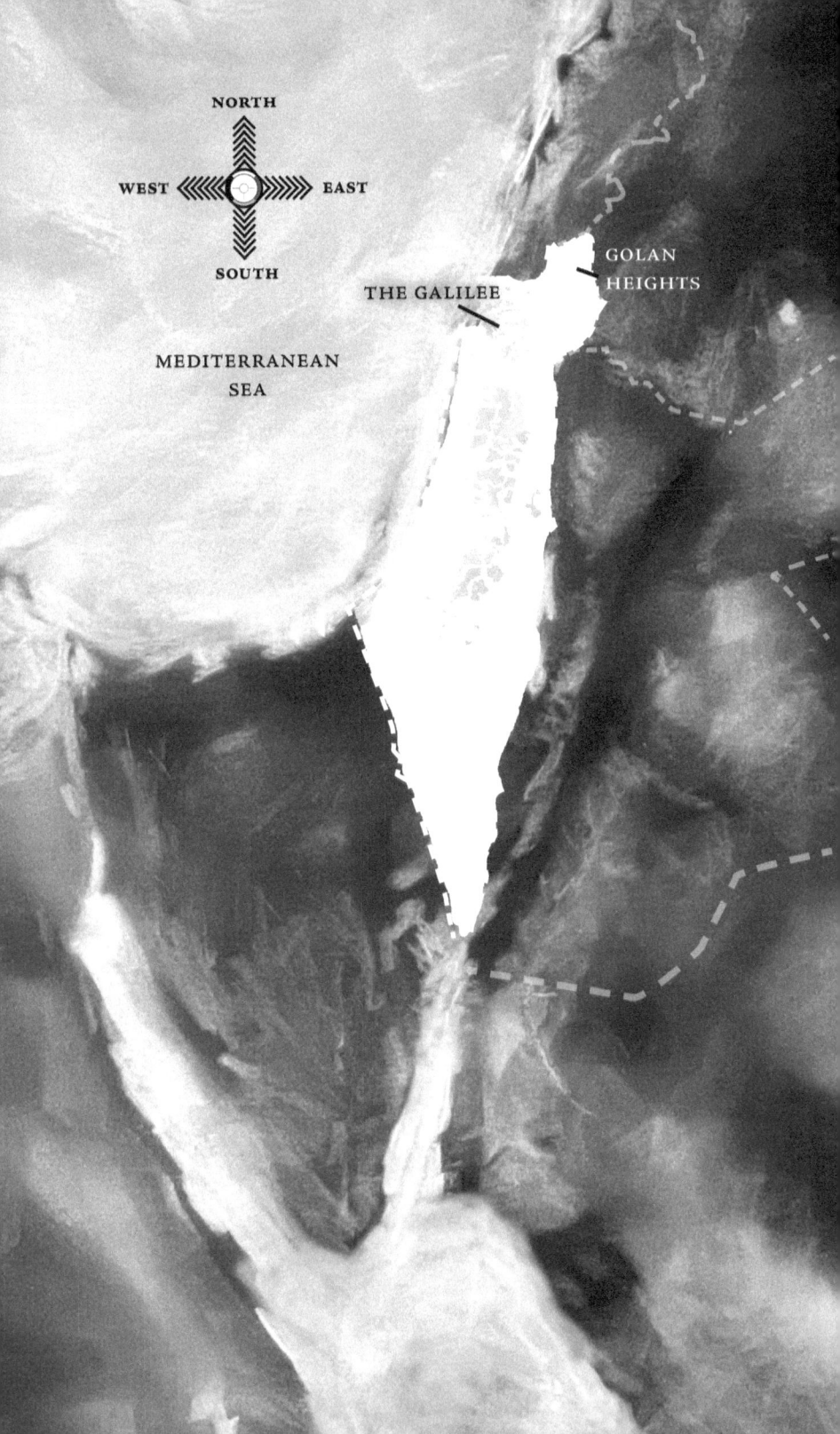

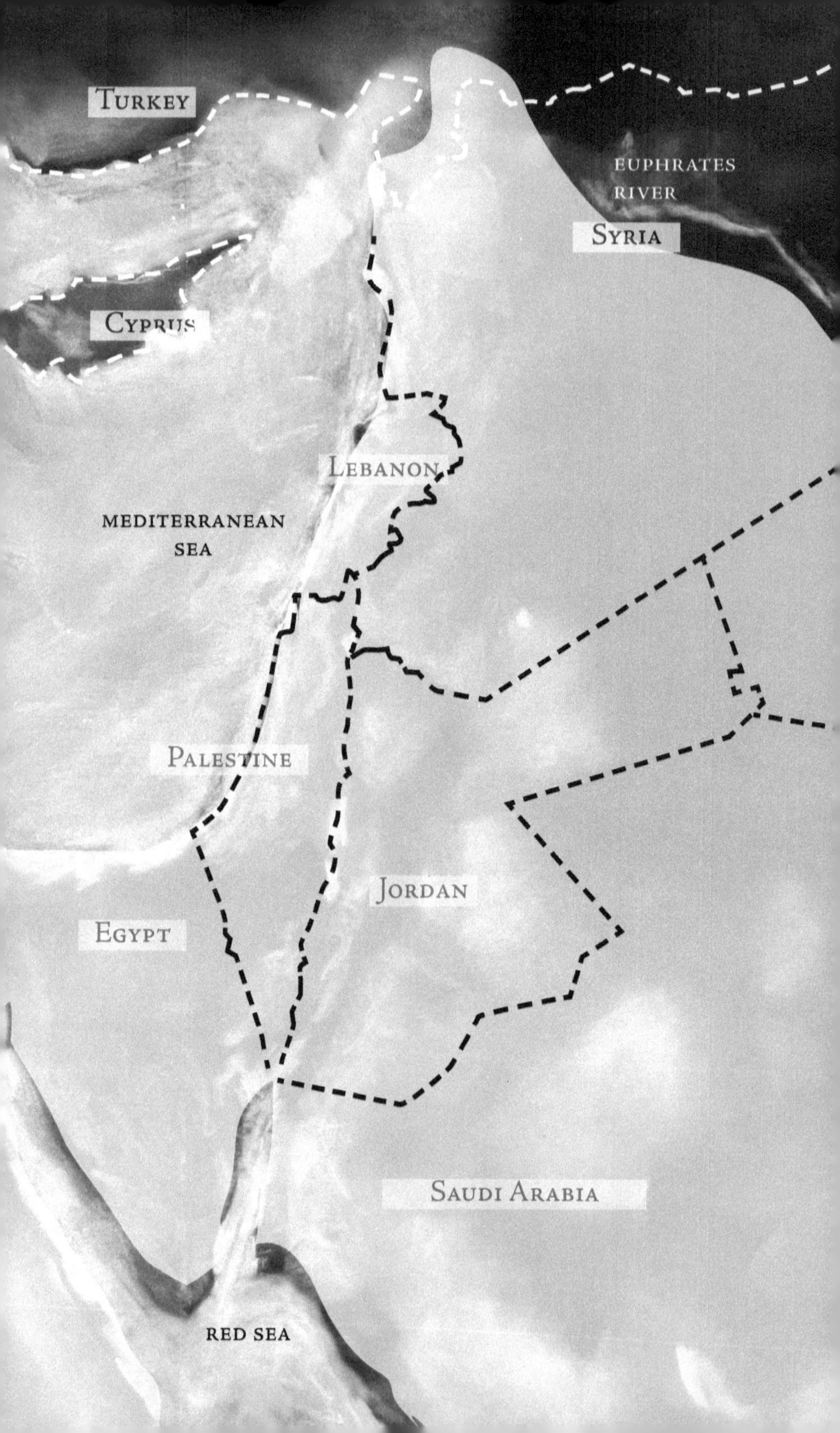

TURKEY

CYPRUS

EUPHRATES
RIVER

SYRIA

LEBANON

MEDITERRANEAN
SEA

PALESTINE

EGYPT

JORDAN

SAUDI ARABIA

RED SEA

ERETZ ISRAEL

TIGRIS RIVER

EUPHRATES RIVER

IRAQ

IRAN

KUWAIT

SAUDI ARABIA

Palestine 1492: A Report Back

II

Palestine Counter-Maps

Maps arise when societies call for them. Those who know the land intimately don't need maps, at least not ones on paper. Before the idea of a State of Palestine was born, Palestinians didn't make statist maps. Nobody did until a couple hundred years ago with the invention of the nation-state.[1]

Every Palestinian geographer I met in Palestine confirmed that the first maps Yasser Arafat signed in the Oslo peace process were Israel's maps. In the disaster that was the peace process from above, Palestinians didn't have their own maps.

Today, Palestinians make a lot of maps and operate their own geography institutions, and still they don't have a state. That Palestinians did not have their own maps is not why they have been displaced. Still, the Palestinian leadership insists that mapping a border between the State of Israel and a State of Palestine will solve everything: a two-state solution. It's not clear if the leadership can admit that the border between Israel/Palestine already exists and it's not a line on the map. The Israel/Palestine border is the line between Peace/War of empire; the line between Europe/non-Europe of colonialism; the architecture of Above/Below of apartheid; the split between Human/non-Human of cannibalism.

---

1. Denis Wood, *Rethinking the Power of Maps* (The Guilford Press, 2010)

None of this is to say the map is useless or should immediately be discarded. As Edward Said put it:

> In the history of colonial invasion maps are always first drawn by the victors, since maps are instruments of conquest. Geography is therefore the art of war but can also be the art of resistance if there is a counter-map and a counter-strategy.[2]

The borders of Historic Palestine are colonial constructions, but Palestinians have long counter-mapped that construction against the colonizer. Maps of Palestine in necklaces, embroidery, and other artwork have helped build a consciousness of a common struggle among everybody within the colonial outlines of that map. Palestinian communities are highly diverse, yet every single one whose lands are within the colonial borders have been marked for extermination. The counter-map of Palestine convokes their collective resistance.

In this popular political poster published by the Palestine Liberation Organization (PLO) in 1964, the map of Palestine appears prominently in the background and is accompanied in the foreground by Palestinian children, a Palestinian woman, and imagery of armed struggle.

The poster reads,

> Palestine Liberation Organization-Palestine Liberation Army.
> For the sake of our land and our children we joined the Palestine Liberation Army as fighters and volunteers.

---

2. Edward Said, *Peace and Its Discontents: Essays on Palestine in the Middle East Peace Process* (Vintage, 1996)

The Fatah emblem above on the official party flag features the map of Palestine behind two AK-47s and a grenade. The text reads *Fatah: the National Liberation Movement of Palestine. Revolution until victory.*

The emblem below of the Palestine Front for the Liberation of Palestine (PFLP) has the map accompanied by the Arabic letter *jim* from the word *Jibha,* or "Front," which takes the form of an arrow into Palestine, symbolizing its insistence on the refugees' return.

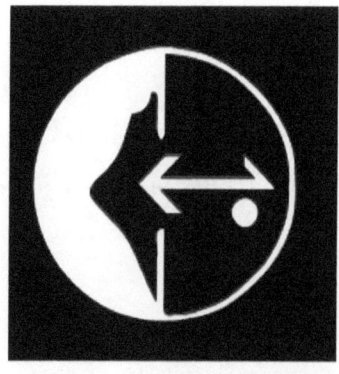

The Hamas emblem shows the map of Palestine above the al-Aqsa Mosque compound's Dome of the Rock where two swords cross in front. The Dome is framed by two Palestinian flags with the statements that comprise the Shahada: *There is no god but God* on the right flag, and on the left, *Muhammad is the messenger of Allah.*

Al-Aqsa regularly appears in Palestinian imagery to symbolize the sacredness of Jerusalem, difficult to communicate in modern cartography, whose tendency is to reduce the Holy City to a mere point on the map.

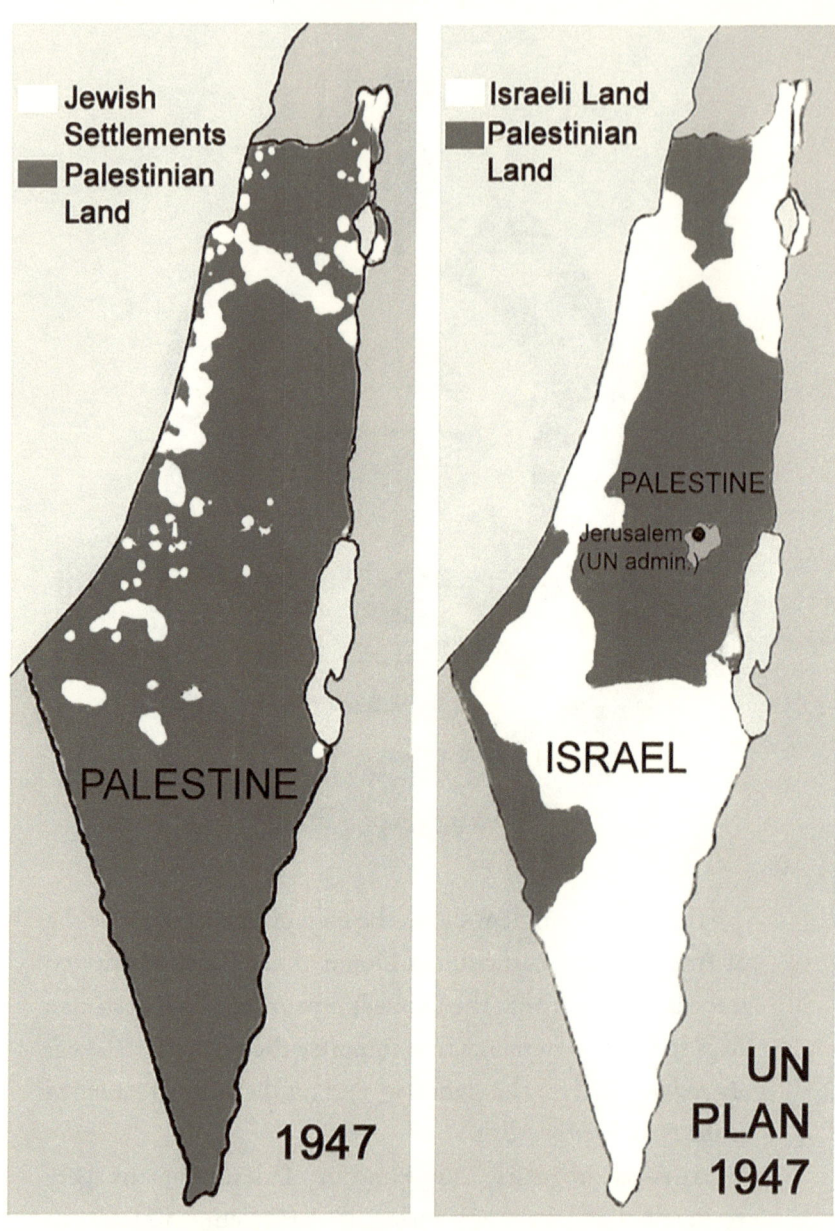

This four-panel map powerfully communicates Israel's ongoing destruction of Palestine. It circulates widely in Palestine awareness campaigns. It doesn't show the Occupied

Palestine Counter-Maps

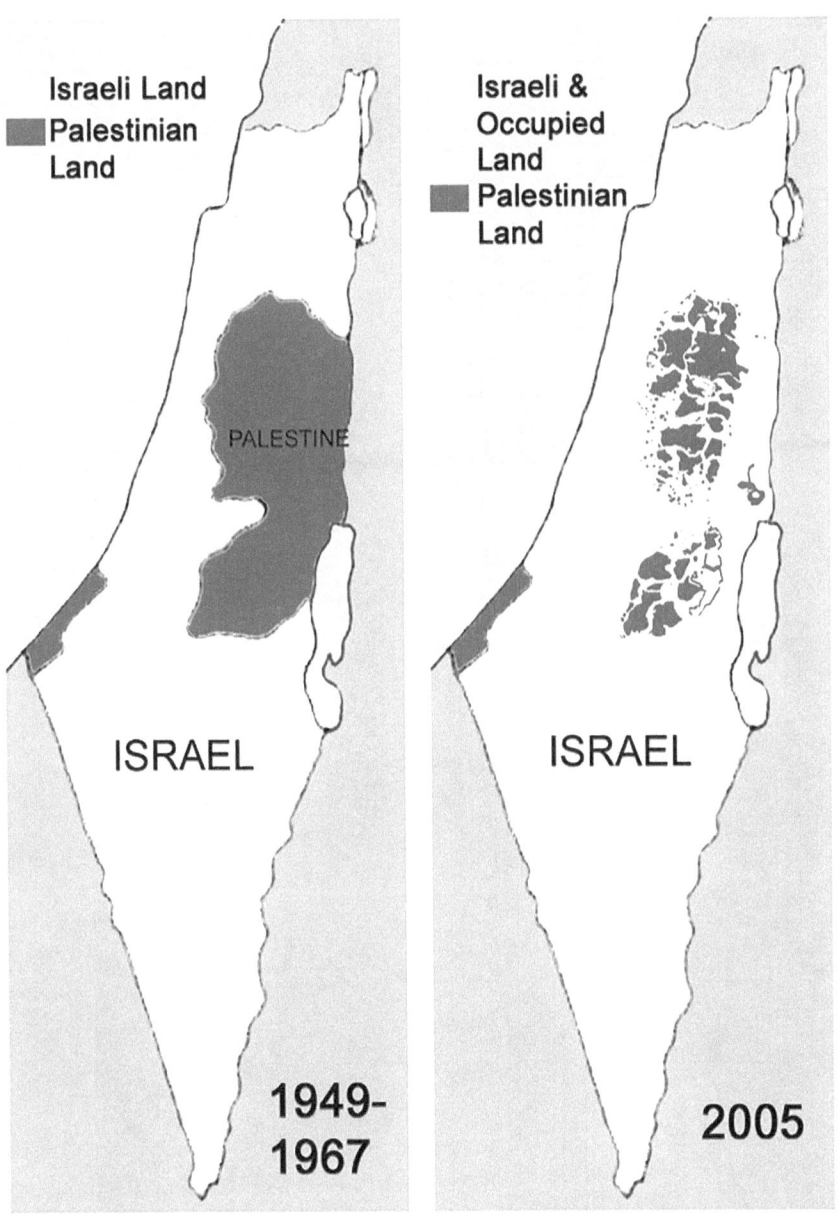

Golan Heights or the presence of Palestinian Citizens of Israel. It takes aim at Israel's growing settlement activity in the West Bank and deliberate sabotage of a two-state solution.

Palestine from Above

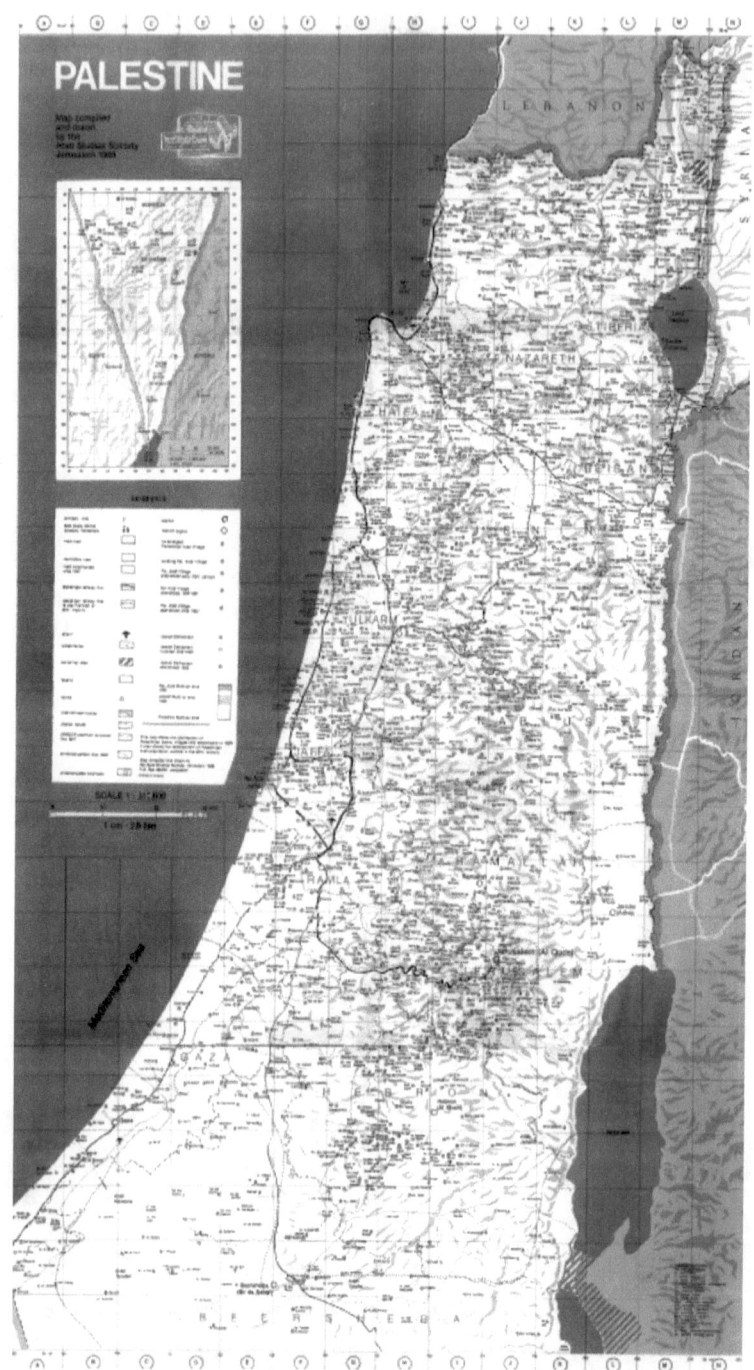

Palestine Counter-Maps

Although Palestinians didn't make many scientific maps before Oslo, ten years before Oslo in 1983, a Palestinian team of surveyors from the Jerusalem-based Arab Studies Society began mapping Palestine, highlighting Palestinian towns and villages and Jewish settlements as they existed on the eve of the Nakba.

(re-emerged) Palestinian Arab Village ⊘

existing Pal. Arab Village ⊙

Pal. Arab Village abandoned early 20th. century ⊙

Pal Arab Village abandoned 1948-1967 ⊙

Pal. Arab Village abandoned after 1967 ⊙

Jewish Settlement ○

Jewish Settlement founded 1945-1949 ○

Jewish Settlement abandoned 1948 ○

The map, republished on the opposite page, was published in 1988 five years after fieldwork first began and would become the first full map of Palestine made by Palestinians. This is according to Palestinian cartographer Khalil Tufakji, who had drawn the map by hand from his offices in Jerusalem's now shut down Orient House, the PLO headquarters in the 1980s and 1990s.

Tufakji gifted me a copy of this map when I visited him for an interview in Jerusalem. I had heard stories of the map throughout the West Bank, that it was everywhere displayed throughout schools and their classrooms. But 1988, the year the map was completed, was also the year the PLO officially adopted the two-state solution as a compromise: a State of Palestine in the West Bank and Gaza Strip next to the State of Israel, the 1949 armistice lines serving as the border.

I asked Tufakji if his maps changed accordingly after 1988, and he confirmed they did. From 1988, as soon as his map of all of Palestine was complete, his future maps would focus only on the West Bank and Gaza Strip, not on Historic Palestine, but on only 22 percent of Palestine.

Salman Abu Sitta's *Atlas of Palestine 1917–1966* doesn't map only the West Bank and Gaza Strip. A large part of the *Atlas* curates the British Mandate's Survey of Palestine as Palestinian villages and place names were before the Nakba. Upon the creation of the State of Israel, Israel immediately began erasing Palestinian presence on the British surveys.[3] The *Atlas of Palestine* counter-maps this erasure.

Abu Sitta's *Atlas* also includes analysis of the various colonial partitions, land ownership and population composition before and after the Nakba, the 1949 Armistice Lines, the border with Lebanon, land exchange with Jordan, historical village photos, the destruction of landscape, the dispossession and confiscation of Palestinian property, water and agriculture's retransformation, and more of Israel's crimes.

And more than that, Abu Sitta's work shows that well over 80% of the land is kept empty by Israel, and there is plenty of space for the Palestinian refugees to return.

---

3. See Meron Benvenisti, *Sacred Landscape: Buried History of the Holy Land Since 1948* (University of California Press, 2002)

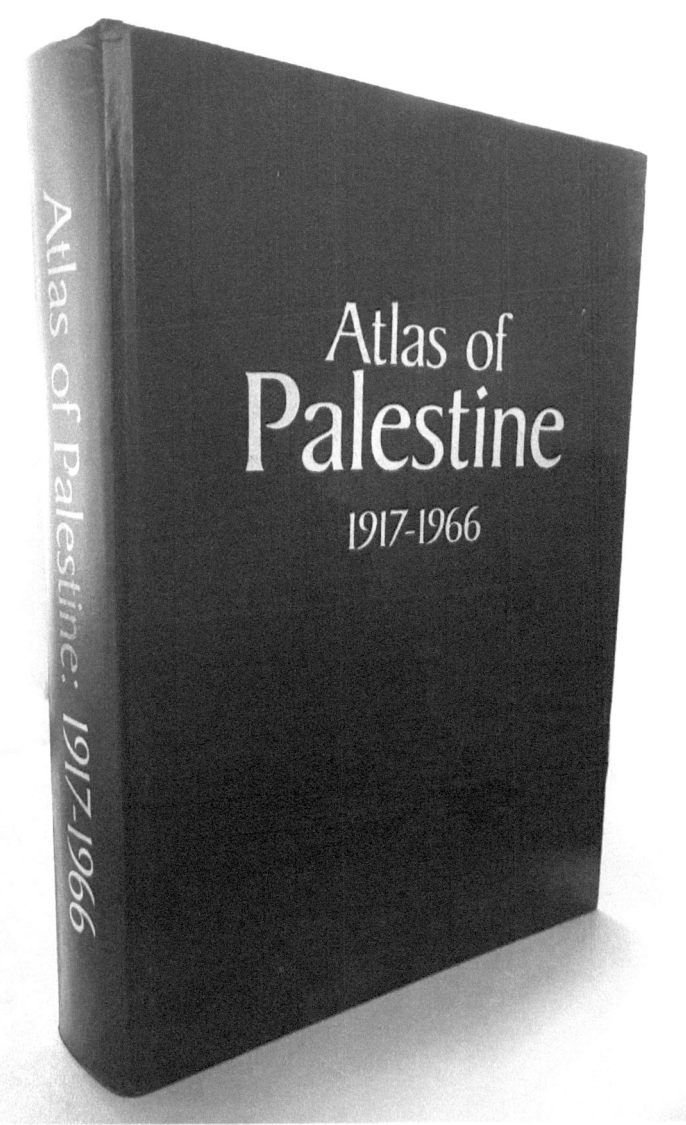

In 2006 when Google Earth was still new, a Palestinian refugee announced a "grand post" on the Google Earth Community Forum. He had created a map of Palestinian villages destroyed or depopulated in the Nakba to be viewed as a layer on Google Earth. Thameen Darby, a refugee from the village of Balad al-Sheikh, described his "Nakba Layer" as a project that would bring joy to other refugees. Promoting it through mass e-mail, he requested the following message be forwarded widely to interested friends and family:

> Do you want to see where your original town or village is in Palestine? If you have Google Earth you can use the attached layer to see the destroyed and existing Palestinian Villages. For those who have not used it yet, Google Earth is a new emerging tool for information exchange based on a three dimensional assimilation of satellite images of the world. Google Earth allows users to add layers to it after they install. There is a layer of all the destroyed Palestinian villages and towns in 1948. This is a big data base that shows the site of each village and directs you to a website that talks about each village in detail.

The layer contained location marks for each village classified by district with links to PalestineRemembered.com for more detail. "The issue of these refugees and their right to their native land," Darby explained on the Google Earth Community Forum, "remains the major obstacle to achieve a long desired peace between the Israelis and Palestinians."[4]

---

4. Linda Quiquivix (2014) "Art of War, Art of Resistance: Palestinian Counter-Cartography of Google Earth," *Annals of the Association of American Geographers*, 104(3): 444-459

"How did they know where the borders were?" I had asked Palestinian geographer Ahmed Al-Noubani during fieldwork in Palestine. "If people didn't have maps, how did they know?"

Al-Noubani had opened his arm out and pointed in one direction and then another. "It was that carob tree to that carob tree." Neighbors, he shrugged. They figured it out.

Al-Noubani and I had met in his office at Bir Zeit University's geography department in January 2011, discussing histories of Palestinian map-making. He had long ago been recruited as part of a Palestinian map-making team at Oslo "to help us with pull" under the framework, he had recounted.

"Land was used for pastures and herders," Al-Noubani continued, recalling a time when maps were rare. "Tribes knew their borders." Claims to property, he had explained, were made through the *Hujja*, a land transfer paper agreement where boundaries were not lines but descriptions of natural landmarks that villagers understood between each other.

"But today," he continued, "the Israeli courts ask, 'What are the coordinates? What are the borders?' You can't say the carob tree is the border. They don't accept it."[5]

Our conversation ended that day with Al-Noubani's declaration of a wish: that more work be done on the social relations people have with borders. And I couldn't stop thinking about the tree.

---

5. Linda Quiquivix (2013) "When the Carob Tree Was the Border: On Autonomy and Palestinian Practices of Figuring it Out," *Capitalism Nature Socialism*, 24(3): 170–189

Palestine Counter-Maps

An olive tree marks Rafah Crossing 100 years ago.

@jehadabusalim

·II

The Wretched of the Empire

One hundred years ago, almost nobody would have believed Europe would become the great defender of the Jews. A Jewish classmate once shared with me a tragic saying among Israelis who recognize this to be true: *Jews had to leave Europe in order to become European.*

It is rational to join the side of the oppressor when empire offers that as the sole option for survival. To say it's rational is to say it's understandable; it's not to say it is ethical. The wretched of the earth's choice to help crush other wretched cannot be fully condemned without condemnation of the world that produces that choice, that produces a people as wretched, a people as condemned. The two choices are to go above or remain crushed below. It's understandable to wish to assimilate, but a below still remains. Again, understandable but not ethical. An imbalance still remains, the trauma remains, the terror of falling remains, extermination remains, genocide remains. Resistance is an inevitability; it is to be expected, not condemned. But resistance is not the same thing as liberation.

The late Jewish liberation theologian, Marc Ellis, spoke of a shift in God's role within Judaism following the Jewish Holocaust in the 1940s. The agonizing question for Jews since that time has been, *How could God allow it?* This trauma has been readily seized upon by Zionism with the promise that the State of Israel would never allow it, never again, at least not for Jews, because for Israel to protect Jews, it has to holocaust Palestinians, which is no protection at all for Jews. The Palestinian resistance to their own extermination is an inevitability, it is to be expected, not condemned. The agreement to serve empire is what is to be condemned. Empire itself is what is to be condemned.

Israel replaced God as an imposter protector; Zionism replaced God with the State. Gesturing to when the Roman Empire co-opted Christianity, Marc Ellis called Zionism a "Constantinian Judaism,"[1] a co-optation of Judaism on behalf of empire. Ellis fought for a Judaism from below almost alone in the United States until he died. The health of the resistance was weak while he was alive. He got to see only glimpses of it in his life, and may he get to see more in the next. Marc Ellis, *presente*.

Non-Europe is a place where Europe's wretched can sometimes become protected as long as they help crush the resistance. The wretched of the earth doesn't simply get to survive within empire, they have to make themselves useful to it. Not everybody is offered that chance, but those who are offered it regularly take it. *How might we resist the decision to take it?*

Israel is that kind of place where Jews can become White or White-adjacent if they can be useful, an offer that makes whoever accepts it inherently anti-Black. About how this plays out in the United States: it's "the price of the ticket" as James Baldwin used to say.[2] James Baldwin, *presente*.

---

1. Marc Ellis, *Toward a Jewish Theology of Liberation* (Baylor University Press, 2007); also see Sara Roy, "Remembering Marc Ellis" *Contending Modernities* (July 31, 2024)

2. James Baldwin, *The Price of the Ticket: Collected Nonfiction 1948–1985*, (St. Martin's Press, 1985)

One hundred years ago, the resistances of non-Europe were debilitating Europe while, at the same time, the Europeans in Europe were eating at each other again. Europe's implosion in the First and Second World Wars lost the neat Europe/non-Europe world map of Peace/War. Empire had to restrategize and reterritorialize, the beast had to grow new heads, heads of whatever color, religion, gender as long as they could be useful.

Desperate for an optics of redemption, a new principle of "Universal Human Equality" suddenly emerged within Europe at its newly created United Nations, the multicultural face of empire. Some of the below were invited now to a seat at the table, but only the ones Europe considered Human-adjacent enough, only the ones Europe could control.

In the framework of human rights today, the Human/non-Human split has since taken emphasis over the Europe/non-Europe split, even though in practice everyone can see the Human/non-Human of international law still maps onto the Europe/non-Europe of colonial law. The "Universal Human" standard itself was modeled by the European, meaning the non-European human is seen as inherently defective and needs to catch up, if the non-European human is seen as possibly human at all.

Frantz Fanon warned about trying to catch up to the oppressor in his final book, *The Wretched of the Earth* (1961), a book about going below, not going above. Everyone seems to reference that work, but not a lot of people can discuss more than its first two pages on violence, which means they miss the part about not becoming the monsters that we fight.

Fanon's first book, which not enough people even pretend to read, speaks about the psychology of the wretched of the empire, although the book isn't called that. It's called *Black Skin, White Masks* (1952), originally entitled "Essay on the

Disalienation of the Black." The book had been Fanon's doctoral dissertation before it was rejected by his French university. He had to write a new dissertation on another subject before They let him graduate.

Black Skin, White Masks discusses the psychological effects of dehumanization and anti-Blackness under colonialism, as Fanon himself experienced while studying psychiatry and medicine in France, as a Black colonized subject of France, from the Caribbean.

In *Black Skin, White Masks,* Fanon shows the internal and social turmoil Black colonized subjects undergo under conditions of dehumanization and the incentives they believe they will acquire by speaking like a European, dressing like a European, acting like a European, impossible in the end because Black skin turns out to be the border of who's allowed to be a European, of who's allowed to be a Human according to the European.

Since the decolonization movements of the 1950s, 1960s, and 1970s, Europe launched an optics of redemption and reterritorialization. Europe is no longer contained to Europe or to the European. One can even leave Europe to become a European.

But Israel is not a place Jews go to become fully European. Israel doesn't let anyone forget the "wretched" part of Jewish history that empire says it is redeeming, "the worst crime against Humanity" as they call it, since the crime happened in Europe. Europe's holocausts in non-Europe it doesn't consider to be crimes.

The part of Jewish history preserved as "wretched" allows for empire's redemption and much as it does for its deflection. Criticism of Israel's imperial errands, for example, are accused of being anti-Semitic by anti-Semites themselves, accused of being the Devil by the Devil himself, an accusation that's only effective when one doesn't know what's going on, and admittedly, not a lot of people know what's going on.

Israel knows that empire as the great defender of Jews might not always be the case, as empire doesn't care first about identity; empire cares first about preserving itself. Israel is for empire today its post-Holocaust redemption. And even Palestine might be its post-Israel redemption once Israel stops being so useful and if Palestinians were to accept that agreement, and there is no shortage of Palestinians who would accept that agreement. There is no shortage of any of us who would accept that agreement.

We must be cautious, and we must not forget, one hundred years ago almost nobody would have believed Europe would become the great defender of the Jews. Empire regularly changes its face so that it can remain the same.

⫸ SOUTH

The Fourth World War

"Not far from here, in a place called Gaza, in Palestine, in the Middle East, right next to us..."

—EZLN
Mexico, 4th of January 2009

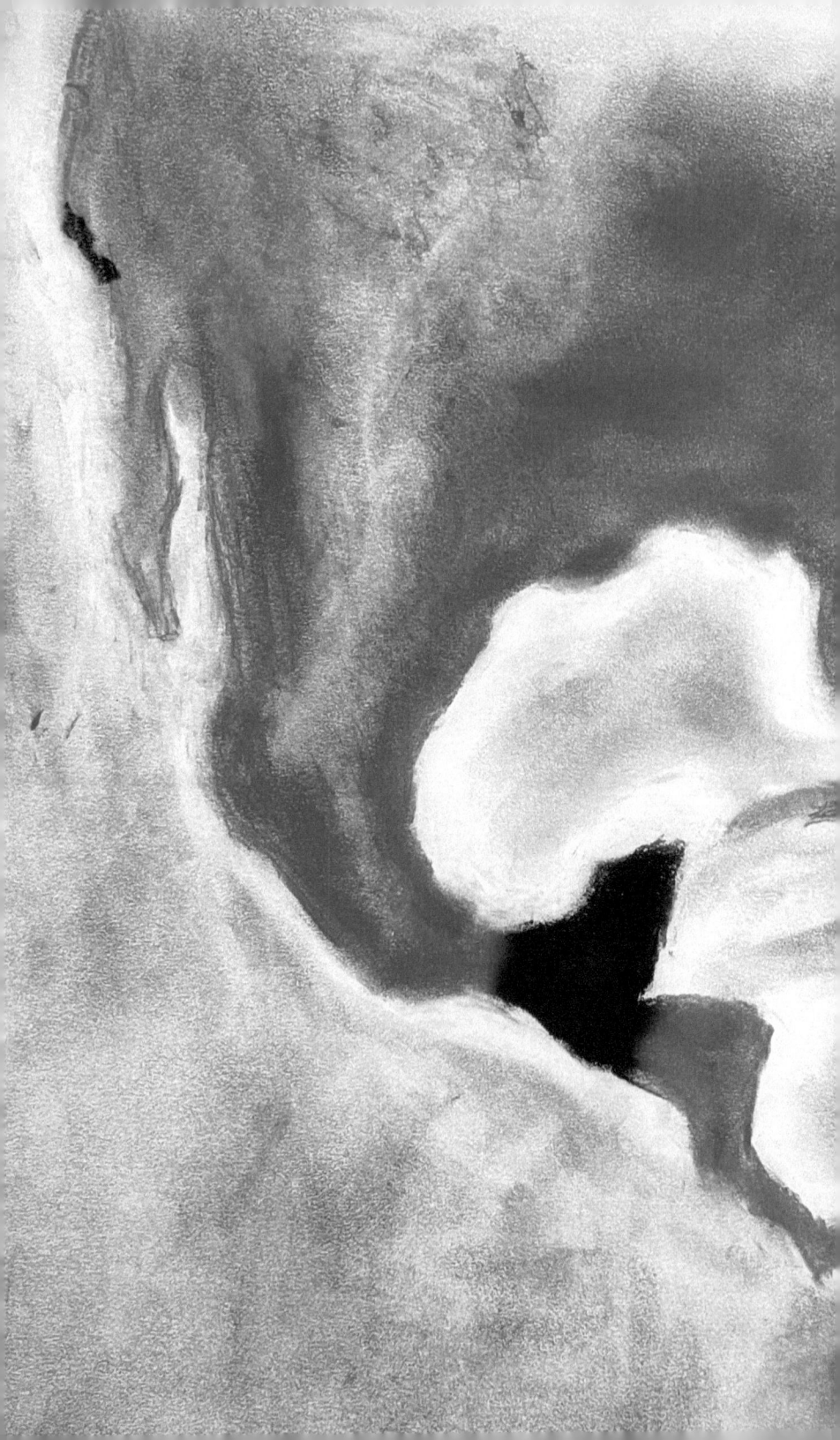

The Third World War

Dedicated to all who will read this brilliant history, so that our children and our *compas* can never say it faded away.

I am writing about the actions and steps I have taken in the struggle, but I am also critical so they can learn from my mistakes and not repeat them. But this does not mean I am not a *compañera*.

I begin with my ancestors and place and day of birth. I am a descendant of the Maya people of *Iximulew*, the Land of Maize, from that corner of earth cut today by the borders of Mexico/Guatemala/Belize/Honduras/El Salvador. I am also a descendant of enslaved Black Afrikans, who I catastrophically know little about. Black is not easily located on a map.[1]

I am also a descendant of Columbus and Them even if nobody seems to know how. We have many Spanish last names in the family, more than we have Mayan names. My beloved grandmother's last name was Mazariegos, the name of the colonizer of Chiapas whose statue in San Cristóbal de las Casas was toppled on October 12, 1992. Is having a conquistador as an ancestor something that has happened through consent? I am learning the bad ones are also our

---

1. William C. Anderson, *The Nation on No Map: Black Anarchism and Abolition* (AK Press, 2021)

The Fourth World War

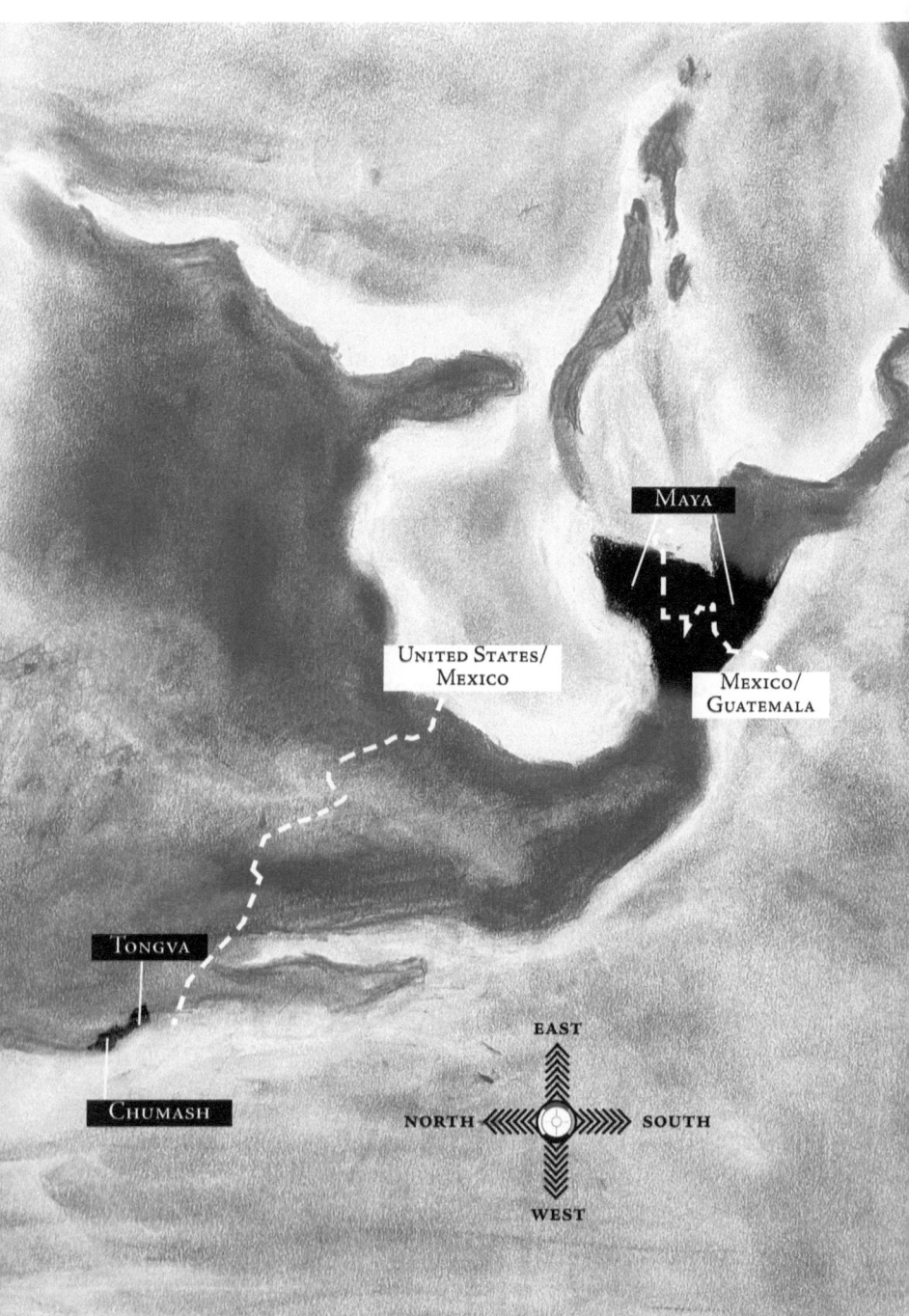

206

ancestors, not only the good ones. The question for each of us now is, *Who are we going to be in this life?*

I took my first breaths in *El Norte*, in The North, to an undocumented Guatemalan family on exactly ⁝∥ B'AQTUN, ⁝∥∥ K'ATUN, ⁝ TUN, ·∥∥ WINAQ, ·∥∥ Q'IJ, ⁝ AJMAQ in the Maya long count, or Tuesday, May 30, 1978.

I was born and raised in Occupied Chumash lands in the fieldworker towns of Oxnard and Hueneme, one hour north of Los Angeles, the colonial settlement built on Occupied Tongva lands first by the Spanish Empire, then by the Mexican Empire, then the American Empire, and now by a global empire. I grew up in the 1980s in last decade of the Third World War in the United States of America (USA), where those who don't listen to the pains of the below still call it the Cold War.

For many years my family did not have *papeles*, papers, documents granting legal permission to live and work in the United States. When I was little, my family regularly introduced me to their friends as *la ciudadana*, the citizen of the family, and everyone would stare as if I would do magic.

I am a first-generation college student, which means the generations before mine did not attend college. A first-generation college student is a sign of reaching the American Dream for an immigrant family, a sign of assimilation that makes the *gringos*, the Americans, be nicer to you. Depending.

In Guatemala, my family on all sides struggled with poverty. Quiquivix is a Mayan name, but we kids didn't know that at first. Pronounced kee-kee-veesh, our teachers were convinced it was French. That used to feel like a relief. Most of my family refers to themselves as *ladinos*, the Guatemalan and Chiapas equivalent of the Mexican *mestizos*, mixed roots of Native, European, and often Afrikan that denies both the Native

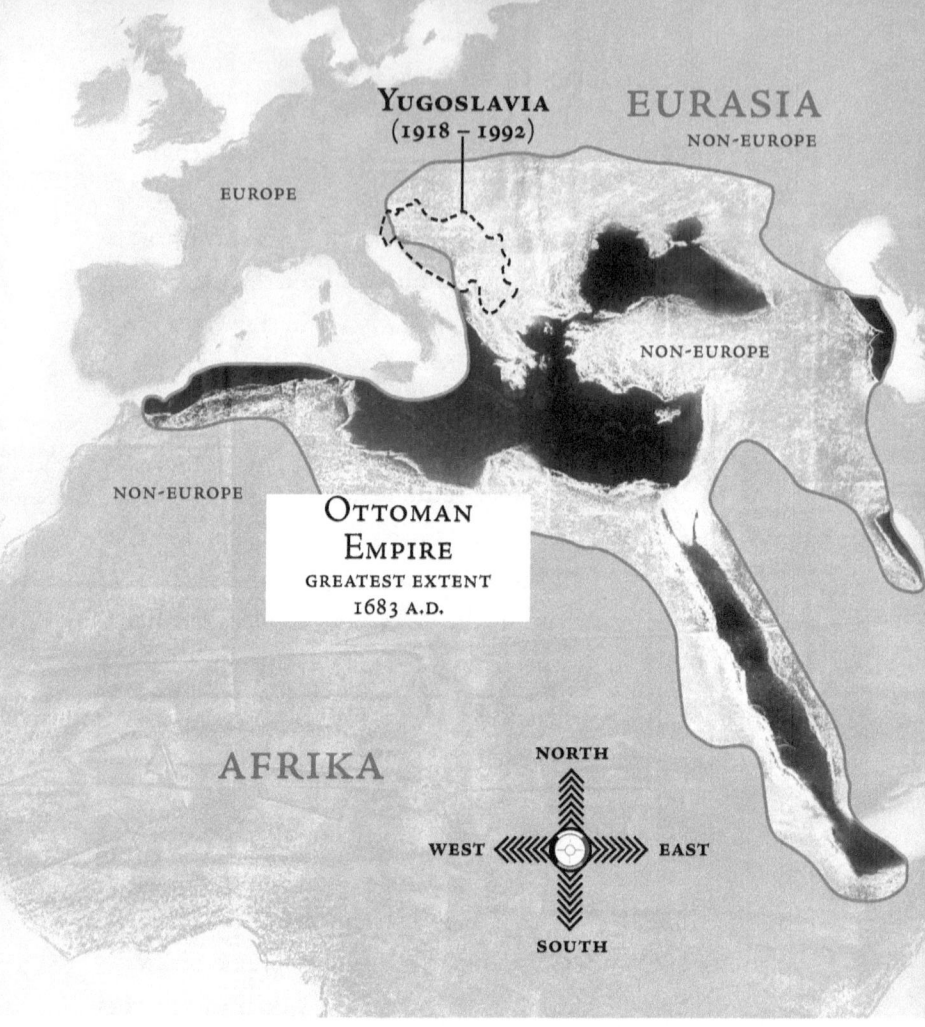

Yugoslavia was a name used between 1918–1992 for a geography in the the western Balkan Peninsula previously controlled by the Muslim Ottomans. The Balkans may be the least European part of Europe for its highly diverse communities of Muslims, Catholics, Jews, Protestants, and Eastern Orthodox Christians. Its diverse worlds disrupt notions of a homogeneous and a racially pure Europe.

and the Afrikan, and whose great wish is to become closer to European. It's like that in Guatemala and Mexico, too. It's like that everywhere the Europeans colonized Abya Yala. Migrants already know before setting foot in the USA that it's like it is back home: the ones in charge are nicer to you when your skin is a lighter color, and that if you can't be White, then at least don't be Black.

In our father's assimilation journey into Whiteness, he had a more difficult time than most hiding his Native because his last name remained Mayan. He used to tell us Quiquivix had been Yugoslavian, originally spelled Kikovic and then changed along the way. Something about pirates shipwrecking in the Caribbean. It was his way of becoming closer to European not knowing he was picking the least European part of Europe, or maybe fully knowing and just happy with whatever part of Europe he could get.

Our mother is a survivor of domestic violence and helped us escape our father when were still little. She is the first who taught me about escape. She took us with her from Los Angeles to Oxnard to live with our grandmother, aunts, uncle, and cousins. Our grandmother knew some Mayan words. She had learned them from the *Inditos* at the *mercado*, she would tell us, the "little Indians" at the market. It wasn't until later as a young adult when I first visited Guatemala that I would learn we had been *Inditos*, too.

As a child of migrants in the USA, *pochas* and *pochos* as we are called, I heard stories of being poor in Guatemala, but I didn't know we were also poor in the United States until I started school and learned our shoes were telling everybody we were poor. In school I earned good grades and awards at first, misbehaved in adolescence when they split me up from my friends, almost didn't graduate high school, and was able to catch up in time to go straight to college, straight to a working-class university.

I enrolled in the California State University Northridge (CSUN) in Los Angeles and began in August 1996, a month before the assassination of Tupac Shakur, *presente*. I majored in Business Administration with a specialization in Information Systems, another way of saying "the internet for business applications." I was good at computers at a time when few people were good at computers. I chose that line of study because I would need to be employable after college to pay back my student loans, and everyone was saying you could land a job without a problem if you were good at computers.

In the business schools of the 1990s, the solution for everything seemed to be "globalization." Globalization was helping everyone around the world get jobs, the professors were saying. Globalization meant the whole world was becoming capitalist now. The so-called alternative to capitalism, the Soviet Union, had just collapsed. The experts were saying this triumph of capital had brought about the "End of History," that there was no longer a fight about the future, no longer a fight between the capitalist "First World" and the communist "Second World." Everybody was now embracing capitalism, everybody including the "Third World."

In 1994, the Zapatistas in Mexico had risen up against capitalism, but none of my professors ever brought it up. My teachers talked instead about the "opening up" of Mexico and China, meaning, the exporting of the manufacturing jobs from where labor was expensive to where labor costs were cheap and environmental regulations hardly existent. Everywhere was opening up, everywhere that had been previously difficult for capital to enter was now opening up for sale.

The Soviet Union, its full name the Union of Soviet Socialist

Republics (USSR), spanned Eastern Europe and Northern Asia and was headed off by Russia since its inception in 1922. Its collapse in 1991 marked the end of the war that was only cold between the USSR and its nuclear counterpart NATO.

NATO stands for the North Atlantic Treaty Organization and is another way of saying "Western Europe and its cross-Atlantic extensions." NATO has been headed off by the United States, Western Europe's most powerful cross-Atlantic extension, since NATO's inception in 1949, shortly after Western Europe's empires imploded in the Second World War. When the United States took over the imperial reigns, it launched a nuclear arms race against the USSR, its European rival to the east promoting communism instead of capitalism.

This badly named cold war was not cold for the Maya peoples in Guatemala. The 500-year-long extermination campaign of Columbus and Them intensified against the Maya during this time, even though the name of the genocider had changed from the Spanish Empire to the State of Guatemala. The State of Guatemala, like all states, is an instrument of force. It was assisted in its genocide by other instruments of force, namely America in the north and Israel in the east.

In 1954, the Central Intelligence Agency (CIA) of the United States helped overthrow the democratically elected president of Guatemala accusing him of communism for instituting land-back reforms. A banana corporation headquartered in the United States, the United Fruit Company, had arranged the government overthrow, launching what the textbooks would call a 36-year-long Civil War, but what my family simply called war.

In 1954, The President of Guatemala had been the second overthrown by the CIA. Iran's President had been the first overthrown by the CIA the year before.

The CIA had been formed in 1947 in the first years of World War III. Its Iran operation had been coordinated with the British, who understood Iran's Prime Minister, Mohammad Mosaddegh, as a threat for seeking to nationalize the Anglo-Iranian Oil Company. Shortly after Mosaddegh's overthrow in 1953, the Anglo-Iranian Oil Company would change its name to British Petroleum, BP.

Presidents all over the world today sell the people and the land at the service of capital. It's no wonder why. The ones who refuse are hunted, overthrown, assassinated. In 1961, the Republic of the Congo's first Prime Minister refused to serve capital and was hunted, overthrown, assassinated. Patrice Lumumba, *presente*. In Chile, the CIA hunted the socialist-leaning president who ended up dead by the end of that day. Salvador Allende, *presente*. That year in Chile was 1973. The day fell on a September 11th.

During the Second World, the Soviet Union, had been fully complicit in intensifying the Third World War. In October 1962, the Soviets used Cuba as a launching pad for nuclear weapons pointed at the United States. From Cuba, the Soviet's medium-range missiles could reach Washington, D.C. Known in the United States as the Cuban Missile Crisis and in the Soviet Union as the Caribbean Crisis and in Cuba as the October Crisis, the 13-day confrontation was regarded as the closest the world came to escalating into a full-scale nuclear annihilation.

Notice the US Navy/Air Base in Cuba at Guantanamo on the map on the opposite page. Decades before the island's colonial overseers would be overthrown by the Cuban Revolution of January 1, 1959, they had long ago leased Guantanamo to the United States with no expiration date.

In addition to serving as a military base, since the September

11, 2001 attacks on the United States, Guantanamo has also served as a detention camp and torture center for hundreds of people kidnapped by the United States in its Global War on Terrorism, a war with no bounded geographies, a war with no limits, a war without end.

Empire's current newspaper of record reports that as of May 2024, Guantanamo has been used to detain about 780 people from 48 different countries. Today, 30 remain, of which only 11 have been charged. Out of the hundreds detained since 2002, only 16 have ever been charged with criminal offenses. [2]

World wars did not stop with the fall of the Soviet Union. The situation has continued to be war everywhere except between the ones with the nuclear weapons, further encouraging others to develop nuclear weapons.

With every war since 1991, those who keep their gaze with the above keep asking if we're on the brink of a Third World War or call the current war a "New Cold War." But is it not still war even when the war is cold for the above but still hot for the below?

---

2. "The Guantanamo Docket," *New York Times* (May 24, 2024)

The Third World War

Palestine 1492: A Report Back

Capital

In business school, it is clear to everyone there that capitalism is a system where money is supposed to make more money. Far more than just about having money, it is about capital, about money that makes more money, and it doesn't matter how. Not everybody says that last part out loud.

People raised by capitalist societies are taught to confuse capitalism with simply using money or with buying and trading at a market, at a *tianquitztli*, at a *souq*, at a *mercado*. These are human activities that have been around for thousands of years, well before capitalism, which they say is only a few hundred years old, younger than Columbus and Them.

Down below the streets know that money is far more than just money. Money is power, an overwhelming power. Capital is about turning power into more power, but not just that. It's about extracting it from others and accumulating it, about taking others' energy and claiming it as one's property. And it doesn't matter how. To do it legally or illegally is merely a question of tactics. The corporate banks and the narcotraffickers who depend on each other today teach everybody this. The deception on behalf of capital is neither moral nor immoral; for capital, the deception is purely pragmatic.

Capital cannot stop itself from wanting to grow. Stealing energy is its defining logic: war. Anywhere where there's energy is its desired domain. Anything that gets in its way is its enemy. Capital compliments societies that believe eating at the top of the food chain should be life's goal. Capital's promises to uplift those on the menu to a seat at the table if they work hard enough can be seductive illusions. When all one knows is that those above live in some kind of stability, control, and even fun while crushing you down below, desiring to be just like Them can be an overwhelming temptation.

It can be difficult to have an intelligent conversation about capitalism among people raised by it. In the United States, the discussion often starts and ends on whether selfishness is human nature, yes or no. The answer is supposed to determine whether capitalism is human nature, yes or no. One looks around. Reality points to yes. The conversation ends.

When our selfish potentials are rewarded and our collective potentials are suppressed, it is difficult to agree that selflessness is also human nature. In capitalist societies, selfishness is not only rewarded, it is made to be envied. Caring for the other is devalued, ridiculed, forgotten, exterminated. Capitalism makes sense among highly traumatized societies forced into scarcity, among those disconnected from land and community, forced to fend for themselves, forced into acquiring food for themselves where it doesn't matter how.

In the United States, most who are made dependent on capitalism and come to defend it are not capitalists themselves, although many wish to be. Most don't have money to invest somewhere to have it make more money; most need that money just to buy some food. It is the type of money that runs out right away rather than reproduce itself. The disconnection to land makes them dependent, so dependent that they defend it. When they see no alternative, the defense of capitalism is for many a basic question of survival, a necessity more than it is an ideology. Displaced from the land, the dependent ones find it impossible to live without also becoming cannibals. A generation later, they forget it's even possible to live differently. Two generations on, they find it easier to imagine the end of the world than imagine the end of cannibalism.

Not everybody who thinks they are anti-capitalist understands it this deep. The anti-capitalist position from above, the one most often amplified in capitalist societies, only talks about the battle between the capitalist and the worker; it does not bring up the greater war between capital and the earth. The anti-capitalist position from above takes aim at the capitalist, not at capital. This position believes the revolutionary subject will be the worker, and by this they don't mean everybody who works. They mean the waged worker, not the rest of the earth. Their ire is directed at the boss for not fully compensating the waged worker, which the boss can get away with because the boss owns the means of production, by which they mean the factory. They don't know much about land as a means of production. They don't know much about land. The anti-capitalist position from above does not see the earth as anything other than an object of property, a resource: a repository of energy, power, food. They see the earth the way the boss sees the earth, not in it or part of it but above it.

Capital's formula where money makes more money is M–M', where M equals Money and M' (Money Prime) equals more money.[1] In addition to this insight, Karl Marx also showed the formula for when the worker serves as an intermediary between money making more money: M–C–M'. This is where the capitalist invests money in a place, such as a factory, and the worker produces commodities, the C. The capitalist will sell those commodities for more than the

---

1. Karl Marx, *Capital Volume I: A Critique of Political Economy* (1867)

worker's wage in order make more money. That the worker is not fully compensated for their labor value is how in theory the capitalist is supposed to make more money.

The C is not always necessary to get to M'. The goal of capital is not to create jobs for the workers; the goal of capital is to make more of itself. M–M' is the more direct path. The labor of the workers, the C of the equation, is a mere intermediary, a partner sometimes, an adversary most of the time. If capitalists could skip over hiring the troublesome C they would, and they increasingly do. Playing the stock market, speculating on real estate, and engaging in other forms of gambling are some of their favorite ways to M' without the troublesome C. Replacing the workers with obedient robots is another.

What happens under capitalism when the worker gets transformed out of existence? Is it still capitalism, or is it something else?

The anti-capitalist position from Above often defines the battle between the capitalist and the waged worker as the main contradiction, the main dialectic of capitalism. They compare it with other exploitative systems in Europe that preceded it:

Slavery: master vs. slave

Feudalism: lord vs. serf

Capitalism: capitalist vs. worker

From here, they conclude the worker will be the revolutionary subject in overthrowing capitalism. Yet in the history of anti-capitalist struggles, it is difficult to find an example of workers overthrowing capitalism.

Under feudalism and slavery, promises that someday the below can become the above if they just work hard enough is not a built-in mechanism. By contrast, under capitalism the worker is constantly made to believe one day they can become the capitalist. The few examples where that happens are over-represented as general reality, but the promise is helpful in encouraging the workers to work harder, a deception that is neither moral nor immoral for capital; the deception purely pragmatic. *It's just business*, as capital likes to say.

Rather than seeking capital's overthrow, we have plenty of examples of workers seeking to improve it through economic reforms. The workers fight for "a piece of the pie," as they like to call it, a piece of capital. That more pie for them will require more wars, not everybody likes to say out loud. Rather than seeking capital's overthrow, we have plenty of examples of workers defending it against the ones defending the earth from capital's wars.[2]

It is built into capital's logic that if one is forced to hire workers into order to get to M', then the more easily exploited workers will be the most desirable. *It's just business*. In business schools, labor is the most tempting place to cut costs. For essential domestic work like agriculture and caretaking, skilled workers with the least rights are the most desirable. In the United States, only a couple of generations ago these jobs were filled mostly by descendants of enslaved Afrikans, who fought bloody battles for their rights and then more bloody battles just to enforce them. They were soon replaced by others who don't have rights: undocumented workers. Labor unions in the United States, the ones who fought for a piece of the pie, in the 1990s witnessed their bosses move the factories to foreign countries, leaving many them now out of the American Dream,

---

2. *Marxism and Native Americans*, edited by Ward Churchill (South End Press, 1983)

as they like to call it. To cope with the loss, they say many are addicted to drugs now. Some politicians tell them everything is fine, and they are the problem. Some politicians tell them things are not fine, and foreigners are the problem. Maybe one politician might tell them the capitalists are the problem. No politician will tell them capital is the problem. Politicians don't get hired or keep their jobs by telling the truth about the boss.

It is built into capital's logic that if the undocumented migrant, the overseas worker, or the robot is cheaper, the capitalist will go with the one that's cheaper. *It's just business.*

There's another saying that goes, *Don't hate the player, hate the game,* but even those who say it aim their ire at other players and not on the game. What happens under capitalism when the big player, the boss, gets transformed out of existence and the worker remains? What happens when the workers take over the means of production and kick out the boss? Is it still capitalism, or is it something else?

Let us illustrate. I produce pencils, you produce paper, and we want to exchange. How do we figure out this exchange? *Time is money,* capital likes to say. It takes me one hour to produce five pencils. It takes you the same amount of time to produce ten sheets of paper. We trade my hour for your hour, my five pencils for your ten sheets of paper, and we've conducted our exchange.

We have carried some familiar assumptions in this transaction that we've learned from somewhere. One, we consider each other equal: one hour of your labor time equals one hour of my labor time. Two, we consider each other property owners: I own what I produce, and you own what you produce. Three, we can make and keep a contract with each other, an agreement: we exchange ownership and can be trusted to respect the transfer.

Is this still capitalism, or it is something else? Whatever its name is, *What about the tree?* Nobody compensated the tree. Nobody consulted the tree.

Didn't the tree also work to help produce those pencils and that paper? What would be the compensation for the tree, and how would we quantify that? A lot of other workers have contributed to making the tree: the soil microbes, the wind, the water, the carbon dioxide, the sun. How do we compensate them, how do we compensate everybody who works?

Capital's answer is to compensate the least number of workers you can get away with. Valuing the work of the earth to zero is its foundation. If the goal is to get to M', compensating everybody sends back their energy and cannot be accumulated. Compensating the earth for its work will not concentrate the earth's energy in the hands of a few.

Like the capitalist, the anti-capitalist position from above does not consider the earth, only the human worker, and by this they do not mean all humans. The enslaved human is considered to be part of the earth and is thus considered to be property, just like the earth is considered to be property. The labor of the enslaved is not considered equal to the labor of the waged worker, the one allowed to freely sell their labor power or refuse to work, the one allowed rights to ownership, the one allowed to engage in respected contracts. The master owns the enslaved's labor power. The enslaved is not a property owner; the enslaved is property. The enslaved does not engage in contracts; the enslaved is forced to work.

In business school in the 1990s, even as the globalization of capital was becoming the answer for everything, we were also being taught that globalization was not sustainable, that there are too many people on earth, they were saying, and if everyone on Planet Earth lived the lifestyle of the United

States, we were taught, we would need four Planet Earths. That statistic is today five Planet Earths.

When this fact was mentioned then and continues to be mentioned today by the above, it is not to blame capital's ravaging of the Earth. It is instead to blame something called "overpopulation," a reframing of the problem as "there are too many people on Earth and not enough energy for everybody." Those who say that do not count themselves among these supposedly "too many people."

This reframe often comes from those who can imagine the end of the world before they can imagine the end of capitalism. This reframe often comes from those so displaced from the land, so traumatized, so broken it is a terror for them to imagine the end of capitalism.

Capital

Palestine 1492: A Report Back

Downward Assimilation

They say the sociologists in the United States are worried the children of today's immigrants are not assimilating like the previous immigrants. By *today's immigrants*, they largely mean Indigenous and Afro-descendants south of the United States border called *Latinos* or *Hispanics*. By *previous immigrants*, they mean the Europeans.

For children of today's immigrants, the sociologists have coined a term of caution: *downward assimilation*. It's what they call Brown people who share their lives and fates with Black people more than they do with White people.

The place where I first learned English was where I first learned I was supposed to upward assimilate into Whiteness. Television taught me I was a Democrat, and I went with that for a while. Republicans had never hid how much they disliked my family and anybody who wasn't White.

The only politics I knew of back then meant "electoral politics," which I found myself following more closely than most people around me. I'm not sure if it surprised anyone that I applied to become a Congressional intern once, but it surprised me that I was quickly accepted. The year was 2001. The Congresswoman's office was looking for somebody good at computers in a sea of Political Science applicants who weren't yet good at computers.

I had submitted my application on a whim after moving to the East Coast for two semesters to see it snow. California State University Northridge was part of a national student exchange program popular with cold-weather students curious about Southern California.

For Fall semester 2000, I traded spots with someone at Rutgers University in New Jersey because my student loans couldn't afford New York City. At Rutgers I took a writing class, a music theory class, and a drawing class where I learned how to work with different types of charcoal.

For the next semester, Spring 2001, I traded with someone at the University of Maryland because my student loans couldn't afford Washington, D.C. I was accepted as an intern by the office of a Latina Congresswoman from California. She was famous for losing elections as a Republican until she switched her party affiliation to Democrat.

Congress is an unpaid internship; getting it on your resume is supposed to be payment enough. I was required to enroll in a Political Science class while at Maryland in order to receive college credit. In that class is where I first heard the name Bernie Sanders, often mocked by the professor as "The Independent Socialist from Vermont" whenever he called on our classmate who interned for Bernie Sanders. She was the only Black student in the class. In 2001, saying the word "Socialist" in public without as much ridicule wouldn't happen for another decade. It would became safer after the housing crisis of 2008 and the Occupy Wall Street Movement that followed in 2011 that made a lot of people hate capitalism for the first time.

In January 2001 when the internship began, the Republican George W. Bush has just been inaugurated as president after a stolen election. The Democrats on Capitol Hill didn't seem to mind that much by the time I arrived. They seemed more worried about their committee assignments in Congress more than about democracy. The Republicans controlled Congress when I was there, which meant they controlled committee assignments, the places granting Congressmembers direct influence. The Congresswoman I interned for was on the committee dealing with "defense" questions, dealing with war, a theme important to her political futures because of the so-called "defense contractors" in her district. Lockheed Martin, the largest weapons manufacturer in the world was in her district, who invited her interns and staff on a Black Hawk helicopter to take a joyride above Washington D.C. when I was there.

The United States finds a gruesome joy in naming its weapons and military operations after Native warriors it has battled. Black Hawk was born Mahkatêwe-meshi-kêhkêhkwa in his native Thâkîwaki language, on Rock river, in the year 1767, a place renamed Rock Island, Illinois by the colonizers following Black Hawk's surrender and imprisonment.[1] Black Hawk was a defense chief of his people, sometimes called the Sauk people. They had allied with the British against the United States in the War of 1812 in the hopes of preventing the United States from colonizing further west.

Without question, everybody thought riding on a Black Hawk helicopter was special, which made me think it was special too, also without question. For this, and not only for this, I have had to learn to forgive myself. For this, I have had

---

1. *Autobiography of Ma-ka-tai-me-she-kia-kiak, or Black Hawk, Embracing the Traditions of His Nation, Various Wars in Which He Has Been Engaged, and His Account of the Cause and General History of the Black Hawk War of 1832, His Surrender, and Travels through the United States. Dictated by Himself.* (1833)

to learn to surround myself with people who always question, with people who pray they never stop being people who always question.

Republicans and Democrats as people are not simply colleagues; they are friends more than they are enemies, sometimes they are best friends, roommates, spouses, lovers. I did not witness existential battles between them, only re-election battles. The work of governing to them seemed to be a sporting event, slinging mud at each other in public, even calling each other evil in public, seeming to be high-fiving each other in private.

One day, the Chief of Staff of the most powerful Republican of the House of Representatives at the time came to give the interns an inspirational talk about a day in his life. He came at us with low energy, holding a drink in his hand, describing these days in Congress as "boring" because "there wasn't very much going on right now," nothing like in previous years with all the wars. After September 11th, I imagined he must have been feeling better.

The September 11, 2001 attacks on New York and Washington D.C. happened shortly after I returned home to California, making my head spin. I was frightened and upset. I considered joining the Air Force but thankfully they didn't call me back.

The television kept repeating something about how Americans can now understand how Israelis feel. A flash of Yasser Arafat donating blood to the victims surprised me. Arafat was the long-time Chairperson of the Palestine Liberation Organization, the PLO. I didn't know much about Palestinians other than Arafat was their leader and that I should be afraid. *They hate Americans*, the television kept repeating, *They hate our freedoms*.

Downward Assimilation

Some months before, I had seen an Arab woman on the news debating a White man. She said Palestinians are suffering. She had used that word, "suffering." And then the news host cut her off. It was the Second Intifada, which had erupted in September 2000, exactly a year before. I added Arafat donating blood to my growing collection of things about Palestine that weren't making sense.

Palestine had been the reason for the September 11 attacks, they were saying on the television. My list of questions was getting long. I couldn't find someone to trust. I didn't know any Muslims. I didn't know any Palestinians. My bosses at the time were Jewish, and they were helpful in how unhelpful they were. We had watched the news coverage together on September 11th while at work. When I asked their thoughts about Yasser Arafat donating blood, they responded, "I spit on his blood." I didn't know Palestinians, but I didn't like how Israel's defenders were talking about Palestinians. It brought a fire to my stomach I couldn't fully understand. I quit that job days later and moved on, curious about what I had just done.

Wikipedia, the online crowd-sourced encyclopedia, was new at the time and became my starting point. The expensive corporate encyclopedias that for generations had been sold in printed sets, like the colonial *Encyclopædia Britannica*, were beginning to lose influence at the time. They had tried to delegitimize *Wikipedia* as a reference, but I had heard of a research study that concluded *Wikipedia* and *Encyclopædia Britannica* averaged the same number of errors. Today almost nobody has heard of *Encyclopædia Britannica* and everybody knows about *Wikipedia*.

Wikipedia was the first to tell me about the creation of the State of Israel, and my heart broke in disbelief. No one had mentioned Israel had been created through the destruction of

Palestine. I had been nine years old when I first learned about Israel when in Spring 1988 at the Oxnard College Auditorium, my *prima*, my cousin, invited me to watch her perform in a play. She had just arrived from Guatemala, sent to live with us by my *tía*, my aunt, who was afraid my prima attending university in Guatemala would turn her into a Marxist.

The play was *The Diary of Anne Frank*, a story with an ending my prima hadn't prepared me for. I had only gone to cheer her on; I had never heard about the Nazis or about Europe's crimes before. On the television, White people were the ones who seemed to have it all together. We hadn't yet learned about Columbus and Them in school.

I was confused that Anne and her family, although light-skinned, were not officially considered White. By the end of the play, Anne and her family were captured by Nazis and taken to an extermination camp because they were not White. It was the first story I confronted with a terrible ending that nobody was going to rewrite. Nobody could tell me why it had happened, only that it had happened, relieving my heart right away by telling me about the creation of the State of Israel, that Jews were safe now with their own state, supported by the might of the United States.

More than twelve years would have to pass before I'd learn the truth: that Palestinians have had to die for Europe's crimes.

Soon after the September 11 attacks, universities across the country reported their U.S. Foreign Policy courses were overflowing. Our Foreign Policy professor often compared us at CSUN to the students in the Ivy League, and not positively, alleging that the Ivy League students did all the readings before class, which I would learn was untrue ten years later when I would teach in the Ivy League.

But the professor did say something I've regularly seen

proven true: states exist only to preserve themselves as states, and that's it. States don't exist for the people, they are not there primarily for the nation; states exist to preserve their own continued existence as instruments of force with internationally granted legitimacy.

Also, there are no friends in foreign policy, only allies.

Also, allies are not the same thing as friends.

I've noticed Republicans and Democrats get along best when it comes to foreign policy, meaning when it comes to waging war on the ones who don't get to vote. I didn't learn that part in class, it's been more of an observation. The politicians teach that everyone outside the United States can be sacrificed as long as the United States is kept strong. Far too often, the voters agree.

The Gulf War of 1990–1991 is officially timestamped this way by History with capital-H to make it look like that war ended. The bombing of Iraq began during the Republican administration of the first George Bush and continued throughout the Democratic administration of Bill Clinton. By the time Clinton left office in 2001 and the second George Bush came in, the war had already killed half a million Iraqi children. When asked if the price had been worth it, the Clinton administration's Secretary of State, a woman named Madeline Albright, affirmed: "The price is worth it."

Shortly after September 11th, a wounded and dangerous United States began retaliating against the people of Afghanistan and the people of Iraq, lands Americans are fine waging war on but cannot point to on a map.

The Fourth World War

DOWNWARD ASSIMILATION

On the opposite page, a map of lands of the peoples and martyrs of Palestine, Iraq, and Afghanistan

Presentes

PALESTINE 1492: A REPORT BACK

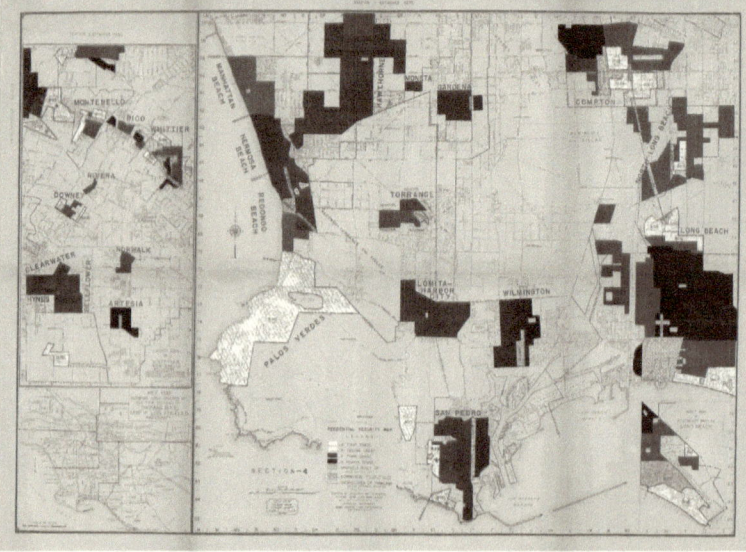

III

Globalization from Below

Maybe it was after visiting other cities, maybe it was after getting a job on the other side of the city that I started to wonder, *Why is Los Angeles like this? Why is Compton Compton? Why is Santa Monica Santa Monica?* It was a new growing feeling, that it was alright to ask *Why.*

In my final semester before graduation, I enrolled in an Urban Geography course on the other side of campus that helped with an answer. "Residential Security Maps," or "redlining," racialized housing discrimination from just a few generations before, systemic in its reach from the politicians in Washington, D.C. to the White neighbors across the street.

Redlining had come out of the New Deal, the economic reforms in the United States during the Great Depression, the first time a Wall Street crash had spread worldwide. The New Deal created jobs for the unemployed and offered Americans a number of socialist programs to help get through tough times.

It does sound nice at first. But the more you learn about the New Deal, the more you remember the struggles of the 1950s, '60s, and '70s hadn't happened yet. Redlining was one of the New Deal's lasting discriminatory legacies still physically present on the landscape today. It was part of a financial aid package to help White people realistically purchase a home through mortgages, by making smaller payments over a longer period of time, denying the same for non-White people, especially denying the same for Black people. The New Deal was legal economic warfare, a shift in American strategy after blatant plantation warfare became illegal.

Compton had originally been a White colony of Los Angeles called Comptonville in the 1860s, named after an American settler who had led a group of some 30 others to Occupied Tongva lands near *Paayme Paxaayt*, the West River, today's Los Angeles River, the place that used to be the Tongva peoples' main source of food. By the time Compton and Them arrived, the river had long been seized as private property by the Spanish Empire before it was taken by the Mexican Empire and then taken by the American Empire, along with the *Pueblo de los Ángeles*.

The Americans kept Los Angeles' name in Spanish, shortened from the much longer *El Pueblo de Nuestra Señora la Reina de los Ángeles del Río de Porciúncula*, The Town of Our Lady the Queen of the Angels of the River of the Porciúncula, first named this way by the Spanish Empire who first seized the land in 1781 and founded the town through enslaved Tongva labor and the destruction of *Tovaangar*, the Tongva world. To accommodate Los Angeles' growth, the river was channeled with concrete so it would stop moving location and not take up so much real estate.

On the redlining map of Los Angeles 70 years after Compton and Them, a chunk of West Compton was colored in Red. Compton was still largely White at the time of redlining, but that Red area on the map was described as *an old blighted laborers district with serious subversive racial influences and threats*. Specifically, the map warned of a *Threat of negro infiltration from areas north*, "areas north" meaning Watts and South Central, both geographies labeled *Negro: 50%*, also colored in Red.

Some 70 years before, at around the time of Compton and Them, enslaved Black people in the U.S. South had just forced the abolition of slavery in the United States.[1] It happened during the Civil War, which ended in 1865 between White people but still hasn't ended against Black people. Many Black people the South fled to Los Angeles for safety but were met with economic and legal warfare.

After the Civil War, the U.S. Constitution had been amended to abolish slavery, but still allowed the enslavement of anyone labeled a criminal. Since then, the United States has been labeling Black people criminals. They say Black people are only 14% of the population in the United States, yet of the incarcerated population in the United States, Black people make up 37%. Black people are only 14% of the population in the United States, yet of those serving life sentences in the United States, Black make up 48%. Los Angeles incarcerates more people than any city in the United States.[2]

Plantation slavery may have legally ended in the United States, but its notions of freedom and slavery keep the White/Black binary mapped onto the Master/Slave relationship, a war that has not ended in the United States.[3] Subjected to continued White-supremacist terror through law, police

---

1. W.E.B. DuBois, *Black Reconstruction in America: An Essay Toward a History of the Part Which Black Folk Played in the Attempt to Reconstruct Democracy in America, 1860–1880* (Harcourt Brace & Company, 1935)

2. Kelly Lytle Hernández, *City of Inmates: Conquest, Rebellion, and the Rise of Human Caging in Los Angeles, 1771–1965* (UNC Press, 2017)

3. Edmund Morgan, *American Slavery, American Freedom: The Ordeal of Colonial Virginia* (W. W. Norton & Co Inc, 1975)

violence, and paramilitary violence often by those same police, between the 1910s–1970, millions of Black people fled the South for safety and for work in cities like Chicago, Detroit, New York, Oakland, and Los Angeles.

The color Red on redlining maps translated to mean *Hazardous*, the worst of the map's four possible colors, geographies that would be readily denied mortgages and insurance.[4] Another chunk of East Compton was Blue, the second-best label, *Still Desirable*, places of *good character* where the *Professional and business people, skilled artisans, Jr. officials, etc.* lived and with *Negro: 0%* and *Nationalities: None subversive*.

Green was labeled the *Best* of the four possibilities. In Los Angeles, these geographies were places where *Executives, retired capitalists, and movie people, etc.* lived. Still live. Beverly Hills was colored Green with *Foreign Families: 0%; Negro: 0%;* and with sometimes only a *Slight infiltration of Jewish people*. The year of the map had been 1939, the year Hitler invaded Poland.

Foreign Families: 30%; Nationalities: Mexicans, the Red chunk of Compton warned in 1939. *Negro: Few %*. Directly south was colored Yellow, not Red. Yellow was the second-worst on redlining maps, labeled *Definitely Declining* but not *Hazardous* like Red. *Class and Occupation: Professional and small business men, white collar workers, etc; Foreign Families: Few %; Nationalities Possibly few Mexicans; Negro: None %* but considered to be *Definitely Declining* because *Threat of subversive racial elements from north*.

---

4. Digitized redlining maps of various cities across the United States are freely accessible to view and download online at the *Mapping Inequality: Redlining in New Deal America* project, put together by Robert K. Nelson, LaDale Winling, et al (2023) https://dsl.richmond.edu/panorama/redlining

Santa Monica is a beach-front settlement that maintains its name from the time of the Spanish Empire, the time of the first European settlers in Tovaangar, the time of the ones who first imposed their world on top of other worlds. The Tongva village of Comicranga was destroyed to create Santa Monica. They say the daughter of the village chief had his daughter kidnapped at the age of six by the colonizers, who sent her to their concentration camp euphemistically called the San Gabriel Mission so she could stop being Tongva and could instead become property.

At the time of the redlining maps, about half of Santa Monica was Red. This surprised me. I was working in Santa Monica at the time and knew it as a very expensive, very White part of Los Angeles. Back in 1939, the map said the Red-colored part of Santa Monica had been *Negro: 10%*. I didn't know that many Black people had once lived in Santa Monica. They had been domestic workers and janitors for the ones who lived on the other side of Montana Avenue, near the Brentwood Country Club, colored on the map Blue, a place offering *many marine and mountain view Homesites* and proximity to the beaches. This blue area was the "sundown" part of Santa Monica where Black people weren't allowed to be after sundown. A freeway was there now, the Red part of Santa Monica where Black people had previously lived.

Maybe the professor noticed me become indignant at this history. When he learned I was good at computers, he said I could change the world by making maps. He meant Geographic Information Systems (GIS) and encouraged me to enroll in the Geography Master's program and begin next semester. I applied and was immediately rejected. My grades during undergrad had sometimes been the lowest in the class, sometimes the highest in the class, depending on the subject and the professor. I barely averaged a C. I successfully appealed my rejection and promised I would do well, which ended up being true. I would graduate the Geography Master's program with honorable distinction, straight As. My thesis would receive a major award, encouraging me to enroll next in a doctorate, also in geography.

I had begun the Master's program in August 2003, and in addition to learning GIS and mapping Los Angeles' freeway pollution and the city's Guatemalan neighborhoods, I also learned geography was about critical thinking on migrations, borders, culture, placemaking, and globalization. "Critical" meaning asking all the *Why* questions, examining the unspoken assumptions. It was different from business school, where I had learned mostly the *How-tos*, not very much of *Whys*.

In a geography seminar entitled Globalization was where I first learned to think critically about capitalism. It was also where I first learned about the Zapatistas and kept seeing the phrase *Free Palestine*. It was the movements themselves who had made the distinction between globalization from above and globalization from below. Above and Below were simply another way to reference the familiar split between "the Haves and the Have-Nots," as everyday people often say. The Zapatistas were credited with launching the globalization from below "movement of movements" with their uprising on January 1, 1994, weaving solidarity across the globe, making clear they were not anti-globalization but were for a different type of globalization, an *alter*-globalization, "a world where many worlds fit," as the Zapatistas were saying then, "a world where all the worlds fit," as the Zapatistas are more precise in saying today.

In that Globalization seminar is when I first saw the name Karl Marx appear in any book I was holding in my hands. The first time it happened I froze, but the professor and the rest of the class just kept going. We were reading *Empire*, a then-recently published academic book that had sold a lot of copies, rare for any academic book.[5] The professor had assigned it because everybody was reading it and so we had to know about it. Few of us understood it, but the little I grasped blew my mind, as they say. It felt everywhere I was looking, I was seeing empire. Or maybe I had already been seeing it, and just needed the concepts. It felt everywhere I was looking, I was now more and more asking *Why*.

A flood of questions beginning with *Why* began to flow on things I hadn't been allowed to question as a Democrat. It felt liberating to shake off the binary Democrat vs. Republican. It was becoming clear all agreed on war and worked to preserve empire, the corporate globalization of death and destruction. I was understanding more now, but I was no longer aligning with most people around me.

Like there exists a globalization from below, there also exists a transnationalism from below. "Transnational" is not only for corporations. Migrants were also transnational, interconnected across borders, not reducible to a single nation. *Just like my family.* Border transgressors, not reducible to any single nation. I smiled at learning this and wrote my thesis on the topic, on what Guatemalan transnationalism looked like between Los Angeles and Guatemala. For the first time I got to visit Guatemala, and for the first time, I got to learn what it felt like to have a parent help with your homework. My own mother was an expert, a transnational migrant before the academics had even invented the phrase.

---

5. Michael Hardt and Antonio Negri, *Empire* (Harvard University Press, 2000)

In a seminar called Geographic Thought was where I first encountered the name Edward Said (pronounced *Sa-eed*). It was September 2003. He had just been killed by cancer, a Lebanese classmate shared with the class. The professor bowed his head. The late Palestinian intellectual Edward Said had not been a geographer, but his critique of Orientalism, the West's geographic imaginations about the East, about Asia, exists as part of the Human Geography critical theory canon, that is, a lot of geographers have built from Edward Said's critique of Orientalism.[6]

Edward Said, *presente*.

When I first learned about Edward Said he had just died, and Israel had just begun construction on the Apartheid Wall, describing it as a security barrier between Israel and the West Bank. Israel's own maps showed the Wall deviating far away from its supposed border, encroaching into the West Bank to take more land from Palestinians, confirming my suspicions about walls and borders everywhere being violent and unnatural, confirming my suspicions about Israel.

---

6. Edward Said, *Orientalism* (Pantheon Books, 1978)

GLOBALIZATION FROM BELOW

PALESTINE 1492: A REPORT BACK

·III

Dying in Order to Live

Israel's military siege on the Nativity Church took place between April–May of 2002. It was the time in Bethlehem when Israel shot up the church built on the spot where tradition holds Jesus of Nazareth had been born. For 39 days, Israel's military trapped hundreds of Palestinian fighters, civilians, nuns, and monks inside the Church while shooting at them through the windows and withholding from them water, electricity, food, and medicine. This happened during the Second Intifada, the Palestinian uprisings across the West Bank and Gaza Strip between 2000–2005, territories that together were supposed to have already become a State of Palestine, according to the lie that was the peace process.

The two-state solution of the poorly named "peace" process had been secretly agreed to in Oslo, the capital of Norway, between Israel and Yasser Arafat and signed on the White House lawn in September 1993. Israel agreed to participate as to prevent it further embarrassment during the First Intifada, the Palestinian uprisings across the West Bank and Gaza Strip between 1987–1993, a previous time, before it happened again in 2023, when the world witnessed Israel as the overwhelming aggressor through widely circulating images.

The Second Intifada had been sparked by Israeli Prime Minister Ariel Sharon's storming of the al-Aqsa Mosque compound in Occupied Jerusalem with a thousand heavily armed police and soldiers on September 28, 2000. By then it was already clear the peace process had been a lie. It had resulted in peace only for Israel, and created the collaborationist Palestinian Authority, the PA, to police Palestinians on behalf of Israel. Israel never stopped occupying, displacing, shooting, killing, and imprisoning Palestinians throughout; Israel never stopped taking more land in the West Bank and Gaza Strip, the 22% left of Historic Palestine.

I had learned about the Nativity Church Siege in a photojournalism course the year after it happened. I was still in the undergraduate program at the California State University Northridge satisfying a long-held curiosity about how dark rooms worked. Studying photojournalism answered that question and left me asking many more. The night we studied the photographs of the Siege, I had known nothing about the Siege or the Church, but I was conscious I was hearing about Palestine again. A staff photographer from the *Los Angeles Times* had snuck inside the Church during the Siege with her digital camera, becoming the only Western journalist to capture the story from inside. She had passed her memory cards to a Palestinian priest for safekeeping before leaving the Church, knowing Israel would seize her equipment. Her photographs would survive, circulated widely, and be nominated for the most prestigious prize in American journalism. As our professor recounted the story, I paid attention to how he spoke about the Palestinians. He was sympathetic.

After graduating from the master's program in June 2005 and about to move to North Carolina for the doctoral program that August, I quit my job and spent my savings and my summer backpacking around the world with my camera, wondering if I could become both a photojournalist and a geographer. That summer of travel began in China, where I had been invited to present my work in an international geography conference on borders. Chinese geographers toured us around the region's Golden Triangle, where the borders between China, Thailand, Myanmar, and Laos meet. After that, I traveled to Cuba, Venezuela, and Argentina without much idea of what I would find, but I kept hearing the resistances there were strong.

When my first semester at the University of North Carolina at Chapel Hill ended in December 2005, I immediately boarded a plane to backpack Syria, Lebanon, Jordan, Egypt, and Palestine, back when I was still referring to the land as Israel/Palestine. I began planning that trip two months before after noticing a travel guidebook for the region had a single paragraph toward the back addressed to "Solo Women Travelers," letting me know it had been done before. As had happened with many people in the United States with the 2003 invasion of Iraq, I was convinced that the corporate media was lying, I just didn't yet know how much.

I landed in Syria one midnight in December with a layover first in Istanbul, where the snowflakes outside the airplane window are still the largest I have seen. At the Damascus airport, I encountered all men. They were all respectful. I took a taxi to a hotel, woke up the next day, and peered out the window, hesitating a little to go outside. I wondered what I should wear. Only in Saudi Arabia and Iran are women forced to cover their hair.

I wandered around in Damascus with my camera trying to blend in, unsure of what I would find, discovering a new world, trying not to photograph too much. The Umayyad Mosque, embroidered dresses, colorful veils, pistachio ice cream. Damascus is one of the oldest continuously inhabited cities in the world, and the Umayyad Mosque is where they say the head of John the Baptist is buried.

Syria's border with Lebanon was so close, I was able to hop on a taxi from Damascus to Beirut, parts of which reminded me of the Los Angeles party scene with the occasional bombed out building next door. From there, a bus to Jordan to hike the pink stone city of Petra. I didn't stay long in the capital city, Amman. The city had a series of hotel lobbies bombed by Al-Qaeda the month before. I asked a taxi driver if we could go see the border between Jordan and Iraq, and he refused right away. From Jordan, a bus to Egypt to see the Nile River and the pyramids. It was now January 2006, only three days would be left after Egypt for Palestine before my return flight from Tel Aviv. I had wished to visit Gaza's border with Egypt but was told it was hard to get in. The bus took the longer way, from Egypt to the southern tip of Palestine before turning north to reach Jerusalem. Throughout the bus ride and our stops in between, the televisions were reporting Israeli Prime Minister Ariel Sharon had just suffered a stroke.

We arrived in Jerusalem at midnight. I slept in the lobby of a hostel and checked in the next morning. In the lobby, an American-Israeli settler talked about the Palestinians the way White people used to publicly talk about Black people in the United States. "Didn't the Israelis take the Palestinians' homes?" I asked him not as a challenge but as a genuine question. The settler frowned at me as if I were ignorant and dumb. He left. Interactions like these helped me become less confused about Palestine. After being racially profiled by Israel at the airport on my way back home and forced to undress helped me become a lot less confused.

I had gone to Palestine to see what I would learn, making no plans other than to see in person the Dome of the Rock, Israel's Wall, and the Nativity Church, not knowing one day I would return.

NORTH
WEST
EAST
SOUTH
LEBANON
Beirut
Damascus
SYRIA
OCCUPIED
GOLAN
HEIGHTS
Haifa
MEDITERRANEAN SEA
OCCUPIED
WEST BANK of the RIVER JORDAN
OCCUPIED '48
Jerusalem
BESIEGED
GAZA
STRIP
RAFAH
CROSSING
Beersheba
JORDAN
EGYPT
Petra
SINAI
PENINSULA
FROM
THE NILE RIVER
&
THE PYRAMIDS
Taba

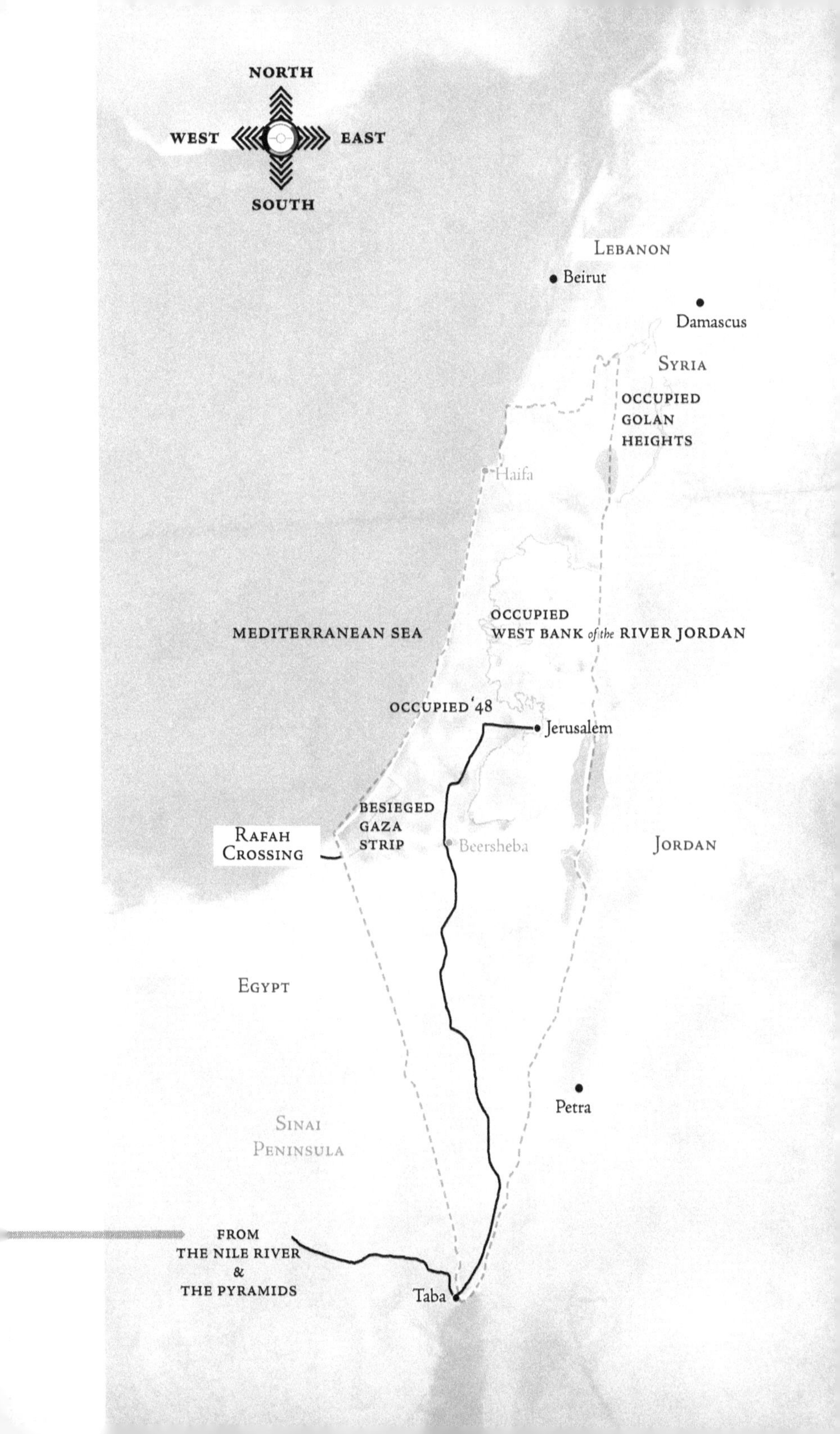

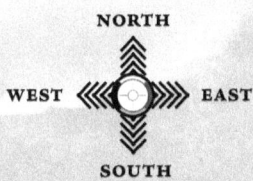

Dying in Order to Live

My first morning in Jerusalem I was greeted by Tupac tagged on a brick, *2Pac*. It became the first photograph of Palestine I would take.

January 5, 2006

The Fourth World War

The Dome of the Rock in Jerusalem is the centerpiece of the al-Aqsa Mosque compound. It was built in the years 691–692 on the site of the destroyed Second Jewish Temple, destroyed by the Roman Empire in the year 70. The Second Temple's western wall still remains, where today Jews still go to pray.

Al-Aqsa is often depicted in Palestinian resistance imagery as a sacred geography that contemporary maps have a hard time depicting. Jerusalem was the first direction Muslims prayed before it shifted to Mecca.

January 5, 2006

The next day, a Palestinian taxi drove me the five miles south from Jerusalem to Bethlehem. Israel's Apartheid Wall was as far as he would go. I'd have to walk myself through and find the rest of my way.

This was in the fourth year of the Wall's construction. Since that time, a more fortified checkpoint with 24-hour Israeli military presence exists. Palestinians are not allowed to cross from the West Bank into Jerusalem.

Aida Refugee Camp is on the other side of the wall, directly to the right. We wouldn't know it yet, that we would soon accompany each other, Aida Refugee Camp and me.

January 6, 2006

Four years later when Salah Ajarma would ask me to map Aida Camp in 2010, I didn't know he had been one of the Palestinians besieged inside the Nativity Church eight years before.

When Rachelle and I found out and shyly asked him, he was happy to meet us at the Church and share the story. Salah showed us the bullet holes that remain on the walls and pointed to the windows Israel shot through; he introduced us to the pillars that shielded them from bullets as they slept; he presented us to the trees that provided their last leaves when food was running scarce; he pointed to the walls from where neighbors tossed bags of food that avoided the soldiers' gaze; he recounted the story of how he and his sweetheart, his soon-to-be wife Rasha, had kept in touch throughout those 39 days.

Salah also shared that the sacred altar down below, the grotto where a star marks the spot of the manger, was the warmest, quietest, safest place and became a healing space, a clinic tending to Palestine's wounded during the siege.

When Israel lifted the siege, it expelled several Palestinians to countries outside of Palestine and many to the Gaza Strip where only five years later in 2007, they would live once again under siege, a siege that still has not ended for the ones who are still living.

This is a photograph I took on January 6, 2006 the day I first met the Nativity Church. I had no idea I would soon return to Palestine and learn to struggle from a Palestinian like Salah Ajarma, *presente*.

Six months later was summer 2006. I was in Guatemala and Southern Mexico preparing for my doctoral research on the Mexico/Guatemala border. On the Chiapas the side of the line, in San Cristóbal de las Casas, I was curious to learn more about the Zapatistas. The old colonial city, literally named after Columbus and Them, was where the statue of the colonizer Diego de Mazariegos had been knocked down that October 12, 1992. The Zapatistas had taken San Cristóbal during their uprising that January 1, 1994. Nobody in San Cristóbal I could find could tell me about the Zapatistas, or maybe they did not want to.

At the outdoor *mercado* of the Maya Tzotzil communities, the Zapatista image was almost everywhere, handmade wool figurines and Subcomandante Marcos t-shirts to satisfy the Zapa-tourists like me, who think they can go to San Cristóbal de las Casas and find the Zapatistas but all they get is a Zapatista t-shirt. It would be a little longer before I learned what the Zapatistas had been doing that summer of 2006, and more of who they really were.[1]

It was July 2006. In my hotel room, *CNN International* was reporting something about Beirut. Israel had just bombed the airport. It hit me different this time, and it went on for days. The coverage on *CNN* in English on my laptop was different from *CNN International* and *CNN en Español*. The Spanish-language channel had invited a professor to provide education, background, history, history meaning the Nakba of 1948, not simply a history of the week before. CNN in English was vilifying Lebanese and Palestinians alike, humanizing only Israelis, repeating Condoleezza Rice's shoulder shrug at war,

---

1. El Kilombo Intergalactico, *Beyond Resistance: Everything, An Interview with Subcomandante Insurgente Marcos* (Paperboat Press, 2008)

the "growing pains of a new Middle East," as she had put it.

I used to struggle to describe that realization as an unbearable heartbreak, to stare at the lie from the face of the ones you used to trust while seeing reality reported from somewhere else. I still struggle to describe it. It entailed a lot of crying. Since then, millions of more hearts have been broken to realize how easily Holocausts can still happen, often do happen and well beyond Palestine.

Congo, Haiti, Sudan, *presentes*.

The world as I had known it died that summer in Chiapas with my gaze to Palestine. Back at school, I couldn't do any of my work. My time was spent researching and learning everything I could about Palestine, speaking about Palestine to everybody I could. My doctoral adviser, Altha Cravey, supported me in doing something few advisers would do. I changed my entire doctoral project to research the borders of Palestine, even though I didn't speak the language and didn't know anybody there. I don't know if I would have finished the program were it not for that change.

A blog in English called Gaza Mom shared a mother's attempts to cross the Gaza/Egypt border at Rafah with her little boy, a border more often closed than it was opened. People would die while waiting for Israel and Egypt to open Rafah, babies would be born while waiting at Rafah. Leila El-Haddad was the writer. Her blog described the devastating conditions in the Gaza Strip and Israel's total control even after removing its settlers from there in 2005 and transferring them to the West Bank to terrorize Palestinians there. The Gaza Strip was already devasting before the Israel began its full siege in 2007, starving Palestinians from food, water, electricity, medicines, "putting them on a diet," as Israel has liked to say, "mowing the lawn" as it described its regular carpet-bombing campaigns.

I wanted to learn as much as I could and attended awareness events and then organized them on campus. I lost a lot of friends; I gained a lot of friends. I began to write publicly, openly critical of Israel and Zionism, knowing full well the consequences. Phone calls were made to my university demanding I be expelled. Emails reached my inbox containing death threats from people who wouldn't show their face and name. In one of the nicer pieces of hate mail, a Zionist let me know they hated my politics but loved my writings. They had read an essay where I mentioned my mother's last name and revealed to me, *Your mother's name is a Jewish Sephardic name from Spain, so mazel tov,* congratulations, *you're Jewish, too!* I thought that part was cool, but it wasn't going to make me a Zionist.

In December 2008, Israel carpet-bombed the Gaza Strip for the first time. Barack Obama had just won his first presidential election. He was silent although they say he had been mentored directly by the late Edward Said. Operation Cast Lead, as Israel called its massacre, lasted well into January 2009. Israel ceased fire days before Obama's inauguration, preventing the Historic moment of a first Black head of the U.S. empire from being tainted by reality.

At the same time in Chiapas, the Festival of Dignified Rage had been convoked by the Zapatistas. The Palestinian people were brought up in every session and roundtable that week. On January 4th, 2009, while Israel's white phosphorus was still raining down on Gaza, the Zapatista spokesperson paused the Festival to speak the following words:

> *Maybe, what I am about to say has nothing to do with the main theme of this roundtable, or maybe it has.*

Dying in Order to Live

Two days ago, the same day in which our word spoke of violence, the ineffable Condoleezza Rice, U.S. government official, declared that what was going on in Gaza was the fault of the Palestinians, due to their violent nature.

The subterranean rivers that run through the world are able to change their geography, but they sing the same song.

And the river we now listen to sings of war and grief.

Not far from here, in a place called Gaza, in Palestine, in the Middle East, just next door, a heavily armed and trained army, from the Israeli government, continues its advance of death and destruction.

The steps it has followed so far are those of a classic military war of conquest: first a massive and intense bombardment to destroy "neuralgic" military posts (so they are called by military manuals) and to "soften up" resistance fortifications; then an iron grip on information: everything that is heard and seen "in the outside world", that is to say, outside of the theatre of operations must be selected according to military criteria; now intense artillery fire over enemy infantry to protect the advance of troops to their new positions: after that an encirclement and siege to weaken the enemy garrison; then an assault to conquer the position by annihilating the enemy; finally, the "cleansing" of the probable "nests of resistance".

The military manual of modern warfare, with some variations or additions, is being followed step by step by invading military forces.

The Fourth World War

We don't know much about this, and it is certain that there are specialists on the so called "conflict in the Middle East", but from this corner, we have something to say:

According to the photos from news agencies, the "neuralgic" military posts destroyed by the Airforce of the Israeli government are houses, huts, civil buildings.

We have not seen any bunkers, barracks, military airports or cannon batteries among what has been destroyed. Then, we think, excuse our ignorance, that either the aircraft gunners have bad aim or in Gaza there are no such "neuralgic" military posts.

We don't have the honor of having visited Palestine, but we suppose that in those houses, huts and buildings used to live people, men, women, children and elderlies, and not soldiers.

We have not seen resistance fortifications either, only debris.

What we have seen, is the so far futile effort to cordon off information and several governments of the world wavering between playing the fool or applauding the invasion, and a UN, already useless way back, publishing lukewarm press releases.

But wait. It now occurs to us that perhaps, for the Israeli government, these men, women, children and elderly people are enemy soldiers and, as such, the huts, houses and buildings where they live in are barracks that need to be destroyed.

And the enemy garrison that they want to weaken with the encirclement and siege of Gaza is none other than the Palestinian population living there. And that the assault will seek to annihilate that population. And that any man, woman, child or elderly person who manages to escape, by hiding from the predictably bloody assault, will then be "hunted down" so that the cleansing can be completed, and the military chief in command of the operation can report to his superiors "we have completed the mission."

Excuse our ignorance again, perhaps what we are saying is, in fact, beside the point. And that instead of repudiating and condemning the crime in progress, as indigenous people and as warriors that we are, we should be discussing and taking a position on the discussion about whether it's "Zionism" or "anti-Semitism", or that it was the Hamas bombs that started it.

Perhaps our thoughts are very simple, and we lack the nuances and the always very necessary marginal notes in the analysis, but, for us Zapatistas, in Gaza there is a professional army assassinating a defenseless population.

Who from below and to the left can remain silent?

_*_

Is it useful to say something? Do our screams stop any bombs? Is our word saving the life of a Palestinian child?

We think that it is useful, maybe we will not stop a bomb nor will our word become an armored shield that prevents that 5.56 mm or 9 mm caliber bullet, with the letters «IMI» («Israeli Military Industry») engraved on the base of the cartridge, from reaching the chest of a girl or a boy, but maybe our word will manage to join with others in Mexico and the world and maybe first it will become a murmur, then a loud voice, and then a cry that will be heard in Gaza.

We don't know about you, but we Zapatistas of the EZLN know how important it is, in the midst of destruction and death, to hear a few words of encouragement.

I don't know how to explain this, but it turns out that words from afar may not be enough to stop a bomb, but they are as if a crack opened in the black room of death for a small light to slip through.

Otherwise, what will happen will happen. The Israeli government will declare that it has dealt a severe blow to terrorism, it will hide the magnitude of the massacre from its people, the big producers of weapons will have gotten an economic break to face the crisis and "world public opinion," that malleable entity, always in tune with the situation, will turn to look the other way.

But not only. It will also happen that the Palestinian people will resist and survive and continue fighting and continue to have sympathy for their cause from those below.

Dying in Order to Live

And perhaps a boy or girl from Gaza will survive too. Perhaps they will grow and, with them, anger, indignation, rage. Perhaps they will become soldiers or partisans for one of the groups fighting in Palestine. Maybe he or she will face combat against Israel. Maybe he or she does it by firing a rifle. Maybe by blowing himself up with a belt of dynamite sticks around his waist.

And then, up there, someone will write about the violent nature of the Palestinians and make statements condemning that kind of violence and there will be another debate about whether Zionism or anti-Semitism.

And then no one will ask who sowed what was reaped.

On behalf of the men, women, children and elderly of the Zapatista Army of National Liberation.

Subcomandante Insurgente Marcos
Mexico, 4th of January 2009.

On my first trip to Palestine, I had noticed a mural on the Apartheid Wall on the Bethlehem side of the checkpoint. The painting had eyes peering through a keffiyeh, surrounded by maize and the words "To exist is to resist, *Viva Palestina libre, abajo el muro fascista, EZLN*" Long live a free Palestine, down with the fascist wall, EZLN.

January 6, 2006

Years later in Zapatista territory with Palestinian compas returning from the Little School we noticed a similar mural on a building in Oventik, in Maya Tzotzil lands. It read "To exist is to resist" in four languages: Tzotzil, Spanish, English, and Italian along with "¡De chiapas a palestina la lucha por la libertad nos hermanece!" from Chiapas to Palestine, the struggle for freedom makes us kin!

January 1, 2014

⟪⟪⟪ NORTH

A World Where All Worlds Fit

"And we aren't referring here to banishing those above. We're talking about destroying the social relations that make it possible for someone to be above at the cost of someone else being below."

— EZLN

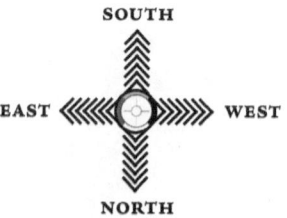

Above vs Below

•

That night on Star Street when I met the *nabi* triplets, the identical ten-year-olds Musa, Issa, and Mohammed, I learned that of the three it had been Issa who didn't like me. All that time I was living in Bethlehem, Jesus had been making faces and trying to whack me.

Moses had been the quieter triplet, very polite. It would be their brother Mohammed, the one whose namesake was the most mysterious to me, who would gift me the flower and help make things right between Jesus and me that night. And not one flower but two, both from the trash.

• •

It was true that Jesus and I had historical tension. I had been raised by a Christian culture of varying degrees of ethics and integrity, getting me into a fight with Jesus. My grandmother had lived as a good role model of what being Christian can be, may she rest in peace. My mother has as well, but she left the church long ago, "For its hypocrisy," she says. She still believes in God though. I have learned much from my mother, not hesitating to leave bad situations, exiting groups and institutions for their hypocrisy, whether it's electoral politics, academia, leftist organizations, sometimes fleeing, sometimes purged. But still, I believe. Still, in love and justice I believe. They are a necessity to me.

In the United States, the loudest voices on Jesus are on TV. Those Christian voices raised me, too. That most of them don't serve others and only serve themselves had made me angry at Jesus even if it hadn't been his fault. I hadn't considered until that night on Star Street that Jesus could be mad at me, too.

• • •

I used to insist for a long time about Israel/Palestine that, "This is not about religion," although I knew better than that. But I was mad at religion and thought I could separate it from politics and economics, as if questions of ethics could be so easily separated from politics and economics.[1] I also didn't know how to talk about religion and still stumble when I do. I never want to insult any religion or keep pitting religions against religions like empires do. I think a lot of people share that, too.

Having been raised by Christianity from above and Christianity from below, I had known a bit about Judaism, more about Christianity, and was both curious and afraid of Islam until Palestine made me more curious than afraid. It was hardest for me to learn about Islam. The loudest Muslim voices in the United States wish to be loved by empire, and I wasn't going to ask them. I also don't trust anyone eager to convert me into their world, whether religious or secular.

Back when I was preparing to live in Palestine, I asked Palestinian friends in the United States how to handle the

---

1. William Cavanaugh, *The Myth of Religious Violence: Secular Ideology and the Roots of Modern Conflict* (Oxford University Press, 2009)

question about my religion. "When people are curious, how should I respond?" I asked. I am neither Jewish, Christian, nor Muslim. My faith is not tied to Palestine's ancestor Abraham, or to any of the other Asian faiths. I am also not an atheist. My ancestors are Maya and Afrikan, and I like very much their worlds when they are from below, both from before and from after. Would Palestinians know how to interpret that?

"They probably won't know what to do with you," a Palestinian friend replied back then. He was raised Christian in the United States and also hadn't known how to talk about religion. In the end, I decided to respond in Palestine whenever asked, "I was raised Christian," which was not a lie and was even nice. It had made me somewhat literate in Christianity, thus a little conversant in Palestine, even if just a little bit.

••••

I was raised Christian because Columbus had been a crusader, imposing empire's version of Christianity on the earth. Empire has a religion even if it calls itself secular, even if it's a co-opted religion, it's still part of that religion. No matter how much it changes its name and face and co-opts our words and worlds, the Devil remains Devil. So how is empire not about both politics and economics and religion, too? How is empire not about imposing one world at the expense of other worlds?

Colonialism may not have a single religion, but it is false to say that colonialism has no religion. People who say that may just not want to insult religions or keep pitting religions against religions like empires do. People who say that just may not know how to talk about religion. If that is the case, it is important for us to study and learn from those who do.

"A world where all the worlds fit" is the remedy to empire,

to extinction, to colonialism, I am convinced. How do we begin working toward that without recognizing that religions are worlds? Secular activists, influencers, academics, politicians, and aspiring politicians don't know how to talk about this, or maybe they don't want to. Many don't have a problem with empire. Often the loudest secular voices wish to be accepted by empire and police others from bringing up either questions of religion or critiques of empire.

Capitalism is called secular, yet it shapes all social relations. So how is capitalism not like a religion? Nationalism is called secular, yet people are willing to die in the name of it. So how is nationalism not like a religion? A world where all the worlds fit is a question of global social relations, a question of sharing the world with all our difference. It is a question bigger than resistance, it is a question of liberation.

—

The Christian liberation theology center in Palestine, Sabeel, held a conference in 2011 where I first met Christian anarchists and Marxists who don't really use those labels of anarchists and Marxists. Among them were Richard Horsley, Ched Myers, and Elaine Enns who didn't seem to get upset if I referred to them anarchists or Marxists, depending. They reminded me that Jesus was not only resisting but seeking liberation against empire, a history I recalled hearing about Jesus before, but which got drowned out by empire.

The labels anarchist and Marxist carry a lot of baggage. But heavy words can be helpful in trying to find others critical of domination and capitalism. Just like the word Christian carries a lot of baggage but can be helpful in finding others who share something important, even if it turns out in the end they want opposing worlds. Words can lose their usefulness fast, especially once they're co-opted. I avoid using labels to describe myself, although I haven't fully given up on the word "leftist," although I'm close to giving up on it. People think they already know you because they think they know what those labels mean.

The way I use "left" is to describe a political horizon that respects difference and "right" as the political horizon that disrespects difference. There exists a below *to the right* that seeks to rise above, desires a seat at the table, hopes to impose their way on others and take the place of the oppressor. There also exists a left from above that pretends to respect difference, one that is fine with people looking different and even acting different, but one that doesn't want people to *be* different. Both the left from above and the below to the right do not seek to undo the relation of domination that is above/below.

"From below and to the left" means, to me, a political horizon that seeks to escape from the above/below relation to share the world together with all our difference. We don't have to call this "left" and can call it something else, but we do need to be clear about our proposals vis-a-vis other struggles, vis-a-vis each other as we're being crushed by this world.

÷

Does it help or does it hurt to call a movement "leftist" anymore? I've borrowed this phrase from the Zapatistas before, "from below and to the left." The word "left" seems to be completely devoid of real meaning today, co-opted like the word Christian before it, like the word Islam before it, like the word Judaism before it. Co-optation isn't sufficient reason to give up on words or to give up on movements. Co-optation becomes part of the reality of the movement and should be part of the story that's told and resisted. Just like with Judaism, Christianity, and Islam. In the United States, where a culture does not exist to talk about how words are used differently, the word "leftist" means the same thing as "liberal" or as "progressive" to many people. Everyone seems to think they know someone by the words they use instead of asking how they're using those words.

When I use the word "left" in "from below and to the *left*" I use it to make a distinction between it and "from below and to the *right*," the tragic dominant posture of the below as I have experienced the below. To be below is to be crushed by the above. To be below and to the *right* is to wish to become the above, to become like the masters, to impose one's world on and crush the other belows. To be to the right is to not respect difference. There exist Christianities from below and to the right. There exist Judaisms, Islams, Buddhisms, Hinduisms, Marxisms, Anarchisms from below and to the right, as well as from above and to the right and from above and to the left.

If not the word "left," is there another word we can use to convoke and to affirm an ethical posture against injustice, a vision of sharing the world with all our difference?

I can be convinced to give up on the word "left," but not without insisting much of the below doesn't want to escape together to create the world anew. So, what words do we use to talk about that part, too, about our common vision and not just talk about the below?

⁙

There is identity, and in the dominant world, there is identity within a context of domination, within a context of above vs below. In a global context, what we each do affects the other. If this context is ignored, a false solidarity grows, a false unity grows, an identity politics grows that wishes instead to crush and use other worlds, to be incorporated into the dominant world, not to create the world anew.

A world anew requires a brave answer to the question, *Could it be another way?* What will it take for the answer to be *Yes* by each of us, and in our own geographies, in our own calendars, and our own ways? What will it take for us to keep finding each other along the way? What will it take for us to really mean it, where we're not simply using words, co-opting words, where we're not replicating the same world of above vs below?

The Time of the No, the time of the Yes[2]

Compañeras, compañeros:

Having defined who we are, our past and present story, our place and the enemy that we face, as laid out in the Sixth Declaration of the Lacandón Jungle, what is left pending is to further define why we fight.

We defined the "no," we still haven't fully delineated the "yes". This isn't the only thing, as we also need more answers to the "how," "when," "with whom".

---

2. EZLN. *Them and Us, Part V. – The Sixth* (January 2013)

A World Where All the Worlds Fit

All of you know that it is not our intention to build a great big organization with a central governing body, a centralized command, or a boss, be it individual or a particular group.

Our analysis of the functioning, strengths, and weaknesses of the dominant system has led us to believe and to emphasize that unified action is possible if we respect what we call the "modos" [manner, way of doing things] of each of us.

And these things we call "modos" are nothing but the knowledges that each of us, individual or collective, have of our own geography and calendar. That is, of our pains and our struggles. We are convinced that any attempt at homogeneity is no more than a fascist effort at domination, regardless of whether it is hidden in revolutionary, esoteric, religious, or any other language.

When one speaks of "unity" they elide the fact that such "unity" occurs under the leadership of someone or something, be it individual or collective.

On the false altar of "unity," not only are differences sacrificed, but the survival of all of the small worlds under the tyranny and injustice they suffer is obscured.

In our history, this lesson is repeated time and again. And every time the world turns, our place is always that of the oppressed, the disdained, the exploited, the dispossessed.

Above vs Below

What we call the "four wheels of capitalism": exploitation, displacement, repression, and disdain, have been repeated throughout our history, with different names up above, but we are always the same ones below.

But the current system has gotten to a state of extreme madness. Its predatory ambition, its absolute disrespect for life, its delight in death and destruction, and its effort to impose apartheid on all of those who are different, that is, all of those below, is taking humanity to the point of disappearance as a form of life on the planet.

We could, as someone might advise, wait patiently for those above to destroy themselves, without acknowledging that their insane arrogance and pride will destroy everything.

In their drive to be higher and higher above, they dynamite the floors below, the foundations. The building—the world—will ultimately collapse and there won't be anyone to hold responsible.

We think that yes, something is wrong, very wrong. But that if in order to save humanity and the badly damaged house it inhabits someone has to go, then it should be, it must be, those above.

And we aren't referring here to banishing those above. We're talking about destroying the social relations that make it possible for someone to be above at the cost of someone else being below.

The Zapatistas know that this great line we have drawn across the

A World Where All the Worlds Fit

world geography is not a conventional understanding. We know that this model of "above" and "below" bothers, irritates, and disturbs some. This is not the only thing that irritates them, we know, but for now, we are referring specifically to this discomfort. We could be mistaken. Quite likely we are. The thought police and knowledge inspectors will surely appear in order to judge, condemn, and execute us... hopefully only in their flamboyant writing and not hiding their vocation as executioners behind that of judges.

But this is how the Zapatistas see the world and its modos: There is machismo, patriarchy, misogyny, or whatever one may call it, but it's one thing to be a woman above and something completely different to be one below.

There is homophobia, yes, but it's one thing to be a homosexual above and something very different to be one below.

There is disdain for those who are different, yes, but it's one thing to be different above and quite another to be so below.

There is a left that is an alternative to the right, but it is one thing is to be on the left above and it is something completely different (we would say opposite) to be on the left below.

Place your own identities within the parameters we are laying out and you will see what we are saying.

The most deceitful identity, fashionable every time the modern state

Above vs Below

goes into crisis, is that of "citizenship."

The "citizen" above and the "citizen" below have nothing in common; they are opposite and contradictory.

Differences are chased, cornered, ignored, disdained, repressed, displaced, and exploited, yes.

But we see a greater difference that crosses all of these differences: that of above and below, the haves and the have-nots.

And we see that there is something fundamental to this great difference: the above is above on the backs of those below; the "haves" have because they dispossess those who don't.

We think that being above or below determines our gaze, our words, what we hear, our steps, our pains, and our struggles.

Perhaps there will be another opportunity to explain more of our thinking on this. For now we will just say that the gazes, words, ears, and steps of those above tend to conserve this division. This does not, of course, imply immobility. Conservatism seems to be very far from a system that discovers more and better forms of imposing the four wounds that the world below suffers. But this "modernization" or "progress" has no other objective than to maintain above those who are above in the only way it is possible for them to be there, that is, on the backs of those below.

A World Where All the Worlds Fit

In our thinking, the gaze, words, ears, and steps of those below are determined by the line of questioning: Why this way? Why them? Why us?

In order to impose answers to such questions on us, or in order to avoid our asking them in the first place, gigantic cathedrals of ideas have been built, more or less well thought out, usually so grotesque that not only is it amazing that someone has developed them and someone believes them, but also that they have also constructed universities and centers for research and analysis based on them.

But there is always a party pooper who ruins the festivities at the end of history.

And that stick-in-the-mud responds to these questions with another: "could it be another way?"

This question could be the one that sparks rebellion and its broader acceptance. And this could be because there is a "no" that has birthed it: it doesn't have to be this way.
Forgive us if this confusing detour has irritated you. Chalk it up to our modo, our ways and customs.

What we want to say, compañeras, compañeros, compañeroas, is that what convoked us all in the Sixth was this rebellious, heretic, rude, irreverent, bothersome, uncomfortable "no."

We have gotten to this point because our realities, histories, and rebellions have brought us to this "it doesn't have to be this way."

This and also because, intuitively or by design, we have answered "yes" to the question, "could it be another way?"

We still need to respond to the questions we encounter after that "yes."

What is that other way, that other world, that other society that we imagine, that we want, that we need?

What do we have to do?

With whom?

If we don't know the answers to those questions we have to look for them. And if we have them, we have to make them known among ourselves...

For our part, we have seen, listened to, and learned from everyone.

We saw who came around only to take political advantage of the Other Campaign, who jumped from one mobilization to another, seduced by the masses, and thus revealing their incapacity to generate anything themselves. One day they are anti-electoral, another day they hang their flags in whichever mobilization is in style; one day they are teachers, the next students; one day they are indigenists, the next they are allied with landowners and paramilitaries. They clamor for the avenging fire of the masses, and disappear when the antiriot

A World Where All the Worlds Fit

tanks arrive with water cannons.

We will not walk again with them.

We saw who appears when there are stages, dialogues, good press, and attention, and who disappears when it is time for the work that is silent but necessary, as the majority of those who are hearing or reading this letter know. All this time our gaze and our ear were not directed toward those on the stage, but rather toward those who built it, who made the food, swept the floors, tended to things, drove, flyered, stuck it out, as they say. We also saw and heard those who climbed over everyone else.

We will not walk again with them.

We saw who the professionals of the assemblies are, with their techniques and tactics for driving meetings into the ground so that only they, and their followers, are left to approve their own proposals. They distribute defeat wherever they appear, facilitating roundtables, sidelining the "yuppie" and "petit-bourgeoisie" who don't understand that at stake in the day's agenda is the future of world revolution. Those who think poorly of any movement that doesn't end in an assembly that they themselves run.

We will not walk again with them.

We saw those who present themselves as struggling for the freedom of the political prisoners during events and campaigns, but who insisted

Above vs Below

that we abandon the prisoners of Atenco and continue the journey of the Other Campaign because they had their strategy ready and their events programmed.

We will not walk again with them...

Opening ourselves to those throughout the world who have pain will not lessen our own. The path will be even more treacherous.

We will battle.

We will resist.

We will struggle.

We may die.

But one, ten, a hundred, a thousand times, we will always win always.

For the Revolutionary Indigenous Clandestine Committee—General Command of the Zapatista Army for National Liberation

The Sixth-EZLN

Subcomandante Insurgente Marcos.

Chiapas, Mexico, Planet Earth.

PALESTINE 1492: A REPORT BACK

Side by Side

Soon after being purged from the Nation of Islam for being a truth-teller, Malcolm X borrowed money from his sister and traveled to Afrika and the Middle East in 1964. For what would be the final year of his life, he came back reporting that "travel broadens your scope," sharing in speeches and interviews his learnings about anti-colonial struggles outside the United States, the place he knew best.

While visiting Mecca in pilgrimage as a Muslim, Malcolm received the Arabic name El-Hajj Malik El-Shabazz. While visiting newly independent Nigeria to deliver a speech, he received the Yoruba name Omowale, meaning "The son who has come home."

While in newly independent Ghana, he met the ambassador to the newly independent Algeria and refined his analysis on Whiteness. To the Algerian ambassador, he had shared his worldview of Black nationalism before realizing the Algerian ambassador, a revolutionary, was white. Of this encounter, Omowale, El-Hajj Malik El-Shabazz, Malcolm X shared:

> *When I was in Africa in May, in Ghana, I was speaking with the Algerian ambassador, who is extremely militant and is a*

A World Where All the Worlds Fit

revolutionary in the true sense of the word (and has his credentials as such for having carried on a successful revolution against oppression in his country). When I told him that my political, social, and economic philosophy was Black nationalism, he asked me very frankly, well, where did that leave him? Because he was white. He was an African, but he was Algerian, and to all appearances, he was a white man. And he said if I define my objective as the victory of Black nationalism, where does that leave him? Where does that leave revolutionaries in Morocco, Egypt, Iraq, Mauritania? So he showed me where I was alienating people who were true revolutionaries dedicated to overturning the system of exploitation that exists on this earth by any means necessary. So, I had to do a lot of thinking and reappraising of my definition of Black nationalism. Can we sum up the solution to the problems confronting our people as Black nationalism? And if you notice, I haven't been using the expression for several months. But I still would be hard pressed to give a specific definition of the overall philosophy which I think is necessary for the liberation of the black people in this country.[1]

In another speech delivered only hours after his house was firebombed on February 14, 1965, and only a week before his ultimate assassination, Omowale, El-Hajj Malik El-Shabazz, Malcolm X again reported back on worlds where people are white only "incidentally," where white does not mean they're The Boss, where white was only a description, an adjective, not a noun.[2]

---

1. Malcolm X, "The 'Young Socialist' Interview" in *By Any Means Necessary* (Betty Shabazz and Pathfinder Press, 1970)

2. El-Hajj Malik El-Shabazz, "The Last Message" (February 14, 1965)

In the dominant world, far more global today than during the time of Omowale, El-Hajj Malik El-Shabazz, Malcolm X, white-adjective continues to be entangled onto White-noun, beings designated as superior within a world structure of superior vs inferior against beings who are black-adjective, against beings marked as Black-noun.

white-adjective vs black-adjective. White-noun and Black-noun together, but above vs below, not side by side. White supremacy and anti-Blackness together, two poles of the dominant world, two poles of the world of 1492, two poles of the world even before, of Asia's world even before. Not the same as Human vs non-Human. White vs Black is Human vs *anti*-Human.

Omowale, El-Hajj Malik El-Shabazz, Malcolm X didn't get to live long enough to develop his overall philosophy. I wonder how much more healing there might have been on earth had he not been martyred when he was. I wonder who are the ones taking up the project he left behind. I wonder if maybe we all should be taking up the project he left. Liberation is at stake.

Is the task of White people, is the task of the ones who believe they're the Boss because they're incidentally white, is the task of White people to split apart *white-adjective* from *White-noun*? Is it the task of White people, is it the task of the ones who want neither the privilege nor the sociopathy, is it the task of revolutionary White people to split apart their *incidental whiteness* from *White-I'm-Boss*?

Can the two split? For a world where all the worlds fit, they must be split. How can they be split? And after the split, after white-adjective's escape, how might white-adjective evade recapture into White-noun? The seductions to remain captive are great. Captive to privilege. Captive to sociopathy. Captive to empire. And everybody knows the Devil's temptations to stay captive are great.

I have heard white-adjective people refuse the label White and think it's enough while the world continues treating them as White, while the hospitals, the schools, the workplaces, the courts, the prisons, the state not only see them as white, they *treat* them as White, and while everyday people *treat* them as White. One cannot say they are not White when the world treats them as White, whether one likes it or not.

The world itself is a problem. It is a problem of the world. It is a problem of an anti-Black world. It is a problem of a system structured by domination, by above vs below, making it difficult for us to share the world together, side by side... by side by side.

Everybody knows the Devil's seductions are great.

• •

The first time I heard about sharing the world side by side as an alternative to above vs below, I was listening to Sylvia Marcos speak in Chiapas for the first time. The Mexican intellectual was quoting the Palestinians on the challenge of hope.

The day was January 1, 2013, the 19th anniversary of the Zapatista uprising. We were gathered with a thousand others from around the world at the Indigenous Center for Integral Capacitation (CIDECI) near San Cristóbal de las Casas, at its Third International Seminar of Analysis and Reflection, "Planet Earth: Anti-Systemic Movements."

Sylvia was speaking alongside autonomous movements from Mexico and around the world, from the Purépecha peoples in Cherán to the Mapuche peoples in Chile. She was joined by other movement elders, including artist Emory Douglas of the Black Panther Party; the late Zapatista intellectual

Pablo González Casanova; and the late architect and militant intellectual Jean Robert, Sylvia's life partner.

When Sylvia spoke that day, she described the march of over 40,000 Maya Zapatista men, women, and children throughout Chiapas that had just taken place on the 21st of December of 2012, the end of the Maya long count. The Zapatistas had marched quietly that day with no single leader, with all of them leaders. Each stepping up on a stage they built and transported with them for the occasion, and stepping down off stage just as quickly, *juntos y a la par*, together and side by side. Sylvia emphasized that part, "together and side by side." I soon learned it is the focus of her work on Mesoamerican philosophies and worldviews.

Together and side by side is a Zapatista women's demand, philosophy, and practice of walking alongside the Zapatista men in struggle, in a complementarity of difference rather than in a competition. That is, they do something very other than repeat the logic and practice inherent to domination, inherent to patriarchy. When Sylvia ended her offering that evening with, "We have to expect to be prisoners of hope, like the Palestinians say," I knew I needed to introduce myself.

I was in attendance as a listener seeking to weave more between Chiapas and Palestine, seeking to organize a Palestinian delegation to Zapatista territory. I had just encountered the right person. When I shared with Sylvia my task, she responded, "I am Palestinian. My grandparents were from Bethlehem." We embraced.

The next year in her home, we gathered with a Palestinian delegation of women, all of us having returned from week-long stays in Zapatista territory as students in their *Escuelita*, their Little School. We exchanged our experiences and remarked on the weavings between Chiapas and Palestine, present in different degrees in both geographies.

Each Little School student had received four textbooks: *Autonomous Government I; Autonomous Government II, Autonomous Resistance;* and *Women's Participation.* We were given time to read them while visiting the Zapatistas' autonomous clinics, schools, food gardens, cooperatives, and justice systems, and while sharing back with them how we were organizing where we lived, what our struggles looked like.

Sylvia shared from her Little School experience by outlining the ways the Zapatista Women's Revolutionary Law of 1993 was being lived in the present, as detailed in the textbook *Women's Participation.* She was writing an essay pulling out the philosophical foundations of the Zapatista women's struggle against patriarchy and emphasized a fluid dualism between men and women, not a binary dualism of Western feminism that responds to patriarchy by reversing the positions of domination, that responds by placing women as superior to men in struggle. The Zapatista women insist that their struggle is to live together and side by side, women and men, not above vs below.

I offered to translate her essay, published that year in 2014 as "The Zapatista Women's Revolutionary Law as it is lived today,"[3] and in the process, I received from Sylvia some conceptual *curanderismo,* some conceptual healing. She helped me shake off the notion that all dualisms were bad, that all dualisms were binary, that all differences were in competition. She spoke of worlds of complimentary opposites and of fluidity in between.

Sylvia's work intervenes against Western approaches

---

3. Sylvia Marcos "The Zapatista Women's Revolutionary Law as it is lived today," *openDemocracy* (July 2014)

to feminist justice that focus on switching the positions of domination between men and women, and on making demands for sameness between genders, for women to become oppressors like the men under patriarchy. Her writings instead emphasize the Mesoamerican worldview of difference existing "together and side by side" and the Zapatista women's practice of walking alongside Zapatista men in struggle while being "the women that we are," an insistence on difference, a complementarity of difference, not a binary competition toward a standard, toward sameness.

The call to respect difference rather than to tolerate difference was still new to me. Sylvia pointed me to another Zapatista phrase to help me shake it off: "We are equal because we are different." I sat with that one, thinking about the definition of equality I had previously been taught: citizenship, and that to attain citizenship, several boxes had to be checked off, meaning a standard had to be met to attain equality, and that once a standard for equality was introduced, inequality was at the same time introduced.

If we begin with "We are equal because we are different," then rather than being weak because of our differences, we are strong because of our differences, not in spite of them. When I asked Sylvia from where this wisdom came, she simply replied "It's in nature." Wisdom is observed all the time in nature.

• • •

The Little School taught me most about the land. It taught me the way I was fighting for the land was all wrong. The land is not just a moral imperative; land is the condition of possibility for the creation of another world. It taught me the struggle is not just about taking back the land but about what kind of life is made possible with the land, about what kind of world can be built together with the land, side by side with the land.

For three days in a Maya Zapatista household, the compas fed me, sheltered me, protected me in the world they had designed to be autonomous from the dominant world. I wouldn't have been able to repeat it back home. I only knew to pay someone for everything I needed back home. I could say I was anti-capitalist all I wanted, but as long as I needed money in order to live, I wouldn't know how to live without capitalism.

I eventually made my way back home to Oxnard, California, in the United States, a country where almost nobody knows how to live without capitalism. A place where almost nobody wants to build together with the land. Land in Oxnard is used for industrial agriculture. We are told as children to stay away from the land. We are told as children to go to school instead, where we learn some more to stay away from the land.

Oxnard is a place where food growing is intensive and back breaking, where each field has only one crop, sameness and sameness for acres and acres, where everything different is -cided: pesticided, insecticided, herbicided; where the relations between plants and animals and between plants and other plants is forced into a competition for life.

Without any access to land, I learned to grow food first in pots and then in a community garden where I experimented growing a small milpa like my grandmother and mother, where maize, beans, and squash grow together and support each other rather than compete against each other.

The maize grows tall, and is the centerpiece of the milpa, a heavy feeder of the soil and is known as the *leader*. The bean plant crawls up the maize fixing food back into the soil, and of the three it is called the *giver*. The squash stays low to the ground, its large leaves covering the soil and is known as the *protector*. All three plants in a complementarity of difference, not a binary competition toward sameness. All three plants complimenting each other, together and side by side. Maybe from observing their wisdom, by learning to listen we might learn how to build the world anew.

We can say we are anti-capitalist all we want, but how many of us know how to live without capitalism?

We can say we are anti-patriarchy all we want, but how many of us know how to live without patriarchy?

We can say we are anti-domination all we want, but how many of us know how to live without domination?

How many of us know how to get to that world of side by side by side by side? And if we don't know, how many of us wish to start?

SIDE by SIDE by
SIDE by SIDE by
SIDE by SIDE by
SIDE by SIDE by
SIDE by SIDE by
SIDE by SIDE by
SIDE by SIDE by
SIDE by SIDE by
SIDE by SIDE by
SIDE by SIDE by

Palestine 1492: A Report Back

Strategy and Tactics

•

Sun Tzu's *The Art of War*, a text written roughly 2,500 years ago, was traditionally kept secret among the generals and the kings who didn't want the soldiers studying strategy; the soldiers might overthrow the generals and the kings. Soldiers were trained only in tactics, meaning they were never trained at reading and managing the bigger fire, only at starting fires, putting out fires, and reporting there's a fire. Today, *The Art of War* is widely available but few seem to read it outside business schools and corporate board rooms, as if more evidence were needed that capital is war.

It's important to note *The Art of War* is a book about a specific type of strategy: military strategy, the zero-sum game of win or die. Reading it can turn your stomach when you realize the enemy it's talking about is you, your community, your world, your planet earth. The challenge when studying military strategy is to learn to defend ourselves, our communities, our worlds, our earth by not becoming the monsters that we fight, to study strategy beyond the military type of above vs below, and study how to circulate power side by side, all while respecting our differences in both collective and individual forms. That is, all while building the world anew as we shake off the old, together at the same time.

The ethics of who we wish to become while in war may be why we need strategy most. Bare survival pits us against each other, and without strategy there's always a fight, never a question of *how* to fight, *when* to fight, or *if* to fight. Without strategy it's just constant fights. Sun Tzu:

> To win one hundred victories in one hundred battles is not the acme of skill. To subdue the enemy without fighting is the acme of skill.

An old mentor used to tell us, Our task is not to express our outrage but to organize against the source of our outrage. Organizing requires strategy. Mobilizing can be a tactic of a strategy, but mobilizing is not a strategy, mobilizing is not the same as organizing. Mobilizing without organizing is just constant fights.

Still left to address: How do we organize without expressing our outrage? Something that also needs to be addressed: How to fight off the one that calls us enemy while our ability to survive depends on it?

Over to questions of when. When to fight? When to not fight? When to pull resources from the one we fight? When do we reduce harm inside the one we fight? When do we subvert and inspire hearts inside the one we fight?

Back to questions of how. How do we prevent being captured by it, how do we engage it without legitimizing it, how do we stay guided by a strategy outside it?

How do we ensure we do not become it?

• •

In *Guerilla Warfare*, written in 1961, Che Guevara teaches about the difference between strategy and tactics. He begins

Strategy and Tactics

the section "Guerilla Strategy" with the following lines:

> *In guerrilla terminology, strategy is understood as the analysis of the objectives to be achieved in the light of the total military situation and the overall ways of reaching these objectives. To have a correct strategic appreciation from the point of view of the guerrilla band, it is necessary to analyze fundamentally what will be the enemy's mode of action.*

He begins the section on "Guerilla Tactics" with:

> *In military language, tactics are the practical methods of achieving the grand strategic objectives. In one sense they complement strategy and in another there are more specific rules within it. As means, tactics are much more variable, much more flexible than the final objectives, and they should be adjusted continually during the struggle. There are tactical objectives that remain constant throughout a war and others that vary. The first thing to be considered is the adjusting of guerrilla action to the action of the enemy.*

Strategy requires analysis and a bigger objective outside and separate from the enemy's objective. Strategy analyzes the enemy's mode of action; tactics adjust to it. Strategy requires reading what the enemy is doing, in order to manage the fire.

At their best, tactics alone can put out small fires or start small fires. At their worst, tactics alone report over and over that there's a fire, there's a fire, there's another fire...

A World Where All Worlds Fit

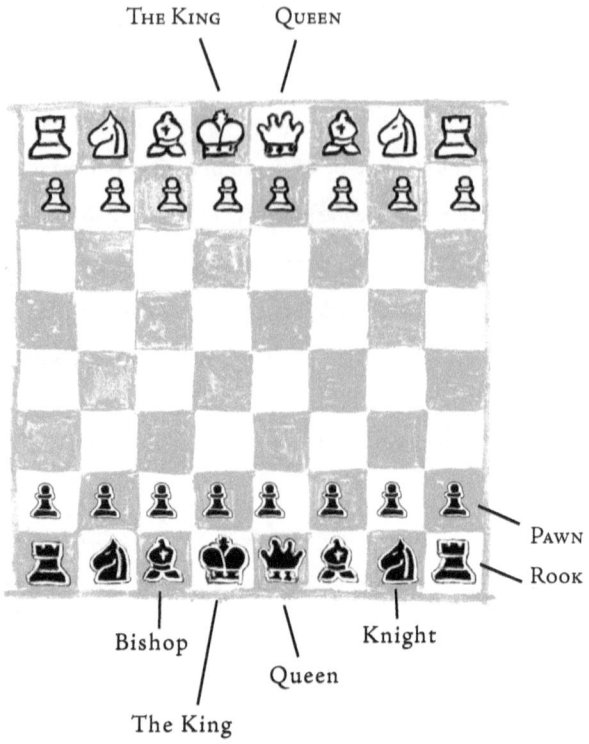

• • •

Chess is a game of war. I know the theory behind it enough to say something about it, but I don't like to play it. I don't like how I feel when I play it. I don't even know if I would be good at it. I didn't even know a chessboard could be sideways until a friend pointed out my chessboards in this book were sideways. They're fixed now.

I only know enough about Chess to critique it, but not because it requires critique, but because the way people talk about Chess requires critique. People seem to believe the chessboard is the only nature of the world, the only possible configuration of the world.

Strategy and Tactics

Chess is a two-player war game where both sides begin with the same military formation and resources. In Chess, each side shares the same competing goal: to capture the other side's King. The loss of the King entails the loss of the game. With stakes that straightforward, everyone on the chessboard is expected to perish on behalf of the King if needed, including the Queen, the Piece with the most capacity, even more capacity than the King.

The capacity of each Piece is measured by its mobility. The Queen possesses the most mobility, able to move any number of squares vertically, horizontally, or diagonally both backwards and forwards, combining the powers of the Bishop, which can move diagonally back and forth, and the Rook, which can move vertically and horizontally back and forth. The Queen does not possess the power of the Knight, the only Piece that can jump. The King can move in any direction but only one square at a time and also cannot jump.

They say the Queen herself is a new Piece on the board. In this more than 1400-year-old game from the lands called India and Persia, the Queen is said to have appeared on European chessboards only 500 years ago, replacing the King's adviser, the Wazir, with a piece inspired by Queen Isabella of Castile.[1] They say the chessboard hasn't changed since then.

About how change takes place, in *Guerilla Warfare* Che Guevara wrote:

> *It is not necessary to wait until all conditions for making revolution exist; the insurrection can create them.*

Guerrilla warfare is a strategy for how a smaller force from

---

1. Marilyn Yalom, *The Birth of the Chess Queen: A History* (Harper Perennial 2005)

below can beat a conventional army from above. The heroes in Guerrilla Chess would be the Pawns, the least powerful, the anonymous front lines, the ones sent out first to fight and first to die, the disposable ones, the least valuable, the ones not even referred to as Pieces only as Pawns. The Pawns can move only one square, two squares if it's their first move, and only forwards. The Pawns cannot retreat, and Pawns cannot jump. They capture only on the diagonal, one square at a time.

••••

I once designed a graduate seminar called "Space and Capital" where I assigned something I'd been wanting to read: writings on war by Gilles Deleuze and Felix Guattari, anarchist philosophers from France who I don't know if they called themselves that.

In *A Thousand Plateaus* (1980), in the chapter "Nomadology: The War Machine" Deleuze and Guattari compare Chess, a tactics game, with a strategy game from China called Go, a game older than Chess and even as old as *The Art of War*.

In Go, the goal is not to capture the King but to capture territory. In Go there is no King. All pieces in Go have the same powers and anonymous identities, reminiscent of the Pawns. Identity, value, and rank does not exist in Go the way it does in Chess. As Deleuze and Guattari put it,

> Chess is a game of State, or of the court: the emperor of China played it. Chess pieces are coded; they have an internal nature and intrinsic properties from which their movements, situations, and confrontations derive. They have qualities; a knight remains a knight, a pawn a pawn, a bishop a bishop...

Go pieces, in contrast, are pellets, disks, simple arithmetic units, and have only an anonymous, collective, or third-person function. "It" makes a move. "It" could be a man, a woman, a louse, an elephant. Go pieces are elements of a nonsubjectified machine assemblage with no intrinsic properties, only situational ones. Thus the relations are very different in the two cases.

Before Deleuze and Guattari, I had never heard of Go. For the rest of the semester, I asked around if anyone knew how to play, but almost nobody had heard of Go. One day I asked my neighbor across the hall who I hadn't known before, sharing about Deleuze and Guattari and the war machine. He said he didn't know about Go, but that one of our neighbors in the same building was a Chess teacher, and he might know.

The Chess teacher turned out to be the 1988 Under-10 World Youth Chess Champion who had beat Bobby Fischer three times, he said, and he had never heard of Go. He spoke Spanish more than he spoke English and had been born and raised in the Maya world. His father was a refugee from Haifa and his mother was from Bethlehem.

I asked if he had visited. He said no. I sensed he wasn't used to talking about Palestine, so I didn't ask that much anymore. Much later he would share that, long ago, he had wanted to compete under the Palestinian flag in World Chess but had been forbidden by forces both from above and from below.

He looked up Go and became curious about it, too. We couldn't find anyone with a board, so we played on a tablet and let the computer inform us when we did something wrong. I can't remember if he beat me every time. We stopped playing the day I made a single move that made the computer flash the board several times. It announced I had just won, and the game was over. We could only stare at the board. Maybe it was what Deleuze and Guattari had written about:

> All by itself a Go piece can destroy an entire constellation synchronically; a chess piece cannot...

―

Sometime later, I came across an illustration from a series *La Vida en el Ajedrez*, Life in Chess. It showed four rows of Pawns against one row of Pieces with no Pawns protecting any of the Pieces. The artist, Eduardo Salles, had entitled the illustration *Revolución*, Revolution. I wondered the backstory: how had the Pawns recruited more Pawns to become 32? Had the other side's Pawns been convinced to switch sides?

I played the artist rendering in real life using only legal moves and found it was true: 32 Pawns on a chessboard can overpower the Pieces and capture the King. Not by changing the power of the Pawns, but by changing their relationship to the Pieces. And by changing their relationship to each other.

In order to shake off the oppressor, the Pawns must stay close together, keeping each other safe while moving forward, knowing some be martyred. Still, while the odds of winning are good, winning is not a guarantee. The sides must be kept closed off so a Piece like the Queen can't take them out from behind.

∸

The other day, I called my old neighbor to get his assessment on whether the 32 Pawns can win. His answer was that my chessboards were sideways. They're fixed now. I thought he

might remark on why my Pawns were all different instead of the same, but he didn't. I thought he might be insulted I had changed the sacred chessboard. He wasn't. He later showed me online drills he gives his students that change the board all the time, including a well-known Chess formation with 36 Pawns instead of 32. It's called Horde.

Since white always makes the first move in Chess, I asked him if it will make a difference that the Pieces are white instead of black, and that the Pawns are black instead of white.

He ignored my question and shared a story of a student who asked him if it was racist that white always goes first in Chess. He said he could only laugh not knowing what to say. I said I wouldn't be surprised with Isabella up there as Queen.

After inspecting the rest of the board, he confirmed the 32 Pawns can overcome the Pieces and take the King. As long as they stay close together and keep the sides closed off from the Queen. To statistically confirm, he showed me how to log onto lichess.org, an open-source Chess platform he uses with his students, and I noticed that next to his username was an icon of a globe and a Palestinian flag.

•⎯•

They say the chessboard hasn't changed in 500 years. If it's true it's not necessary to wait for the conditions to change, as Che Guevara taught, that the insurrection can create the conditions, then what if the Pawns change the chessboard's conditions? What if the least powerful, the anonymous front lines, the ones sent out first to fight and first to die, the disposable ones, the least valuable ones changed the conditions?

What if the ones below could change the landscape of battle by changing their relationship to the above, by changing their relationship to each other?

Strategy and Tactics

Palestine 1492: A Report Back

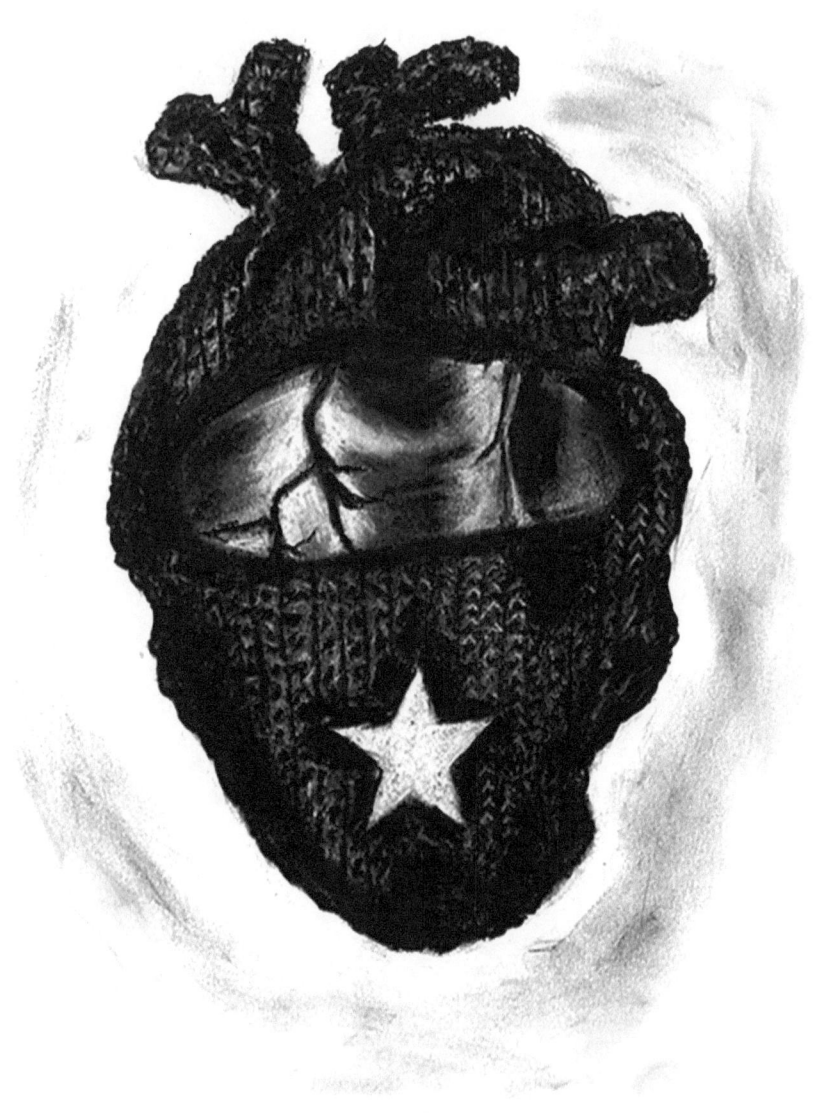

The Common

•

That night in West Jerusalem, George Jackson taught me the importance of knowing when to lose a fight. He had even prepared me for my loss, helping me understand that losing can help make you stronger. On page 130 of *Blood in My Eye*:

> *It is not defeatist to acknowledge that we have lost a battle. How else can we "regroup" and even think of carrying on the fight. At the center of revolution is realism. To call one or two dozen setbacks defeat is to overlook the ebbing and flowing process of revolution, coming closer to our calculations and then receding, but never standing still.*

Knowing when to lose a fight means knowing when to accept reality, when to accept the truth. That night in West Jerusalem, watching Israelis in willful shopping delusions with Palestinian blood under their feet, I recognized a familiar yet younger face of fascism before me.

The following year, I found myself losing again and quickly expressed gratitude. I was battling the Afropessimists, opponents whose great concern is the health of the resistance, specifically the health of Black liberation. Losing to them taught me that if we're serious about "a world where all the worlds fit," we need to first begin with those who do not fit.

A World Where All the Worlds Fit

. .

Afropessimism as I have encountered it is critical thought, specifically Black thought analyzing the foundational requirement for Black liberation: the world needs to be dismantled for the creation of the world anew. Afropessimism doesn't spend a lot of time, even spends no time, talking about the creation of the world anew, which seems to bother people. Admittedly, it is nice to hear stories of resistance and creativity and love under even the worst circumstances, as if the good eventually balances out the bad in the world. Afropessimism points out that for Black people there exists no such eventual balancing out in this world. This world is set up as a great imbalance of White social life at the cost of Black social death.

Usually, this is where people get triggered most, at "Black social death." It forces us back to slavery time, which History says is over now. Afropessimism argues that it's not. The whips and chains may have pulled back, but the structure persists of master vs slave. Indeed, the truth of the structure of above vs below is that the structure of master vs slave persists. Master vs slave is the primary relation of above vs below.

Reality is usually the part that triggers. Afropessimists don't seem to be saying something different from what every Black person already knows, and from what every person paying attention already knows. They're just saying it out loud, using precise words. Afropessimism insists we first admit the world itself is a problem for Black life before moving on to questions of solidarity and resistance. It insists we admit the reality before us: that the world itself is deadly for Black life. That's it. And maybe that's Afropessimism's entire project, to get us all to admit reality, a worthy project in times of genocide and willful delusions.

Nicholas Brady, John Murillo III, and Omar Ricks were the fighters I encountered in 2012, a time when Afropessimism was still more underground than it was above ground. Black Studies and Africana Studies departments at most universities were discouraging their students from reading the Afropessimists. Something about how they didn't like the Afropessimist focus on ontology, the study of being. I was long ago convinced the dominant world is the problem, and all I did was think about ontology, the study of how the world is and how I wish it to be, the study of who we are and who else we might be. Encountering the Afropessimists was generative for me.

Brady, Murillo, and Ricks were patient, respectful, and strong while I lost almost every round, some of the fiercest defenders of Black people I have known. About the world, none of them lied to me that it was going to be alright. I found hope in that.

They were graduate students at the time studying with Jared Sexton and Frank B. Wilderson III, who I have sparred with only through their writings and lectures. All of them introduced me to the writings of Hortense Spillers and Saidiya Hartman, all of whom in my mind are part of the Afropessimist current, although I don't think everyone calls themselves that.

• • •

Afropessimism looks at the chessboard and points to the capacity granted to the Queen and the capacity granted to the Pawn before the game even begins. That's all. Afropessimism looks at the world and points to the different capacities granted to people who are white-adjective and to people who are black-adjective, and the capacities granted to those in between. Their analytic points out that the structure of the world's antagonisms is foundationally anti-Black.

The Afropessimists didn't make the term up, but it was in their writings where I first encountered the phrase "anti-Black." I had thought it was harsh. We were already in agreement well before our encounter that the world needs to be dismantled for the creation of the world anew. It was their insistence on the specificities of Blackness that called me in, their insistence that Black was different from People of Color.[1] They were not wrong. I just had never heard anyone say it out loud before. Since then, the term Black Indigenous People of Color (BIPOC) has arisen, in an attempt to give both Black and Indigenous struggles more specificity.

My instinct had been to disagree about the specificities of Blackness until I realized they were describing not a theoretical reality and not every possible reality; they were describing *this* reality, a White-supremacist reality whose opposite pole is anti-Black, a world that tells you every day that if you want to survive and if you can't be White, then at least don't be Black.

I was challenged by how the category of the slave is different from the category of the colonized; how the Black condition was not legible by even People-of-Color struggles who fight only against White supremacy, not also against anti-Blackness. A struggle against only White supremacy is a struggle to stabilize one's own condition within a world that keeps crushing Blackness. A struggle against only White supremacy is a struggle to stabilize one's own condition on a foundation of anti-Blackness.

---

1. Jared Sexton (2010) "People-of-Color-Blindness: Notes on the Afterlife of Slavery," *Social Text 103*, 28:2

I was challenged by their argument at first that the Black condition was not the same thing as a colonized condition; that Black remained instead an enslaved condition; that the Black condition was not in the realm of the *non*-Human but of the *anti*-Human. I was challenged by their argument that while the non-Human can complement Human life, the anti-Human is the enemy of Human life; that whether captive or escaped, the slave is a terror to the master's psychic life.

The master's identity as master is possible because the master has the capacity to enslave. If the slave were to escape, there would be no more master, a terror to the master's psychic life, a terror to the master's sense of self. If the master would become another self, one who does not enslave, the world comes undone and a new world is born. The commitment to the capacity to enslave is the problem; the commitment to *being* a master is a problem, a question of ontology; the commitment to being a master means the slave is not granted the capacity to escape.

The non-Human has more capacity for protection from the Human, more capacity for assimilation into the Human. The anti-Human has neither. *If you can't be White, then at least don't be Black* is what the dominant world says to People of Color, even to People of Color who are also Black. In this world, many Black people don't wish to be Black. To be Black is to be the truth of this world, and it's not easy to be the truth of this world. It is a terror to the psychic life of this world to be its truth.

••••

Without their own legibility, Black liberation struggles are forced to use the concepts and words of others in order to be heard just a little bit, an amount not sufficient enough and a grammar not specific enough to listen to Black suffering.[2]

Non-Human is not a grammar specific enough to listen to Black suffering.

Racism is not a grammar specific enough to listen to Black suffering.

People of Color is not a grammar specific enough to listen to Black suffering.

Worker is not a grammar specific enough to listen to Black suffering.

Civil Society is not a grammar specific enough to listen to Black suffering.

Refugee is not a grammar specific enough to listen to Black suffering.

Immigrant is not a grammar specific enough to listen to Black suffering.

Colonized is not a grammar specific enough to listen to Black suffering.

Indigenous is not a grammar specific enough to listen to Black suffering.

Here in Abya Yala, in the lands Black people were brought as the White Man's property across a whole ocean, Black people do not qualify under the dominant world's category of Indigenous to make their claims to rights. To be Indigenous means you can point to your ancestral lands on a map. To be Indigenous means you can prove you were there before the White Man's time. To be Indigenous means you can make a claim of sovereignty on the map.

I can point to my ancestrally Indigenous lands; I cannot point to my ancestrally Black Afrikan lands. Blackness does not

---

2. Hortense Spillers (1987) "Mama's Baby Papa's Maybe: An American Grammar Book," *Diacritics*, 17: 2

exist on any map.³ Blackness is not limited to land. Blackness, black-adjective mapped onto Black-noun, exists on the body, whether on water or on land.⁴

Enslaved is a grammar more specific to listen to Black suffering.

Property is a grammar more specific to listen to Black suffering.

When Black people were kidnapped as the White Man's property across a whole ocean, enslavement on water and not only on land, they were stripped of their genealogies, their languages, calendars, geographies, and kin, disappearing any possible map of home in this world, becoming a stranger even when returning to Afrika in this world.⁵

In the Caribbean, unlike in the United States, Black slaves were allowed to keep their language, their families, their religion, their drum. They say Black slaves in Haiti organized a successful rebellion because of this cultural continuity. "Successful" is what official History calls a slave rebellion where the formerly enslaved are forced to pay reparations to their former masters rather than the other way around.

Reparations not for the masters but for the enslaved requires something very simple that everyone seems to resist: dismantling the world built on enslavement. That's it.

It is clear that a new world would be the true justice. For what is justice if not the work we do to ensure the crime doesn't happen again *to you, to me, or to anybody else.*

---

3. William C. Anderson, *The Nation on No Map: Black Anarchism and Abolition* (AK Press, 2021)

4. Frantz Fanon, *Black Skin, White Masks* (1952)

5. Saidiya Hartman, *Lose Your Mother: A Journey Along the Atlantic Slave Route* (Farrar, Strauss and Giroux, 2008)

A World Where All the Worlds Fit

But not a lot of people are talking about a new world or of this world as a problem. Instead, it seems everyone else wants to stabilize their own position within this world, within a foundationally anti-Black world.

—

I wonder if we might have a conversation about Black liberation and this world, a conversation about Palestinian liberation and this world, about Jewish liberation and this world, about all our liberation and this world.

An invitation from years ago from Frank B. Wilderson III:[6]

> One of the things we need to deal with is the ways in which right reactionary white civil society and so-called progressive colored civil society really works to sever the Black generation's understanding of what happened in the past. So right now, pro-Palestinian people are saying, 'Ferguson is an example of what is happening in Palestine, and y'all are getting what we're getting.' That's just bullshit. First, there's no time period in which Black police and slave domination have ever ended. Second, the Arabs and the Jews are as much a part of the Black slave trade—the creation of Blackness as social death—as anyone else. As I told a friend of mine, 'yeah we're going to help you get rid of Israel, but the moment that you set up your shit we're going to be right there to jack you up, because anti-Blackness is as important and necessary to the formation of Arab psychic life as it is to the formation of Jewish psychic life.'

---

6. Frank B. Wilderson III, "'We're Trying to Destroy the World': Anti-Blackness and Police Violence After Ferguson," *Ill Will* (November 23, 2014)

The Common

I believe that looking at it from an anti-capitalist perspective, from an anti-White supremacist perspective, the Palestinians are right—provisionally—until they get their shit, then they're wrong. So this is a historical thing: what we have to do is remind each other, to know our history in terms of slavery and our resistance to it, but also to be able to have x-ray vision, and say that just because we're walking around in suits and ties and are professors and journalists doesn't mean we're not slaves. That is, to understand things diachronically. And that will allow us to be in a coalition with people of color, moving on the system with them, but ridiculing them at the same time for the paucity — the lameness — of their desire and demand. And for the fact that we know, once they get over [their own hurdles], the anti-Blackness that sustains them will rear its ugly head again against us. So that we don't fall into a sort of genuine bonding with people who are really, primarily, using Black energy to catalyze and energize their struggle.

⁂

Black liberation struggles have powerful historical moments that other struggles adopt as their own without a lot of care: Apartheid, Jim Crow, Civil Rights. Most who adopt those words don't seem to study those struggles, learn from them, disagree with them, agree with them, disagree again. The words were made powerful by Black struggles as examples of injustice and the attainment of justice. The words were made powerful by Black struggles and still Black Lives Matter quickly becomes Muslim Lives Matter, Native Lives Matter, Immigrant Lives Matter, White Lives Matter, All Lives Matter, taking away the specificity of Blackness again.

Many who speak about Palestine with a lens from above bring up the racial segregation of South African Apartheid as a comparison to Israel's Apartheid but can't tell you about who Steve Biko or Chris Hani were.[7] They can tell you about Nelson Mandela and quote Desmond Tutu saying Israel's Apartheid is worse than South Africa's ever was. They rarely also quote Tutu saying life in post-Apartheid South Africa is also worse than South Africa's Apartheid ever was. Instead, the end of South African Apartheid is celebrated rather than analyzed. Instead, what happened in South Africa after Apartheid is supposed to be the model of justice for what should happen in Palestine.

Those with a lens from above can't tell you that the end of South African Apartheid came at the beginning of the Fourth World War. Those with a lens from above can't even tell you about the Third World War. They're still calling it the "Cold" War. Those with a lens from below, from the below of the below, can tell you it's been one long war, even before the First World War, even before 1492 when the already existing war on Blackness became a globalized war.

•••

Patriarchy is often described as the struggle of the masculine against the feminine, seen as humanity's oldest contradiction. In a global war on Blackness, the enslaved fits differently in that gendered contradiction: disposable, unnecessary, undesirable, an anxiety, a terror for the reproduction of the Human species. Under patriarchy, women are exploited but have the capacity

---

7. See Steve Biko, *I Write What I Like* (1978); on Chris Hani, see *Incognegro: A Memoir of Exile and Apartheid* by Frank Wilderson III (South End Press, 2008)

for protection; for reproduction, they are a necessity. In this world, Blackness does not have the capacity for protection. For reproduction, Blackness is disposable, unnecessary, undesirable, an anxiety, a terror.

Capitalism is often described as the struggle between the boss against the worker, seen by some as modern society's main contradiction. The enslaved fits nowhere in that contradiction. The worker is the owner of their own labor power; the enslaved does not own anything, the master owns the enslaved and the enslaved's labor power. The worker consents to work for the boss; the enslaved has no capacity for consent. Both boss and worker are rights-bearing subjects; the enslaved has no capacity for rights.

The enslaved is like the tree in capital: no capacity to own; no capacity for consent; no capacity for rights.

The enslaved is *un*like the tree in capital: the tree is the non-Human, an important distinction from the anti-Human, an important distinction to keep in mind in times of eco-fascism, in times of diagnosing this world's problem of ecological catastrophe as a problem of "overpopulation."

To dismantle this world and to create the world anew, to build a world in common where all the worlds fit, side by side with all our difference, we need to start first with those who do not fit. We need to start first with those this world wishes did not fit, each in their own geographies, each by their own calendars, each in their own ways.

In times of extinction, genocide, and willful delusions, I will not lie to you that this world will be alright.

Maybe you will find some hope in that.

Did you listen?
It is the sound of your world crumbling.
It is the sound of our world resurging.
The day that was day was night.
And night shall be the day that will be day.

Gracias Madre Padre,

Linda Quiquivix

Linda Quiquivix

⦀ B'AQTUN, ◉ K'ATUN, ·⦀ TUN, ·⦂ WINAQ, ⦀ Q'IJ, ⋮ TZ'I'
SEPTEMBER 19, 2024

OCCUPIED ABYA YALA

WILD OX BOOKS

OCCUPIED CHUMASH LANDS

www.ingramcontent.com/pod-product-compliance
Lightning Source LLC
Chambersburg PA
CBHW030536080526
44585CB00014B/972